Social Studies Discoveries on the Net

Social Studies
Discoveries on the Net
An Integrated Approach

Anthony D. Fredericks

2000
Libraries Unlimited, Inc.
Englewood, Colorado

Libraries Unlimited, Inc.
P.O. Box 6633
Englewood, CO 80155-6633
1-800-237-6124
www.lu.com

Library of Congress Cataloging-in-Publication Data

Fredericks, Anthony D.
   Social studies discoveries on the net : an integrated approach / Anthony D. Fredericks.
      p. cm.
   Includes bibliographical references and index.
   ISBN 1-56308-824-X (softbound)
    1. Social sciences--Study and teaching (Elementary)--United States--Computer network resources. 2. Social sciences--Study and teaching (Elementary)--Computer network resources. 3. Internet in education--United States. I. Title.

LB1584 .F6597 2000
372.83'044--dc21
                                                                00-055847

Contents

Chapter 10: Our World: Yesterday and Today *Continued*

Preface

I remember when I first started teaching. In those days, social studies education meant a couple of textbooks, lots of ditto sheets and ditto masters, and some antiquated supplementary materials such as ancient filmstrips, "older than dirt" films, and (if we were lucky) a few children's books. The social studies program was sometimes piecemeal and often played "second fiddle" to the reading or math program.

Social studies for most students was, I suspect, a less-than-exciting subject. Many students probably thought "social studies" was an extension of the reading program simply because they spent so much time reading dull textbooks and memorizing endless tables of information. Undoubtedly, students did not see much relevance between the information they were learning in social studies and the "real world" outside the classroom. Unfortunately, what resulted may have been a less-than-enthusiastic response to social studies as a subject.

Today, our thoughts about learning social studies and teaching social studies are dramatically different. We know that social studies learning, if it is to be both effective and meaningful, must involve children in numerous *interactive experiences*. By this I mean that children must be offered multiple opportunities to ask their own questions, pursue their own answers, and investigate corners of their world simply because they are interested and because they are encouraged to participate. In fact social studies offers unique opportunities for children to take an active role in their own learning, whether that learning takes place in the classroom or the living room.

Indeed, social studies is one of the most dynamic subjects youngsters will encounter in their lives; thus, it stands to reason that it must be joyous, exciting, and purposeful to them while they are in school. Helping children achieve a measure of self-initiated direction is a challenge for teachers, not in terms of the vast amount of social studies information children need to memorize and regurgitate, but rather in terms of assisting children in investigating their own unique questions and reaching their own personal goals.

The Internet has provided classrooms with magical opportunities to enhance and expand the social studies curriculum in a plethora of ways. No longer do we have to assign dull worksheets: Students can "surf" the Web for up-to-the-minute ideas and information. No longer do we have to require the reading of insipid textbook chapters: Students can chat online with experts around the world. No longer do we have to demand the completion of insipid worksheets that must be accomplished within a single class period: Students can communicate with youngsters around the country to design and follow through on a host of long-term investigations. Indeed, the Internet has provided us with educational possibilities throughout the entire social studies program that are unbounded by curriculum guides and unfettered by distance, time, or experience.

In many ways, the Internet connects classrooms with the real world. It taps into the budding investigator within each student and provides "real time" connections with an incredible array of social studies knowledge and adventures. In short, the Internet has not only empowered teachers and their classrooms, it has equally empowered students. It affords students resources unavailable in traditional ways: It is their key, their passageway, their portal, and their supersonic transport through which they can achieve a personal investment in their own learning.

This book is designed to help you integrate the Internet into your social studies program and enhance the discoveries of your students. It is also designed to take advantage of the natural curiosity of children and the inherent researcher inside each and every youngster. In many ways, this is a book of change, from tiresome worksheets, outdated textbooks, and mundane activities and "ho-hum" projects done year after year. I hope you will consider this book invigorating, exciting, joyful, amazing, magical, and delightful—all characteristics that can, and should be, part of any classroom social studies program.

—Tony Fredericks

Part I

Social Studies and the Internet

Chapter 1

Introduction

An Adventure of the Mind

Social studies is fun. Social studies is an exploration of and an investigation into the unknown. Social studies is learning more about what we don't know, filling in gaps in our knowledge base, changing old ideas, modifying concepts, and discovering that we don't necessarily have all the answers just because we know a bunch of facts. In some ways, social studies is a testament to our own innate ignorance, an ignorance born of a desire to know more about ourselves and our world, not one signifying a complete lack of knowledge.

For children, social studies can and should become a dynamic and interactive discipline. It should allow them to examine new ideas, play around with concepts and precepts, and discover that there is no such thing as a body of finite knowledge. What does this mean for teachers? It means that students must be given a multitude of opportunities to probe, poke, and peek into the mysteries of their world, whether that world is their own backyard or a country far away.

Social studies should also give children a host of opportunities to think, instead of just memorize. Knowing the capitals of European countries or various forms of transportation means very little unless youngsters are provided with opportunities to use that information in some useful way. Asking students to store that information in their minds is not helping them *learn* social studies, but rather is asking them to *parrot* social studies. Little appreciation of the wonders of the worldwide community grows from this procedure, and little application of the facts and figures of social studies comes about through this "traditional" way of presenting social studies. Indeed, social studies is more than numbers, charts, and graphs—it is a venture and an *adventure* of the mind—constantly learning and relearning new data and new ideas. Providing youngsters with opportunities to pose questions about their world, question basic assumptions, or actively seek solutions to various mysteries places a value on the power of the human mind—particularly the minds of children.

Principles of Social Studies Instruction

Students need many opportunities to make sense out of their world as well as lay a foundation from which future discoveries can emanate. The following guidelines should be considered as markers from which kids can grow in social studies:

1. Students need to be provided with a basic body of knowledge that will form the foundation for future discoveries. Being able to identify goods and services may be important in helping students gain an appreciation of the community in which they live. Knowing the geography of the West provides a basis for students to comprehend the trials and travails of early pioneers. Yet meaningful social studies programs must move beyond these facts. In short, an accumulation of facts is no more social studies than a collection of bricks is a house.

2. Children need to use social studies information in a practical and personal sense. Social studies instruction should be geared toward offering youngsters many opportunities to put their knowledge into practice, to see social studies as a daily human activity, and to increase their appreciation of the world around them.

3. Children must take some responsibility for their own learning. They need opportunities to make their own choices or select learning opportunities based on their goals and interests. Kids who are given those choices begin to assume greater control over their personal learning and are more willing to pursue learning for its own sake. In short, social studies is *learned* more than it is *taught*.

4. Students need to understand the interdependencies and interrelationships that exist among all elements of the world around them. They need to grasp the role of social studies in promoting those understandings.

5. Children are naturally active. The very nature of social studies implies an action-oriented and process-oriented approach to learning. By this I mean that children need to "get their hands dirty" in social studies, to manipulate objects, try out different approaches, look around them, and get involved. Kids do this all the time; it's part of the cycle of learning.

6. Children need to be stimulated in diverse ways. The social studies curriculum is enhanced when students have multiple and varied learning opportunities. Students need to know that the skills they have previously relied on can be used to foster a better understanding of new areas of discovery and exploration.

7. Students need to use social studies information in practical and personal ways. Possessing the skills of social studies is one thing; being able to use those skills in a meaningful context is quite another. Elementary social studies instruction should be geared toward offering youngsters a myriad of opportunities to put their knowledge into practice.

8. Children need to be engaged in intellectually stimulating encounters with their world. Social studies provides children with a host of opportunities to question and think about their world. They must be provided with critical thinking opportunities and challenging situations that allow them to set their own learning goals and satisfy them through self-discovery.

These principles support the notion that social studies education, to be productive, requires a partnership between teachers and students, the joy of learning, and youngsters' developing curiosity about their environment. Helping students appreciate their potential for contributing to not only their personal knowledge base but also the world around them can be the basis of a lifelong appreciation of social studies.

Six Key Ingredients

What distinguishes "good" social studies instruction from "average" social studies instruction? Well, through several years of study in "real" classrooms with "real" students, researchers have discovered that the following six "key" ingredients are essential elements in every social studies lesson or unit. These keys are based on the latest research available about how kids learn and specifically about how kids learn social studies.

What is most distinctive about these ingredients is that they are all embedded in well-designed social studies lessons. In short, the mastery of social studies concepts is enhanced when these key ingredients are promoted and emphasized.

- **Hands-on approach**—Children need active opportunities to manipulate social studies, to handle social studies, and to "get down and dirty" with social studies. A hands-on approach to social studies has long been promulgated as one of the most effective instructional strategies for any elementary teacher.

- **Process orientation**—Focusing on the processes of social studies (e.g., observing, classifying, inferring, predicting, and communicating) helps students appreciate social studies as a "doing" subject, one that never ends, but rather offers multiple opportunities for continual examination and discovery.

- **Integration**—When social studies is integrated into all aspects of the elementary curriculum, students begin to understand its relevance and relationship to their daily lives outside the classroom. Children begin to comprehend the impact social studies has on daily activities, both in the present and in the future.

- **Cooperative learning**—When children are provided with opportunities to share ideas, discuss possibilities, and investigate problems together, they can benefit enormously from the background knowledge of their peers as well as the strength that comes from a group approach to learning.

- **Critical thinking**—One of the issues classroom teachers have wrestled with for many years concerns the need to help students become independent thinkers. In other words, effective social studies instruction is not dependent on helping students memorize lots of information but rather on assisting them in being able to use data in productive and mutually satisfying ways.

- **Authentic assessment**—Weaving together formal and informal assessment procedures naturally and normally throughout all aspects of a lesson (beginning, middle, end) is the crux of good instruction. Students should be provided with active opportunities to take a role in their own assessment; this is both motivating and stimulating.

Social Studies, the Internet, and Your Classroom

The Internet can be a natural and normal part of students' experiences with social studies. Internet resources provide youngsters with valuable opportunities to extend and expand their knowledge of the world around them. The Web helps kids develop a rich appreciation for the social studies concepts, values, and generalizations contained within the social studies curriculum. The Internet underscores the idea that social studies is much more than a dry accumulation of facts and figures. Youngsters will learn that Web resources allow them to explore and investigate their immediate and far-flung environment in an arena that has no limits.

By sharing technology with the students with whom you work you are helping to promote their natural curiosity and inquisitiveness and encouraging and stimulating them in the following ways:

1. The Internet provides youngsters with an ever-expanding array of information in a welcome format. Youngsters realize that social studies is not relegated to the pages of a textbook, but can be found in both the near and distant corners of their world.

2. Internet sites extend and expand specific social studies concepts beyond information typically presented in textbooks. Social studies Web sites allow students to explore a topic in greater depth and develop a greater appreciation of its nuances.

3. Well-designed Web sites offer students a variety of information from several angles or points of view. Youngsters learn that social studies knowledge is never static—it's always growing and changing.

4. Web resources help students understand the many ways in which knowledge can be shared, discussed, and evaluated. A variety of related Web sites helps youngsters comprehend social studies as a dynamic subject.

5. The Internet provides children with new information and knowledge unobtainable in any other format. Topics in which new discoveries are being made at a rapid rate (e.g., exploration of ancient civilizations, changing land forms, geopolitical shifts) can be shared through up-to-the-minute reports on the Web.

6. Social studies Web sites open up the world and assist students in making their own self-initiated discoveries. In many ways, the Internet encourages kids to ask their own questions and provides them with the impetus to initiate their own investigations. It stimulates their natural inquisitiveness and enhances their appreciation of the known and the unknown.

7. Learning social studies via the Web is fun. Technology gives students a vehicle with which they can explore, discover, investigate, and examine the world in which they live.

The Internet can be a powerful motivator for the elementary classroom as well as for the natural activities that teachers and children can share. You are encouraged to use this book as a stimulus to youngsters' natural tendency to seek answers to their innumerable questions. You are further encouraged to use the Web sites cited in this volume as "instigators" for scientific discoveries and investigations throughout the months and years ahead. The Internet is a vehicle for stimulating social studies teaching and promoting authentic social studies learning. The benefits are many and the possibilities unlimited.

Chapter 2

The Internet and Instruction

The Internet is a powerful, worldwide communications system. Often referred to as a "network of networks," it connects thousands of computer networks all over the world. It does this through data lines that can transmit information at high rates of speed.

It is an equally powerful resource for classroom teachers and their students. In many ways, it has reshaped our curriculum and the ways in which knowledge is shared with youngsters. That it has redefined our responsibilities is a given; it has also redefined the ways in which children learn and in which we can facilitate that process.

Researching the Internet

Consider the Internet as a very large library. In a large library the researcher has myriad resources, books, periodicals, microfiche, and the like at her or his fingertips. In a large library there will be excellent research materials as well as materials that are barely appropriate or are far out of date. Some of the materials will be easy to find, but it will take an intensive search to locate others. As in most libraries, there will be individuals who can assist in the search process and there will be times when the researcher will be on her or his own in tracking down leads and locating appropriate materials.

Just like a large library, the Internet has its advantages and its disadvantages. Researchers (in this case, students) need to know how to get around this enormous library, whom to ask for assistance, and the validity of the information they seek. Some of the information they collect will be accurate, up-to-date, and precise; other information will be out-of-date, incomplete, or inappropriate. Just because it's online doesn't necessarily mean that the information is useful any more than a book being in a library means that that reference is needed or necessary to one's search for information.

The information on the Internet is but one tool in a researcher's arsenal. It is as good as the researcher makes it or as poor as the individual who put it together. In short, just because something is online doesn't make it valid, appropriate, or necessary.

The Internet Research Paradigm

To assist students in the appropriate use of the Internet, I have developed a modification of the six-step research cycle for information problem solving (Eisenberg and Berkowitz, 1990). This paradigm forms the basis for the activities and projects described in Part II of this book. You may wish to describe and discuss the components of this paradigm with your students prior to initiating these units in your classroom.

- **Questions**—Good research emanates from good questions—particularly self-initiated questions. It is always appropriate for students to generate their own questions at the beginning of any research project. This helps them focus on the nature and intent of the project and frame it in terms that are meaningful to them. To assist you in this process, each of the units includes selected research questions you can ask students in groups or individually. These questions should encourage students to ask their own questions and pursue answers to those self-initiated queries.

- **Site investigation**—The research questions provide students with a structure. They must then assemble a list of Internet sites with which to investigate the questions they posed. Checking search engines for appropriate sites and listing and/or eliminating inappropriate sites are all part of this process. The units in this book provide you and your students with selected Web sites to investigate. As stated elsewhere in this book, other sites may be added to this list as they become available or as others are modified or eliminated.

- **Data gathering**—At this stage in the process students go online to obtain the information they need to answer the questions they have generated. It is here that students should have knowledge about the appropriateness of a site to determine its worthiness as a research tool. Making quick evaluations of sites is an important skill at this stage.

- **Data analysis**—After students have accessed the necessary information from selected Web sites, they must analyze it. They must eliminate unnecessary or inappropriate information and keep pertinent and relevant data. This stage may take a substantial amount of time depending on the amount of preliminary information gathered.

- **Compare and contrast**—Students should have sufficient opportunities to compare and contrast the information collected from the Internet with other information sources. For the units in this book, students can accomplish this comparison process through the use of relevant children's literature. Students will be able to contrast print resources with online resources to determine the depth and breadth of their information and to gauge its validity. Although literature is promoted as a natural mechanism for this evaluation process, students should also be encouraged to utilize other print resources (e.g., monographs, flyers, brochures) for validation purposes.

• **Extending**—Collecting information from one or more Web sites is a valid activity. Students should be offered sufficient opportunities to put that information to work. Each unit in this book contains a variety of "hands-on, minds-on" activities that stimulate intellectual pursuits and offer numerous extensions for comprehending the material collected. Students can use their newfound knowledge in productive, meaningful, and personal extensions. They will see the relevance of Internet resources as "promoters" of intellectual curiosity and investigation. The Internet becomes a valid tool in students' lifelong quest for information and the "gainful employment" of the data in personally satisfying quests.

This paradigm is illustrated in figure 2.1. Note that it is a continuous process: After students have engaged in an appropriate number of extending activities, they will undoubtedly generate additional questions about the topic. From those questions the process begins all over again. The Internet becomes but one tool in a student's search for information, purpose, and comprehension. Most important, that quest is student-initiated and directed. Teachers become information facilitators, offering learning opportunities and encouraging students to pursue topics via multiple resources.

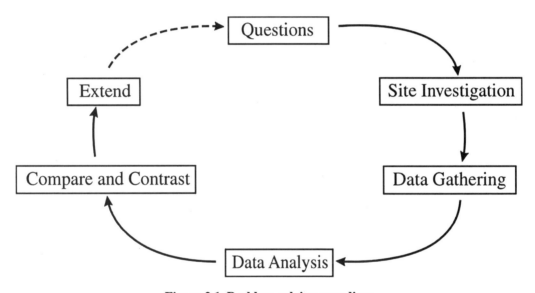

Figure 2.1 Problem-solving paradigm.

A Process of Implementation

This book has been designed for busy teachers. It offers you and your students a plethora of activities, projects, and investigations into every topic and subject in the elementary social studies curriculum. It is both a resource and a tool. For you and your students to achieve the maximum benefit from this book, follow these procedures:

1. Become familiar with the hardware, software, and systems that you plan to use in your classroom. It is a fact of classroom life that the unexpected should always be expected, particularly in areas of technology, so be prepared.

2. Check each site before assigning it to your students. The Internet is always changing, always evolving. It is quite possible that an address has changed or is no longer current. Pages may have been eliminated and new pages may have been added. As always, knowing what your students will be using will eliminate problems later on.

3. Plan to check any sites for their grade appropriateness. Each unit in this book offers several sites that have been selected for their content and appropriate grade levels. You need to know if the sites you assign your students are appropriate to their varying reading levels and/or intellectual sophistication.

4. Emphasize to your students that the Internet is only one research tool at their disposal. Make sure students understand the relevance and connection between any Internet projects and the regular curriculum.

5. Set up specific Web sites as "Bookmarks" or "Favorites." This will enable your students to organize their searches more efficiently within a content area. Refer to your browser help screen or manual for directions on how to accomplish this.

6. Have a backup plan available if certain Web sites cannot be accessed. You probably know that it is not always possible to access selected Web sites. Popular sites (such as those maintained by NASA) are frequently busy during regular school hours. Sometimes the system may be off-line, refusing connections, or the receiving modem may be busy. The recommended children's literature and accompanying activities for each unit in this book will provide you with a variety of options to teach a selected concept. Thus, if sites are busy, you will still be able to engage students in meaningful activities.

7. Be sure your students have sufficient opportunities to learn and practice basic computer and Internet skills. Technology is changing so rapidly that not only is it essential that teachers keep up-to-date on the latest innovations, it is equally important that students be provided with necessary instruction and constant practice in computer literacy skills.

8. Check the sites students are accessing and the materials available on those sites frequently. This book, and other similar resources, is designed as an instructional aid. This does not imply that students should be given a task and left to fend for themselves. Student work must be constantly and consistently monitored.

Web Searching

As of the writing of this book there are approximately 900 million pages of text on the Internet, and that number is growing at the rate of about 500 pages every day. To say that there is a lot of information on the Internet would be an obvious understatement. Anyone who has listed a topic on a search engine knows that there can be an unlimited number of pages for any single subject (list "Transportation," for example, and you'll get more than 16,000 Web pages).

Search engines are the primary research tool for discovering information on the Internet. A search engine is nothing more than an indexing service of Web sites. These indexes are updated frequently and are organized according to the cataloguing procedures of each search engine. Some Web sites are indexed according to their titles; others are listed according to the full text of the site.

Search engines are accessed by clicking on the Search button on the menu bar of the Web browser or by typing in the URL. When the search program is displayed, a search can be initiated by typing a key word or phrase related to the topic desired. Table 2.1 lists some of the more common search engines.

Table 2.1
Search Engines

AltaVista ....http://www.altavista.com
Deja News...http://www.deja.com
Dogpile ....http://www.dogpile.com
Excite ....http://www.excite.com
Google ....http://www.google.com
Goto..http://goto.com
HotBot..http://www.hotbot.com
Infoseek ....http://infoseek.go.com
LookSmart...http://www.looksmart.com
Lycos...http://www.lycos.com
Magellan ....http://www.magellan.com
Northern Light ....http://www.northernlight.com
Profusion ....http://www.profusion.com
SavvySearch...http://www.savvysearch.com
Snap..http://www.snap.com
Yahoo! ....http://www.yahoo.com

There are also search engines devoted exclusively to Web sites that are appropriate for children. Each of the Web sites listed on these engines has been pre-screened and is considered child-safe for all students. Teachers and parents can rest assured that these search engines prevent access to adult or inappropriate materials. Table 2.2 presents some of the best.

Table 2.2
Child-Appropriate Search Engines

Lycos Kids Guide...http://www.lycos.com/kids
Magellan ....http://www.magellan.com
Searchopolis ....http://www.searchopolis.com
Yahooligans...http://www.yahooligans.com

For complex topics you can save a lot of time by utilizing a metasearch engine. A metasearch engine submits a request for information to several different search engines at the same time. The results are then arranged on a list from high frequency citations to low frequency citations. Metasearch engines are time-saving and labor-saving ways of obtaining lots of information in a very short amount of time. Table 2.3 lists some of the more popular metasearch engines.

Table 2.3
Metasearch Engines

All in One ....http://www.allonesearch.com
Beaucoup Search Engines ....http://www.beaucoup.com
C/NET Search ....http://search.cnet.com
Internet Search Sites ....http://www.refdesk.com/newsrch.html
Metacrawler http://www.go2net.com/search.html
Webcrawler..http://Webcrawler.com
W3 Search Engines.........................http://osiris.sunderland.ac.uk/rif/W3searches.html

Lesson Plans

You can enhance any lesson in social studies by accessing a wide variety of lesson plans on the Web. As you might imagine, the quality and content of these lessons vary, but most do offer some unique ways of updating and reinvigorating portions of your social studies program. Consider the Web sites listed in Table 2.4 as positive adjuncts to your curriculum.

Many of the listed sites also offer course outlines, updated reference and resource materials, curriculum guides, standards-based units, and specific projects and experiments. A careful and judicious review of these materials can add sparkle to "tired" lessons and reinvigorate many areas of the social studies program.

Table 2.4
Lesson Plan Resources

Address	Description
http://www.cln.org/cln.html	The Community Learning Network is designed to help classroom teachers integrate technology into their classrooms. They have over 250 menu pages with more than 5,400 annotated links to educational World Wide Web (WWW) sites. Truly a magnificent resource!
http://server2.greatlakes.k12.mi.us/	This incredible collection of teacher resources is available for downloading. Included are lesson plans, computer software, Hypercard files, new resources, thematic units, guest speakers, field trips, and student-created material resources.

(continued)

Table 2.4 *Continued.*

Address	Description
http://www.teachers.net/lessons	Take a lesson, leave a lesson at the Teachers Net Lesson Exchange. The lessons cover all subjects and grade levels and include links to the teachers who posted the lessons. This is an excellent Web site that will energize the overall classroom curriculum.
http://www.pacificnet.net/~mandel	This is a wonderful place to share ideas, concerns, and questions with educators from around the world. The material is updated weekly and you'll be able to obtain lesson plans in every curricular area. Also included are teaching tips for both new and experienced teachers.
http://cccnet.com	This site assists teachers in taking advantage of the vast resources of the Internet. It includes teacher discussion and bulletin board areas as well as online projects teachers can do with their classes.
http://www.teachnet.com/lesson/index.html	This site offers classroom teachers an array of lesson plans in every curricular area. This is an easy-to-use resource.
http://www.education-world.com	Education World claims to be the "world's educational resource on the Web." Its database contains more than 120,000 URLs, many of which are annotated. Teachers can search by keyword or by selecting topic areas.
http://www.ceismc.gatech.edu/busyt	The Busy Teachers' Website provides classroom teachers with a host of educational Web sites in a wide variety of curricular areas. Lots to search here.
http://encarta.msn.com/schoolhouse/default.asp	This incredible resource taps into the power of Microsoft. Here you'll find loads of lesson plans and a wide range of updated resources for every aspect of your classroom curriculum.

(continued)

Table 2.4 *Continued.*

Address	Description
http://www.gsn.org	The Global School House offers a diverse collection of Internet sites, videoconferencing opportunities, professional development activities, contests, and discussion lists for teachers and parents.
http://www.scholasticnetwork.com	The Scholastic Network bills itself as "The best Internet research tool for kids." At this all-inclusive site you'll discover an amazing variety of resources for you and your students. There's simply too much to list here, but you won't be disappointed!

Online Experts

Wouldn't it be great if students could have experts in particular areas of study visit the classroom to offer their expertise on a subject? Well, they can! Experts are available online to answer questions posed by students and supply them with necessary information.

Students can access the expertise of scientists and other experts within and throughout any social studies project. Various Web sites (see Table 2.5) provide students with opportunities to pose questions to working scientists and receive answers in return. Scientists and experts in fields as diverse as geography, economics, political science, history, and anthropology can be contacted via e-mail to obtain up-to-the-minute answers to questions.

Querying working experts in a particular field provides youngsters with relevant data about specific topics. Students should understand, however, that the experts are all working individuals. Every attempt is made to transmit a response back to students in a reasonable amount of time (usually two to three days), but the nature of experts' daily work obligations or field research may prevent that from happening. The experts utilized on each of the sites in Table 2.5 have been carefully selected as responsive to student questions; however, students need to know that they are working social scientists first and that the time they have available for answering questions may be limited.

Many of these sites also maintain lists of some of the most frequently asked questions along with their accompanying responses. Invite students to search these lists before posing a question. Often, the question will have been asked (and answered) previously.

Several sites are also appropriate for teacher use. Posing a question to a working social scientist can provide you with fresh ideas and new perspectives on a specific topic. It's a wonderful way to stay up-to-date on the latest advancements and discoveries and reinvigorate tried-and-true lesson plans.

**Table 2.5
Online Experts**

Address	Description
http://www.ajkids.com	Ask Jeeves for Kids allows students to pose their own questions (in their own language). This site will then provide youngsters with kid-friendly Web sites through which they can obtain the answer(s) to their questions. This is a great resource for any area of the elementary curriculum.
http://ericir.syr.edu/Qa	AskERIC's question and answer service utilizes the diverse resources and expertise of the national ERIC system. The Ask ERIC staff will respond to your question within two business days with ERIC database citations and publications, Internet resources, and referrals to other sources of information. They state that they respond "to EVERY question with personalized resources."
http://www.xpertsite.com	Wow, what a site! Loads of expert connections in a wide variety of subjects and topics. This is the ideal research tool for teachers.
http://www.askanexpert.com	This site connects students with hundreds of real world experts, ranging from astronauts to zookeepers. These experts have volunteered to answer student questions for free.
http://www.vrd.org/locator/subject.html	The AskA+ Locator is an all-inclusive expert site in a wide variety of topic areas. More than 100 expert sites are listed here (with hyperlinks to each). Ideal for both teachers and students.

Informing Parents

As teachers have long known intuitively and as has been validated with a significant body of research, parents play a major role in the education of any child. It has been proven that the bond established between teachers and parents is also a significant factor in the scholastic achievement of students.

For many parents the "inclusion" of technology in the classroom is both exciting and frightening (just as it is for teachers). It is imperative that parents be informed about Internet use in any classroom—such information helps ensure their participation in and support of the overall academic program.

To assist you in that regard, the following "Parental Agreement Form" can be duplicated and sent home to parents at the beginning of the school year. The form tells parents about the utilization of technology in the affairs of the classroom and solicits their support and permission. This ensures that parents are "recruited" as educational partners in your Internet projects.

Parental Agreement Form

Dear Parent/Guardian:

Our class is about to begin some exciting new discoveries and adventures in social studies. We will be examining Internet Web sites in many different areas. This will be a valuable learning opportunity for your child—one that will expand and enhance the entire social studies curriculum.

Your child will be assigned several projects and activities related to the Internet. Please be assured that we will carefully monitor and supervise all computer activities. Like you, we do not wish any student to have access to inappropriate materials.

Our guidelines for using the Internet are quite specific and detailed. All students have received the following instructions:

• Students may not list their names or addresses on any outgoing e-mail or subscription services.

• Students may not access inappropriate materials or Web sites not approved by the faculty or staff.

• Students may not use inappropriate language.

• Students have been advised that e-mail is not considered private mail and may be checked as warranted.

Please talk with your child about using the Internet at school and at home. Afterwards, please sign and return the form at the bottom by _____. (Date)

- -

My child and I have discussed appropriate uses of the Internet. Although the school will make every attempt to restrict controversial materials, I understand that it may be impossible to filter everything. By my signature below, I give my child permission to engage in appropriate Internet activities at school.

Parent/Guardian: _____ Date: _____

I have discussed appropriate uses of the Internet with my parent/guardian. I fully understand my responsibilities and know that any violation may result in my computer privileges being revoked.

Student: _____ Date: _____

The Internet can be a powerful teaching tool and a powerful learning tool. Its utilization within and throughout your social studies curriculum can provide your students with a wealth of learning opportunities available in no other format. Equally, it can offer you an enormous variety of teaching opportunities that go far beyond curriculum guides and teacher manuals. In many ways, it is a resource that "breaks down" the four walls of the classroom and opens kids' eyes to the far corners of the world.

References

Eisenberg, M., and R. Berkowitz. 1990. *Information problem-solving: The big six skills approach to library and information skills instruction.* Norwood, NJ: Ablex Publishing.

Chapter 3

How to Use This Book

The units included in Part II of this book emphasize key concepts throughout the social studies curriculum. In addition, the activities and projects included in each unit integrate skills from a variety of areas to ensure a unique, multidisciplinary, and interdisciplinary study of social studies.

Using a Unit

The units are designed to be complete and thorough guides. However, you are not required to use any single unit in its entirety. You may elect to use selected portions of a unit, combine one section of a unit with other classroom curricular materials, or eliminate some sections of a unit due to lack of materials or time. The true value of these units lies in the fact that they can be easily adapted, modified, or adjusted according to the dictates of your social studies program, your "level of comfort," or students' interests.

The units (which can be used alone, in conjunction with a corresponding thematic unit, or in concert with another unit) offer engaging literature, activities, and Internet projects for a specific social studies concept. Each unit includes activities, questions, Web sites, and related works of literature to provide you with a variety of choices through which to develop targeted content objectives and skills.

Each unit is divided into five separate, yet inter-related, sections, described next.

Introduction

Each unit is prefaced with a brief introduction. These introductions are designed to provide you with basic factual information necessary to an understanding of the social studies concepts and ideas promoted in various activities in the unit.

Each introduction is addressed to the teacher using the unit. However, you may choose to share these introductions with your students as a preliminary activity. Students should understand that the introduction provides only a modicum of information and that more in-depth data will need to be accessed via the Web sites and literature. After students have had sufficient opportunities to gather their own data, invite them to prepare and write their own introduction for a selected unit. These introductions, framed in "kid language," may be just the ticket for stimulating other groups or classes of students to pursue a topic later in the year or in succeeding years.

Research Questions

The second section of each unit includes carefully designed research questions that can be posed to students prior to the start of a unit, while the unit is in process, or at its conclusion. They are not intended to be evaluation questions, but rather opportunities for students to think about some of the basic concepts behind the designated topic.

Many of the questions for a specific unit can be answered via the Web sites and/or the selected literature. This offers youngsters opportunities to research specific aspects of a topic in some detail. It also offers task-oriented queries through which you can monitor student progress.

The questions listed in this section are suggestions only. You are not obliged to use all of them. You should invite your students to generate their own list of questions and add them to the ones suggested here. Maintain those additional questions in a "question bank" and share them with other groups of students or with classes in succeeding years. A collection of student-initiated questions infused into these units can be a powerful stimulant to further exploration and discoveries.

Web Sites

Each unit includes a selection of specific Web sites. These sites are designed to provide you and your students with a broad range of experiences, discoveries, and explorations in various aspects of the topic. Some sites will be general, others more specific.

Please note that the Web site addresses included in any single unit were current and accurate as of the writing of this book. The evolving nature of the Internet is such that some addresses will become defunct, others will change, and new ones will be added to the Internet on a daily basis. You should feel free to add your own favorite sites to the ones suggested here. By the same token, feel free to eliminate those sites that are no longer current or operational.

To assist you in selecting those sites that will be most useful for your students, each site has a brief annotation. These summaries will guide you in selecting those sites that offer important background information as well as those through which students can gather necessary information. The coding system in Table 3.1 is provided to help you select the most appropriate sites for any particular topic.

Table 3.1
Coding System

S: K–3..Site is appropriate for students in Grades K–3
S: 4–6..Site is appropriate for students in Grades 4–6
S: All..Site is appropriate for all students
T: K–3..Site is appropriate for teachers in Grades K–3
T: 4–6 ....Site is appropriate for teachers in Grades 4–6
T: All...Site is appropriate for all teachers

Literature Resources

The literature listed for each unit is designed to offer you and your students multiple opportunities to investigate aspects of the topic in greater detail. Books listed come from a variety of sources and "recommended literature" lists. As you might imagine, some topics have a profusion of related literature sources, whereas for others there is a dearth of relevant books. I have tried, whenever possible, to provide you with the most up-to-date and easily accessible literature available.

The literature reflects a range of reading levels. You should feel free to select and use literature that best meets the needs and abilities of your students in addition to promoting specific social studies concepts. An "energized" social studies curriculum will include literature selections throughout its length and breadth. You will discover innumerable opportunities for developing, expanding, and teaching social studies principles based on the literature in these units. Remember that the readability or difficulty level of a single book should not determine if or how it will be used; rather, the emphasis should be on whether students are interested and motivated to pursue literature-related activities that promote learning in a supportive and holistic social studies curriculum.

You are encouraged to substitute and/or include in any unit books that you have found to be particularly noteworthy, those that are old-time favorites or new releases, or recommendations from colleagues or professional resources. The utility of a unit lies in the fact that the literature used can come from a variety of sources and is not relegated to the suggestions made here. Keeping these units "fresh" and updated with new literature resources can be a powerful stimulant for both teacher and student interest.

Activities and Projects

Each unit contains a wide scope of activities designed to promote growth in critical thinking, creative thinking, problem solving, and social studies research. This gives students unlimited opportunities to process and interpret information while learning relevant knowledge and concepts. I have suggested a variety of activities. You are encouraged to select the ones most appropriate for your students and your social studies program objectives.

You are not expected to use all those activities nor all parts of any single activity. Instead, you and your students should decide on those activities, Web sites, and literature that best serve the needs of the social studies program and of the students themselves. You will discover activities that can be used individually, in small groups, in large groups, or as a whole class. Providing students with opportunities to make some of their own selections can be a powerful and energizing element for the entire social studies program. When youngsters are given those opportunities, their appreciation of social studies and their interest in learning important concepts grows tremendously.

As students become involved in the various units, I suggest that you guide them in researching and/or developing other activities based on classroom dynamics and teaching/learning styles. For learning to be meaningful, it must have relevance. I encourage you and your students to adapt the activities included in the units to create a challenging learning environment that will arouse each student's natural curiosity and encourage students to pursue new ideas and formulate their own connections.

I hope you will make these units your own. Add to them, adapt them, and allow students to help you design additional activities, experiments, and projects that will challenge them, arouse their natural curiosity, and create a dynamic learning environment.

Implementing a Unit

Teaching social studies with these units is not necessarily an "all or nothing" proposition. That is, it is not necessary to use a unit for a full day or a full week. You have several options to consider depending on how you want to present a unit to your class, how much you want it to dominate your daily curriculum, and how involved you and your students want to be. Obviously, your level of comfort with the Internet and the scope and sequence of your classroom or district social studies curriculum may determine the degree to which you utilize a unit. Following are some options for using the units in your classroom:

1. Teach a unit throughout a school day and for an extended period of several school days.

2. Teach a unit for one-half day for several days in succession.

3. Use a unit for two or more subject areas (e.g., social studies plus language arts) in combination and the regular curriculum for other subjects.

4. Use a unit as the "curriculum" for social studies and the regular curriculum for other subjects.

5. Teach a unit for an entire day and follow up with the regular curriculum in succeeding days.

6. Use a unit as a follow-up to information and data presented in a textbook or curriculum guide.

7. Provide students with a unit as independent work upon completion of lessons in the basal textbook.

8. Teach cooperatively with a colleague to present a unit to both classes at the same time. (This can be done with two classes at the same grade or two different classes, each at a different grade level.)

9. Use a unit intermittently over the span of several weeks.

How you use a unit may be determined by any number of factors. It is safe to say that there is no ideal way to integrate a unit into your classroom plans. This list is only a partial collection of ideas. Your own particular teaching situation, personal experience, and students' needs will suggest alternatives to this register of ideas.

Part II

Internet Social Studies Units

Chapter 4

My World

I Am Special

 Introduction

Children need to belong; they need to know that they are important—not only to others, but to themselves as well. This sense of belonging helps instill a basic feeling of self-worth, a feeling that carries over into everyday life as much as into later life. Letting children know that they are special is a natural "duty" of teachers and parents alike. The feelings of worth engendered in children in their early years have a significant impact on the academic, social, and emotional development they experience throughout their school years and beyond.

 Research Questions

1. What can be done to make someone feel special?

2. How does it feel to be special?

3. How do people act when they feel special?

4. Can we tell people they are special without words? If so, how?

5. Are you special? Why?

 Web Sites

http://www.dadsanddaughers.org/
Wonderful suggestions are provided at this site to encourage children to perceive themselves based on the qualities they have and their personality rather than on their physical features. The main focus is body image; without a positive body image, children won't be as happy as they should be. (S: 4–6)

http://www.lil-fingers.com/
This site is designed for parents and young school-age children. It has links to different stories for parents and children to read together. Tips are also provided for parents on how to most effectively read with their children. Recommended links are also present for books, music, and videos for children. (S: K–3)

http://www.pburg.k12.nj.us/Thematic%20Curriculum/I_Am_Special_K01.html
This thorough Web site takes the topic "I Am Special" and integrates it with subject areas in the classroom. It provides literature sources for teachers and children to explore, along with songs and activities to complement them. Questions are presented for children to answer after they have completed their activities. (T: All)

Literature Resources

Choi, Sook Nyul. (1993). *Halmoni and the Picnic*. Boston: Houghton Mifflin.
This book provides wonderful ideas about how to make people feel more comfortable in new areas; the best part is that it beautifully illustrates how children can make adults feel special. In return, this makes the child feel even more special for playing such an important role in life.

Hoffman, Mary. (1991). *Amazing Grace*. New York: Dial Books for Young Readers.
An African American girl is told that she cannot play the part of Peter Pan in an upcoming play. Her peers tell her she cannot play this part not only because she is a girl but also because she is an African American, and Peter Pan was white and a boy. Luckily, Grace ignores their comments and follows the advice of her grandmother to give it all she's got.

Parton, Dolly. (1994). *Coat of Many Colors*. New York: HarperCollins.
Despite the ridicule of other children, a less-fortunate girl wears a coat that was made out of rags by her mother. She is very proud of her coat and doesn't let her classmates bring her down because she knows her coat was made with love.

Thiesing, Lisa. (1998). *Me and You*. New York: Hyperion Books for Children.
This book is illustrated like a photo album. Through the photos, a mother explains how much her daughter is like she was when she was a girl. It brings back beautiful memories for a mother and draws a deeper connection between a mother and daughter.

Zolotow, Charlotte. (1980). *Say It!* New York: Greenwillow Books.
This fun book introduces children to different ways that love is expressed. It is terrific in depicting how the love of a mother for her little girl permeates a walk they take together on an autumn day. Although the little girl doesn't realize what her mother is doing, she is thrilled in the end when her mom says the three special words she's been waiting to hear all day.

Activities and Projects

1. Have students construct a big book that contains pictures and information about how to make people feel special. Ask each child to contribute as many ideas as possible to the book. Ask the children to read books and check out the Internet sources available to them during a selected time in the classroom. Provide each student with large sheets of paper to construct the data and pictures. When everyone is finished, bind the pages together and display the book where the class can refer to it throughout the school year.

2. Place each student's name in a hat and ask each child to pick a name, making sure it is not her or his own. Ask the students to keep their person's name a secret. Ask the students to use the books and Internet sources to list in their journal ways to make people feel special. During the week, encourage each student to refer to the journal for ways to make the selected person feel special. If possible, the students should also try to keep their own names secret. As the week progresses, give the students time at the end of each day to write about what they did to make their partners feel special and what

someone did to make them feel special. At the beginning of the following week, ask the children to share with the class one thing that their partners did to make them feel really special during the previous week. After sharing, the person who made another feel special should stand up and reveal herself or himself.

3. Provide the class with literary resources and Internet sites on the topic "I Am Special." Ask the class to design and participate in a skit about why each student is special. Encourage the students to share with their friends what they feel is special about that person. Choose a day for the students to perform their skit for the school. After their performance, ask the students to encourage people in the audience to stand up and tell what makes them special. When you and your students return to the classroom, ask the students to express on posters their feelings about the skit and what other people said. Display these posters in the room and the hallway.

4. Provide examples of greeting cards that make people feel special. Ask the students: "Who are some special people in the school building?" Create a list of these people and include what makes them special. Have students use the greeting cards as models to make cards for one or more of the people on the list, expressing why that person is important and special to them and the school.

5. Encourage students to go home and ask their parents to tell them why they are special. Ask the children to record what their parents say. While creating something that demonstrates how they felt about what their parents said, students should keep referring to their recordings so thcy remains fresh in their minds. Ask the students to bring their finished projects to school to share with the rest of the class.

6. Ask the students to choose a date for a "Make Someone Feel Special Day." Have the students create posters, banners, invitations, and pamphlets using the Internet, books, friends, and family. Their informative pieces could include an agreed-on color scheme for the day and suggestions about what people can do to make other people feel special. Encourage the children to display their banners and posters and pass out their invitations and pamphlets throughout the school building a week before the big day. Urge students to try to get everyone to participate in this special day. Once the "Make Someone Feel Special Day" passes, encourage the students to get together a petition to make this day a holiday every year for the school.

My Family

Introduction

Families come in all shapes and sizes. Some are traditional, having a mom, dad, and children, and others are non-traditional. Non-traditional families include adopted, single parent, or stepparent families. Some children live with their grandparents and others may have a family member with a disability. No family is the same, but a family is any group of people that live together and care about each other.

Research Questions

1. What is a family?

2. What are some things a family does together?

3. What is special about your family?

4. What are some different kinds of families?

5. Are all families the same?

Web Sites

Note: There are dozens of Web sites that feature individual families around the world. Children may enjoy logging onto these sites to see how different families live as well as learn about their lifestyles. Check out some of the search engines listed earlier in this book.

Literature Resources

Berstein, Joanne & Bryna, Fireside. (1991). *Special Parents, Special Children*. Morton Grove, IL: Albert Whitman.
   This book is about people with special needs and the children they have. It looks at a variety of families that have different exceptionalities, from deafness to blindness.

Brown, Tricia. (1995). *Someone Special, Just Like You*. New York: Henry Holt.
   Black-and-white photos with large-print captions show disabled kids playing and learning in their own environment. The book shows that they aren't much different from others. It emphasizes the fun they have, not their differences.

Rogers, Fred. (1994). *Let's Talk About It: Adoption*. New York: Putnam.
    This book deals with the feelings that adopted children have. They are special people who are cared for and loved in a very special way.

Rylant, Cynthia. (1985). *The Relatives Came*. New York: Bradbury Press.
    This book is about one family's adventure when the relatives from out of town come. It illustrates the look, the smells, and all the fun that come along when out of towners come to stay.

 # Activities and Projects

1. Ask students to interview a family member to describe what type of family they have. Students may want to ask each of several different family members the same questions to see if they all give the same answers. Ask students to record their collected information on a large sheet of newsprint posted along one wall of the classroom ("A Family Graffiti Wall") .

2. Divide the class into several small groups. Ask each group to design a set of questions to be used in interviewing the family of a student from another class. Work with a teacher in a grade higher than yours to arrange a cooperative family interview project in which designated groups of students interview designated families. What kind of new information do they learn about families? How are families similar and different?

3. Ask individual students to construct a brochure entitled 'Welcome to Our Family." Ask youngsters to imagine that a new person (e.g., a baby) is about to join their family. Encourage each child to put together a welcoming document that would introduce the family to the new individual, with particular emphasis on the special features and characteristics of the family.

4. Ask students to create a family tree. Each child may wish to interview family members and relatives about the individuals who make up that family. If possible, children should bring in photos of family members to post on a sheet of construction paper or oaktag. Display family posters along one wall of the classroom.

Friends Share

Introduction

Although many younger children have difficulty understanding the importance of sharing, they need to grasp its importance early in their schooling experience. Sharing makes events and projects more enjoyable. Sharing also helps learning take place. There are numerous advantages to sharing, and it is vital that students learn this early so that the classroom is a more enjoyable and cooperative place.

Research Questions

1. How can we share with our friends?

2. What are the advantages of sharing with friends?

3. Why is it important to share with your friends?

4. What happens when you don't share?

Web Sites

http://www.unicefusa.org/
This Web site discuses the UNICEF Program and how children can use it to help others. Children are given opportunities to volunteer in this program and parents and teachers can find educational materials, including activities, from UNICEF. (S: All, T: All)

Literature Resources

Christelow, Eileen. (1993). *The Five Dog Night*. New York: Clarion Books.
An old man doesn't like his neighbor coming over and bothering him. She is always checking in on him. Finally he becomes extremely angry at her. She stops seeing him. He becomes lonely, then decides to go over and share some cookies with her; they are then friends.

Hoberman, Mary Ann. (1997). *One of Each*. New York: Little, Brown.
This book is about a dog that has one of each of everything and thinks that is perfect, until he has a guest who has a terrible time there. The dog doesn't share with the guest. When he learns that she was not having a good time at his house he goes out and buys more of everything so he can share.

Munsch, Robert. (1999). *We Share Everything*. New York: Scholastic.
    Two children are starting out in kindergarten and they fight for everything. Every time they fight the teacher comes over and tells them they have to share everything. They finally learn this and end up sharing their clothing.

Pfister, Marcus. (1992). *The Rainbow Fish*. New York: North-South Books.
    The most beautiful fish in the entire ocean discovers the real value of personal beauty and friendship when he decides to share his special scales with other fish in the sea.

Silverstein, Shel. (1964). *The Giving Tree*. New York: HarperCollins.
    This book is about a boy and his love for a tree. As he grows up he leaves the tree and comes back whenever he needs something from the tree. The tree happily gives things to him. The tree shares everything it has with the now grown man.

 # Activities and Projects

1. Plan time to discuss the concept of sharing with your students: What does it entail? What are some examples of sharing? What does it feel like to share something with someone? What does it feel like when someone doesn't share something with you? Have students post an oversized sheet of newsprint along one wall of the classroom entitled "Times We Share." Plan time to discuss the entries on the sheet.

2. Ask students to discuss events and times in their own families when they share or when other family members share with them. How do they feel? Why do family members share? Is it easier to share in a family or in a classroom? Ask students to interview their parents about events or incidents in which family members shared ideas or things with each other. Conduct an appropriate discussion in class.

3. Ask students to keep a journal for a week detailing the moments when they share or see others sharing. At the same time, have students notice incidents when sharing does not take place. At the end of the week, have students discuss what they have learned and what they feel are the greatest advantages to sharing or refusing to share.

4. Ask students to create a list of ways they can share with one another in the classroom. Then ask them to create a classroom board game using the list. For example, certain spaces may require the player to share a story with a classmate. After the board game is complete, allow children to play it.

We Need Rules

 ## Introduction

Rules are important to everyday living. They help maintain order and ensure that all individuals perform and behave in appropriate ways. Rules provide order and structure to our everyday lives: We know what to expect and others know what to expect of us. In short, we all play by the same rules.

Children also need to understand that there are consequences when rules are broken. Because society expects us to follow certain rules in certain ways, there are implications when those rules are not followed. Sometimes the consequences are severe, sometimes less so. The important thing for children to understand is that following rules is a part of everyday life, whether one is young or old.

 ## Research Questions

1. Why are rules important in our classroom?

2. Who enforces rules?

3. Why do people need to follow rules?

4. What happens when rules are broken?

 ## Web Sites

http://www.ci.eugene.or.us/dps/police/trfbikes.htm
This site, maintained by the Eugene, Oregon police department, is great for teaching bicycle safety tips. (T: All)

 ## Literature Resources

Cole, Babette. (1996). ***The Bad, Good Manners Book***. New York: Dial Books.
This is a silly book that teaches do's and don'ts through rhymes. Good intentions and the Golden Rule are taught in an unconventional and fun way.

Parish, Peggy. (1994). ***Mind Your Manners!*** New York: Mulberry Books.
This book is recommended for younger children, complete with simple sentences and illustrations. Slightly old fashioned, the etiquette discussed is still very important to life today.

Activities and Projects

1. Ask students to brainstorm different rules of the classroom. Help them formulate a set of rules. Then have students write rules on large sheets of paper, to be posted in the classroom so everyone can see them throughout the school year. This is a great project for the first week of school when setting up the "Students' Classroom."

2. Ask students to pretend that they are the principal of the school. Brainstorm with them about an appropriate set of rules for the school: Should all children be expected to behave in the same way? Should older children have a different set of rules than younger children? Should teachers have a different set of rules than students? Plan appropriate time for small groups of students to design a new set of rules for the school. Later, allow various groups to discuss any similarities and/or differences they may have discovered in their sets.

3. Plan time for students to discuss the people in a community who enforce rules (e.g., police, firefighters): Why are these people needed? What are some of the ways in which they enforce rules? If possible, invite a local law enforcement officer to visit your classroom to talk about rules in the local community and the importance of following those rules as well as enforcing them. Afterwards, have students assemble an informative bulletin board entitled, "Why we follow rules."

4. Ask students to "collect" rules from their families. Have the children assemble the rules into various categories or classifications (e.g., "Rules for Kids," "Rules for Adults," "Rules for When Company Comes," "Rules for the Dinner Table"). Which of the categories has the greatest number of rules? Why? Which group has the fewest number of rules? Ask students to suggest new rules for any "gaps" in the charts.

Community Helpers

Introduction

Community helpers are important to our community. They provide valuable services that help us all function efficiently in society. Community helpers may be visible (police officers, firefighters, sanitation workers) or they may be rarely seen (clerks, administrators). Suffice it to say, most communities need a variety of individuals to make sure services are provided to community residents and that the community functions effectively. This is true whether the community is large or small, rural or urban, mountainous or coastal. It is important for students to know that there are many community members dedicated to serving the needs of the populace in an efficient manner.

Research Questions

1. Who are some community helpers in your community?

2. What does a police officer do for the community?

3. Why are doctors important for the community? How would life be different without doctors?

4. What various responsibilities do firefighters have in the community?

5. Why is it important to volunteer in the community?

6. Why are community helpers so important?

Web Site

http://www.ncpc.org/10act10.htm
   This Web site is wonderful for young students learning about helpers in the community. Students fill in the blanks under each community helper, then use the numbers under the letters to decode the hidden message in the world scramble. (S: K–3)

Literature Resources

Burton, Virginia Lee. (1943). *Katy and the Big Snow*. Boston: Houghton Mifflin.
   This book is about a tractor that has many jobs. One day there is a big snowstorm and she has to plow all the roads so that the people in the community can get through.

Kalman, Bobbie. (1997). *Community Helpers from A to Z*. New York: Crabtree.

In this book readers meet people who make our communities cleaner, safer, more pleasant places to live. Included are agricultural workers, firefighters, recycling workers, and veterinarians.

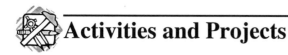 # Activities and Projects

1. Ask students to research selected community workers in your own community. They should check out selected Web sites, read appropriate literature, or interview specific community workers. After students have gathered sufficient information, ask them to take on the roles of specific community workers. Make arrangements with a teacher in another grade to bring students into your room for a "Job Fair." Your students can be interviewed by students from another class regarding the dimensions and responsibilities of their jobs in the local community. Plan time after the fair for students to share relevant information.

2. Invite local community helpers, including parents, doctors, firefighters, police officers, librarians, etc., to discuss their responsibilities with the class. These individuals can be invited into the class on a regularly scheduled day and time (e.g., Friday is "Community Day"). After each visit, encourage students to assemble the information shared into an informative brochure or booklet that can be displayed in the school library.

3. After they have acquired information from classroom guest speakers, the Internet, and literature resources, have students choose a community helper and write a short story detailing one day of their lives without the help of this particular individual. Plan time for students to discuss the short-term and long-term implications of not having that particular individual or position available to the community.

4. Take a class trip to one of the following places: fire department, hospital, library, or veterinary hospital. Have the students take a tour of the area and have them ask the community helpers various questions about their work. Upon returning to school, ask the students to draw pictures showing the information they gained. Display the drawings around the room.

Emotions/Feelings

 ## Introduction

Emotions are distinct qualities of consciousness, such as sadness or joy. Our emotional state is determined and affected by the events occurring in our lives. Major types of emotion are excitement, guilt, sadness, anger, shame, interest, disgust, surprise, fear, and happiness. Our emotions develop during infancy and childhood. It is important to teach children both to recognize the emotions they are feeling and to share, in an appropriate fashion, these emotions with others.

 ## Research Questions

1. Why is it important to share our emotions with others?

2. What are some emotions?

3. What is one situation in which you might feel jealous?

4. Which part of your body shows emotion the most?

5. What are five things you could do to make yourself feel happy if you were having a bad day?

 ## Web Sites

http://www.kidsHealth.org/kid/feeling/
   This Web site explores the many emotions young children have and how to deal with each of them. It is concerned primarily with feelings that arise when growing up and gives examples of places and things that can cheer up children. It also contains a "Kids' Only Closet," packed with easy-to-play games. (S: K–3)

http://www.death-dying.com/child/
   Kids Only is dedicated to helping children recover from the loss of a loved one. Children are encouraged to share art, stories, and feelings. The site also contains games, a special place where questions can be asked, and a book list related to the topic. (S: All, T: All)

 ## Literature Resources

Conlin, Susan & Friedman, Levine. (1989). *All My Feelings at Home: Ellie's Day*. Seattle: Parenting Press.
   This is a book about the feelings that five-year-old Ellie experiences in a single day. Children will relate to Ellie when she feels worried, sad, and excited. Talking about feelings is modeled in this book.

Jahn-Clough, Lisa. (1994). *Alicia Has a Bad Day*. Boston: Houghton Mifflin.

This story is about a little girl who has an especially grumpy day. Her anecdotes to cure her bad mood will amuse children.

Kipfer, Barbara Ann. (1994). *1,400 Things for Kids to Be Happy About: The Happy Book*. New York: Workman.

This book is about everything that children have to be happy or thankful about. Children will realize that they really do have a lot and that the "little things" count.

Sanchez, Enrique O. (1995). *Abuela's Weave*. New York: Lee & Low Books.

This multicultural story from Guatemala teaches about trust, love, and independence. Family pride is also discussed as a grandmother and her granddaughter weave together.

Walsh, Ellen Stoll. (1993). *Brunus and the New Bear*. New York: Harcourt Brace.

This story for younger children discusses Brunus's feelings of jealousy when a new bear appears. This story discusses the feeling of jealousy in a way children can really relate to.

 # Activities and Projects

1. Ask students to express feelings through charades. Prior to playing the game, have the class brainstorm different emotions and how they are most commonly conveyed to people. Students should guess what emotions their peers are acting out, and they must tell what clues were given to them (facial/body expressions).

2. Have each student pick a recent "good" or "bad" day she or he has experienced, then write about that day, including feelings, why she or he felt that way, and how she or he dealt with them. Have students combine stories with illustrations to create a new classroom book.

3. Ask students to create their own classroom bulletin board. They should cut pictures from magazines and place them on the board, to describe things that make them "happy," "sad," "angry," "worried," etc. Divide the bulletin board into sections and ask students to collect appropriate photos and words that can be placed in each category. Plan time to discuss with children their reasons for placing selected words or photos in a specific grouping.

4. Read *Alexander and the Terrible, Horrible, No Good, Very Bad Day* to your students. Afterwards, discuss with them any similarities between Alexander's day and a day that they have experienced. You may wish to post a sheet of newsprint along one wall of the classroom and ask students to list their terrible, no good, very bad experiences. Post a second sheet of newsprint and ask students to list their "Very Good, Outstanding, and Incredible" experiences as well.

Chapter 5

Families and Friends

My Friends

Introduction

Friendship is the relationship between two people who share good times and bad times and are accepting of each other no matter what the circumstances. Friendships are universal: They transcend time, distance, and circumstances. People throughout their lives experience various friendships and various types of friendships. It is important for children to understand that friends don't just happen, however. Good friendships are always a work in progress. They must be nurtured and sustained. Being a friend may be one of the most important "skills" youngsters learn during their early years.

Research Questions

1. What is a friend?

2. How do you become someone's friend?

3. What do friends do for each other?

4. What does it mean when someone is your "best friend?"

Web Sites

http://www.circle-of-friends.com/fun.htm
This Web site discusses people around the world and their different characteristics and personalities. Various characters representing different countries are illustrated. The site also includes coloring sheets, word finds, maze games, and quizzes. (S: All, T: All)

http://www.mamamedia.com/activities/webcards/
This Web site is a place for children to go to make or send cards over the Internet to their friends. (S: All, T: All)

Literature Resources

Aliki. (1979). *The Two of Them*. New York: Greenwillow Books.
This book is about the friendship between a little girl and her grandfather. The book captures the bond that forms between a grandfather and grandchild. It paints a vivid picture of the relationship that forms.

Lobel, Arnold. (1970). *Frog and Toad Are Friends*. New York: Harper & Row.

This book is about two animals who demonstrate the meaning of friendship. It is a short chapter book that describes adventures that frog and toad go through.

Marshall, Edward. (1982). *Fox and His Friends*. New York: The Dial Press.

In this book are three separate episodes in which Fox wants to play with his friends, but duty in one form or another interferes.

McLerran, Alice. (1985). *The Mountain That Loved a Bird*. Saxonville, MA: Picture Book Studio.

In this book the bird, Joy, stops to rest on a mountain that is very harsh and dry. She becomes friends with the mountain and promises to return every spring. Because mountains live longer than birds, Joy promises to send her daughter, and each daughter after that. Over time the mountain undergoes great changes.

Silverstein, Shell. (1964). *The Giving Tree*. New York: HarperCollins.

This book is about a little boy who would visit a tree to eat its apples, swing from its branches, or slide down the trunk. As the boy grew older he wanted more and more from the tree, and the tree gave and gave. The story illustrates the gift of giving and the beauty of unconditional love.

 # Activities and Projects

1. Read the story *The Giving Tree*. Discuss as a class how the tree and the boy had a friendship. Create a tree on a bulletin board. Ask the students to collect pictures, words, or other sentiments that illustrate the individual meaning of friendship. Have the students post two or three of their findings on the tree.

2. Ask the students to review the Web site The Symphony of Friendship. Ask the class to write "Friendship" on the chalkboard. Ask students to volunteer words or ideas that are related to friendship. Have them write a short essay or poem about one of the topics on the board. Have children share their finished products with partners.

3. Have the class sit in a circle to discuss what each child feels is a good way to show a friend appreciation. Then ask students to use an Internet greeting card site to create a greeting card for a friend.

4. Ask students to find the Web site about the two elephants. Afterwards, read the story *Frog and Toad Are Friends*. Discuss with the class whether animals are capable of being friends. Ask the children to write a short paragraph about an animal they know is a friend, such as a pet or in a story they have read.

5. Ask the students to write, illustrate, and share what a best friend is to them. Suggest that it could be a family member, an animal, or a person they know. Ask them to create a biography about this person, including pictures and a timeline of events. When the biographies are completed have the children read them aloud.

6. Create a class friendship chain. Ask each child to write down a quality that is important for being a friend on a strip of colored construction paper. When each child is done, staple the ends together to create a link, then add the links together to create a chain. When it is finished, hang the chain around the classroom.

Family Rules

Introduction

Understanding how families function is an important step in building an understanding of the world. Students need to know what limitations are set by their families, and why. Rules are influenced by the culture of the family. People's culture shapes what is important to them and provides them with values, morals, and beliefs, all of which contribute to the setting of certain rules. An understanding of a person's culture will lead to a better understanding of the rules that person adheres to.

Research Questions

1. Why do families have rules?

2. What is the most important rule in your family?

3. What is the most difficult rule to follow?

4. How do families decide on their rules?

Web Sites

http://www.rainbowraccoons.com/h.htm
The rainbow raccoons list some basic safety and health rules that all children should adhere to. They also illustrate the benefits of following these rules. (S: K–3)

http://www.zstarr.com/doctor/
Family Visits the Doctor is a health education guide for children to color. It presents important medical information for students on annual physical examinations. (S: K–3)

Literature Resources

Gellman, Marc. (1990). *Always Wear Clean Underwear*. New York: Morrow Junior Books.
This book is about "The List," the rules children should live by, not simply because they hear them from their parents but because they are practical. This is an excellent book to use in discussing family rules for any household.

 Activities and Projects

1. Put students in pairs and assign the roles of parents. Ask each pair to compile a list of rules and responsibilities for their children. After they have compiled their lists, ask the pairs to discuss the rules they generated. Plan adequate time to discuss any similarities or differences in those lists. If you wish, ask students to decide which pair of "parents" they would like to have based entirely on the rules that pair generated.

2. Put students in groups of four and ask them to discuss their families' rules. Each group should compile one list of rules that covers all the rules from each of the four group members' families. Once they have compiled that list the group must decide which of the rules is the most practical.

3. Ask students to compile a list of the chores or jobs they perform at home every week. Plan time to discuss how those chores came to be, the duties and responsibilities of the jobs, and the consequences if the jobs are not done. If possible, post individual sheets of newsprint around the room listing the different chores and the responsibilities of each.

4. Ask children to discuss the single most important rule in their individual families. Compile a list of those rules on a sheet of oaktag or on a bulletin board. Encourage discussions about "The Rule." Have students identify or create "The Rule" that governs life in your classroom: How is that mandate similar to or different from "The Rule" that governs family life? Afterwards, ask youngsters to create a list of rules that would be appropriate for every family or a list of rules that would be appropriate for every classroom. Discuss those lists.

School Rules

Introduction

Teachers know better than anyone how crucial it is to have a set, posted list of classroom or school rules. To maintain the correct level of control in the classroom, a teacher must address and explain these rules, remain constant in discipline, and reinforce good behavior in an appropriate manner.

Examples of rules suitable for both the classroom and the entire school include, but are not limited to:

1. Respect others and their belongings.

2. Share.

3. Think about how your behavior affects other people.

4. Be aware of your safety as well as the safety of others.

5. Do your best at all times.

6. Always be a learner.

The best classroom rules are those in which students have ownership. Rules imposed or mandated by a teacher will be significantly less effective than rules designed and created (with appropriate modifications) by students themselves. It is important for students (at any age) to understand that rules are not designed to punish or demean individuals but rather to ensure that everyone has the same set of expectations about behavior. A democratic classroom and facilitative learning environment should be created.

Research Questions

1. What are the basic rights of students in school?

2. What are a student's duties in the classroom?

3. What rights do teachers have in the classroom?

4. What happens when people break the rules?

5. What are the differences between school rules and classroom rules?

Web Sites

http://www.legalpadjr.com/kids.htm

This site was specially designed for children. It explains some basic laws concerning schools. The site also solicits responses from children on current issues involving school law. It then asks children to contribute to creating the laws for a global classroom. A colorful, imaginative way to present information on school law to children, this site offers students a chance to speak out on issues that are important to them. (S: 4–6)

Literature Resources

Dakos, Kalli. (1990). *If You're Not Here, Please Raise Your Hand*. New York: Simon & Schuster.

In this book 38 poems on all aspects of school life provide classroom teachers with some wonderful read-aloud moments and kids with lots of grins and chuckles.

Duffey, Betsy. (1993). *How to Be Cool in the Third Grade*. New York: Viking.

In this book the author focuses on two typical concerns of kids: the need to be somebody special and problems with a school bully.

Howe, James. (1986). *When You Go to Kindergarten*. New York: Mulberry.

This book provides an in-depth look at what it is like to go to kindergarten. The simple text, illustrated with photographs, depicts each step in a typical kindergarten day.

Hurwitz, Joanna. (1990). *Class President*. New York: Morrow.

Julio would love to be class president, but he settles for campaigning for a friend instead. The final results are not what he expected.

Romain, Trevor. (1997). *How to Do Homework Without Throwing Up*. New York: Free Spirit.

In this book is lots of information, presented in an easygoing style for young readers, on how to survive the most dreaded part of any grade.

Schneider, Meg. (1995). *Help! My Teacher Hates Me*. New York: Workman.

For older students, this book offers some common-sense advice on a host of school-related problems, including cheating, grades, and harassment.

Activities and Projects

1. Conduct a class discussion on the importance and purpose of rules, then divide students into groups of four. In these groups they should discuss what rules they feel are necessary for the classroom and brainstorm a list of these rules. Each group should then choose the five to ten rules they feel are most important for the classroom. After they have decided on what rules are the most important, ask them to explain why their rules are important. Then have them write their rules on a large piece of paper and hang it on the chalkboard. They should try to sell the class on their rules. The class should then vote on the ten most important rules. Record these on a poster to be hung in the class.

2. Divide the class into four groups and tell them to pretend they are all members of the board of education. As members of the board of education, they must construct a student handbook for their district. The handbook should include the following: a mission statement, student rights and responsibilities, teacher rights and responsibilities, rules for students and teachers to adhere to, and policies on important information (such as weapons, attendance, drugs/alcohol, sexual harassment). The handbooks should also include consequences of violating the rules and policies. Ask students to share their handbooks with the school principal for comments and suggestions.

3. After studying the importance of rules, discussing the various types of school rules in class, exploring Web sites, and using literature, place students in groups of five to seven to create a skit about what would happen if there were no rules in school. Provide opportunities for students to discuss the implications of their skits within the larger school community or all schools in general.

4. After they have become familiar with the rules of their school by reading the school handbook, ask students to write friendly letters to the members of the school board. These letters can address a rule that students feel is inappropriate and should be changed or a rule that they feel is especially important. Students can write individual letters or letters can be prepared by small groups of students working together. Encourage students to send their letters to the school board and to politely request a response.

Food

Introduction

Civilizations have risen and fallen based entirely on a single staple of life—food. Food has caused countries to send fleets of ships across great oceans and enormous armies into battle. The consumption, transportation, and economics of food have been part of every culture, every country, and many historical events since the beginning of time.

Food is an important concept for students to understand. Not just the nutritional requirements of the food we eat, but also the ways in which history has been shaped and cultures have been influenced by food. Through a study of food, students will learn about social studies, science, language arts, reading . . . . in fact, food is a topic that embraces all curricular areas and provides learning opportunities in a wide variety of disciplines.

Research Questions

1. Why is food important?

2. What are the basic food groups?

3. How does food vary from country to country and family to family?

4. Where does the majority of our food come from?

5. Can anyone create her or his own recipes?

Web Sites

http://www.fsa.usda.gov/edso/ca/agforkids.htm
This Web site describes U.S. farms, in terms of location, crops grown, and animals raised. There are also activities for children to participate in, such as unscrambling the names of California crops, fun facts from the farm, word search, and coloring sheets. (S: 4–6, T: All)

http://ificinfo.health.org/brochure/10tipkid.htm
This Web site includes tips about eating breakfast, exercising, snacking, balancing food choices, and physical activity in school, in a fun and interesting way. (S: 4–6, T: All)

http://www.kidsfood.org/
This site offers students opportunities to choose different activities involving food. There is also a teachers' corner with more information and lesson plans. There is also a parents' corner where parents can learn constructive ways to help their children eat better. (S: All, T: All)

http://www.scoreone.com/kids_kitchen/

Children around the world submit their favorite recipes for the "yummiest" and "messiest" foods to this site. There is a link where kids can swap recipes and ideas. Every month a recipe is selected for creation of the month. (S: All, T: All)

Literature Resources

Blumenthal, Deborah. (1996). *The Chocolate-Covered Cookie Tantrum*. New York: Clarion Books.

This book illustrates a child's ill-mannered outburst over her desire for a cookie, and how her mother sensibly handles her. The story is vibrantly told through illustrations and colorful text.

Cook, Deanna F. (1995). *Kids' Multicultural Cookbook*. Charlotte, VT: Williamson Publishing.

This book discusses kids, from Australia to the Americas, and their favorite recipes. The book includes comments from children who spoke to the author. There are also games, cultural traditions, and customs around the world.

DePaola, Tomie. (1978). *Pancakes for Breakfast*. Orlando, FL: Harcourt Brace.

This book describes a little old lady's attempts to have pancakes for breakfast. She has problems because of a lack of supplies and the participation of her pets.

Hausherr, Rosemarie. (1994). *What Food Is This?* New York: Scholastic

This book discusses 18 wholesome foods. It describes where they come from, how they grow, and what they look like. It introduces foods that many children may not recognize as being edible.

McMillan, Bruce. (1991). *Eating Fractions*. New York: Scholastic.

This book provides a creative, fun way for children to learn about food while learning math. It illustrates fractions using various foods such as bananas, pies, and pizzas.

Mountfield, Anne. (1988). *Looking Back at Food and Drink*. Needham, MA: Schoolhouse Press.

This book explores where food comes from, what people drink, ways of cooking and baking, food from other countries, buying and selling, and a variety of other topics.

Activities and Projects

1. Ask students to select a country. Then have them investigate through Web sites, books, and encyclopedias various foods eaten in that country. Ask students to put together a small party involving their country. Have the students select a certain dish from that country, create it at home, and bring the finished product and the recipe to class. Also have them decorate according to the country chosen and select a food craft taken from their country to demonstrate to the class.

2. Ask students to investigate how certain foods, such as butter, cornmeal, honey, and apple sauce, were made before we could buy them. Assign children to work in groups, using the Internet, books, and encyclopedias, to discover where the recipes originated, how they're made, and what group of people created the recipe. Ask each group to prepare a sample of the food they have chosen and bring it into class, including a recipe and a short presentation about the materials they found.

3. Ask students to cut out several pictures of various foods from old magazines. Have them bring the pictures to class. Hand out a wide assortment of construction paper. Each paper should be labeled with one of the basic food groups. Have the children work in groups and share each other's pictures. Request that the children glue the pictures according to the food groups. After they are done, punch holes in the papers and tie them together to create a booklet.

4. Ask students to investigate selected Web sites and literature from the lists above to trace the route selected food items takes from their growth to our homes: Where are potatoes grown? How are they harvested? How are they shipped to market? How are they packaged? What happens to them when they are purchased? How can they be cooked or prepared? Students should create a series of posters describing the routes various food items take in their journey from field to pantry.

5. Ask individual children to work with their parents to make a list of the top ten food items most often consumed by the family, such as milk, bread, and potatoes. Ask each student to make a chart of her or his top ten items and post all the charts on a bulletin board. Ask the class to note any similarities in the lists. Are there food items that appear on only a few lists?

Clothing

Introduction

Every morning children get out of bed and put on their clothes, but few give thought to how those clothes were manufactured, where they were manufactured, the raw materials that went into making those clothes, how they were distributed or purchased, or a thousand other features and facts that involve the shirts, dresses, socks, and shoes we put on every day. A lesson or unit on clothing can be multifaceted and expansive, involving many curricular areas, such as science (growing various plants), math (number of selected clothes sold during a period of time), health (protection from the elements), social studies (clothing styles in various countries), art (decorations and designs), and language arts (stories about clothes from various cultures). A study of clothing can be an important part of many different social studies units.

Research Questions

1. Why are clothes important?

2. What are some clothing styles of Americans throughout history?

3. How do clothing styles vary from season to season and year to year?

4. Why are shoes important, and what are the styles in various countries throughout history?

Web Sites

http://www.siue.edu/COSTUMES/history.html
This Web site is a book illustrating and defining historical dressing. The various time periods are Victorian perspective, European, Asian, and African countries. Students are also able to click on pictures to see a more vivid detailing of particular styles of dress. (S: 4–6, T: 4–6)

http://www.pconline.com/~tomdolan/costume/costume1.htm
At this site students will be able to learn about costumes down through the ages. Lots of information and lots of visuals compliment this site. (S: 4–6; T: 4–6)

Literature Resources

Bates, Artie Ann. (1995). *Ragsale*. Boston: Houghton Mifflin.
This book beautifully illustrates a family tradition of going to ragsales on Saturdays. The family is looking for things such as mittens, books, and clothing.

Berson, Harold. (1977). *Kassim's Shoes*. New York: Crown.

This is a Moroccan folktale about a man named Kassim who loves his old pair of shoes. However, all the people laugh at the shoes until Kassim is forced to get rid of them. Throughout the story the shoes follow Kassim around the town until he is forced to take them back.

Gould, Deborah. (1989). *Aaron's Shirt*. New York: Bradbury Press.

This book is about the changing seasons and how clothing styles are different in each season. It tells the story of a young boy who has an overwhelming love for a certain shirt. He wears it day in and day out until the weather changes and his mother has to put it away.

Perl, Lila. (1990). *From Top Hats to Baseball Caps, from Bustles to Blue Jeans*. New York: Clarion Books.

Through this book readers travel from the late 1800s to present-day clothing styles of U.S. dress. The book also goes into detail about the secret language of clothes, why we dress the way we do, and who wears pants, shoes, skirts, and hats.

 # Activities and Projects

1. Divide the students into several small groups. Assign each group an item of clothing, such as hats, pants, shirts, shoes, and skirts/dresses. Ask each group to investigate the origination, history, materials used to make it, and various styles of each item. The students can use the Web sites and literature listed above. Ask each group to organize the information they found into a resource book, including table of contents, pictures, and explanations.

2. Read *Aaron's Shirt* to the class, then discuss how styles of clothing change with weather patterns and seasons. Post a silhouette of a student on a bulletin board. Ask students to create various items of clothing, ranging from winter wear to summer wear. Post the items of clothing next to the silhouette. Throughout the year select a different student each week to change the clothing of the silhouette according to the weather.

3. Divide the students into small groups. Ask each group to select a certain time period in history, such as, the early 1900s, the 1930s, the 1960s, and the present. Ask each group to investigate their time period using the Web sites listed above. Ask them to create a fashion magazine of their era, including illustrations or photographs, explanations, and reviews of the clothing. Encourage groups to present their magazines to the class.

4. Ask small groups of students to draw a series of pictures showing the making of wool cloth. Suggest that they connect the illustrations with arrows to show how the wool-making process flows from raw material to finished product. They should show factories near water, tracks transporting wool, and warehouses and stores.

Families Around the World

Introduction

If there is one universal truth in social studies, it is that families are different and families are the same. Although that concept may seem contradictory to some children, it reflects the fact that we enjoy certain expectations within our own family structure, as do other individuals in other families. To say that the family unit is the staple of culture and civilization around the world would be to state the obvious. What may not be so obvious to students is the fact that family life in any country has unique similarities to family life in the United States as well as some unique and interesting differences that make any study of family life around the world a fascinating unit for discovery and exploration. Children have a frame of reference (their own family) in which to compare and contrast the lives of other children and other adults in a wide variety of cultures and countries.

Research Questions

1. What is a family?

2. How are families similar?

3. How are families different?

4. How is your family similar to a family in Mexico, Japan, China, Peru, France, or Kenya?

Web Sites

http://library.advanced.org/50055/jamain.htm
A brief look into Japanese family life, this page is a link from a larger Web page that explores cultures all over the world. This Web site has illustrations to complement the text and is an excellent starting point for exploration into the family lives of the Japanese. (S: 3–6)

http://www.kidlink.org/KIDPROJ/projects.html
Lots of projects, activities, and curricular materials by and for kids. This is a wonderful site maintained by a group of classroom teachers offering an array of fascinating and interesting ideas on the lives of kids worldwide. (T: All)

Literature Resources

Grifalconi, Ann. (1990). *Osa's Pride.* Boston: Little, Brown.

After young Osa alienates her friend with wild tales about her father, who went to war and never returned, her grandmother tells her a tale of foolish pride. The girl's grandmother asks her how she should end a story quilt of a foolishly proud young girl. Osa realizes her own pride is out of hand. This beautifully illustrated book shows the way families communicate and teach their young in an African tribe.

Griffin, Michael. (1988). *A Family in Kenya.* Minneapolis, MN: Lerner.

Ever wonder what life would be like if you lived in Kenya? In this book students can follow 11-year-old Salaama through her typical day. Salaama lives in Mombassa, the second largest city in Kenya. The story of this young girl and her family is used to illustrate the customs and everyday activities of a typical family in Kenya. The text is complemented by stunningly clear photographs.

Hermes, Jules. (1993). *Children of India.* Minneapolis, MN: Carolrhoda Books.

This book is a richly detailed portrayal of life in India. Each page is full of beautiful photographic images, paintings, or drawings of Indian culture. The book covers each region of India with a vivid description.

Miller, Joy. (1996). *American Indian Families.* New York: Children's Press.

This resource is a compact source about the American Indian family. Names, children, marriage, and growing old are discussed in this book.

Peters, Sonja. (1998). *A Family from Germany.* Austin, TX: Steck-Vaughn.

After a brief description of Germany as a country, the book introduces the Pfitzner family, an average German family. The book introduces us to different aspects of Germany through the members of this family. Customs, traditions, special events, and information on everyday life (including school, jobs, etc.) are covered.

Pitkanen, Matti. (1990). *Children of China.* Minneapolis, MN: Carolrhoda Books.

The book begins with a simple introduction to China. Each page offers a glimpse into the life of a child from a different region in China. Beautiful photographs illustrate the text. An excellent way for children to begin to relate to life in other cultures.

Activities and Projects

1. Ask students to work in small groups, with each group focusing on a specific country of the world. Ask each group to investigate selected Web sites as well as appropriate literature to discover basic facts and information about family life in that region of the world. Encourage students to assemble their collected information into a series of brochures or leaflets that can be displayed on an appropriate bulletin board.

2. Encourage students to correspond with an international pen pal. (You can find these at http://www.axessweb.com/users/alllworld/penpals.htm or any one of several other pen pal sites.) Encourage students to collect information about their correspondents'

family life (religious aspects, roles and responsibilities of each family member, traditions, customs, fun activities, etc.). Students should prepare special diaries in which they record selected information on family life in another country. Provide sufficient time for students to share and discuss their diaries.

3. After students have had sufficient opportunities to collect relevant data from one or more Web sites, ask them to take on the role of students in a selected foreign country. Ask each student to imagine she or he is corresponding with students in the United States. Ask students to tell the U.S. pen pals about their family life, where they go to school, holiday celebrations, customs and traditions, or any other pertinent information. Plan time to discuss this "correspondence" on a regular basis.

4. Ask students to form several small groups. Encourage each group to investigate the culture and customs of a particular country through selected Web sites. Afterwards, ask each group to create a newspaper about family life in that particular country. Students may wish to focus on traditional family customs, places families visit, daily family life, family games or sports, as well as other aspects of family life. Using a word processing program, students can "publish" their newspaper and share them with other classes at your grade level.

Chapter 6

Neighborhoods and Communities

Maps

Introduction

A map is a pictorial representation of an area or an object. Maps can serve purposes aside from illustrating the location of certain places. Some maps show the physical makeup of the land, including mountains, rivers, oceans, hills, plains, valleys, etc. A physical map may also show the elevation of the land or depth of the oceans. Maps can also show the population of cities and countries, important natural resources found in that location, products manufactured there, animals that live there, the religion of certain areas, languages spoken in different areas, or the climate of a region. Maps can also show changes over the years. Historical maps can show us the changes in territories owned by countries. Maps have many resources and are an excellent way to link art, anthropology, science, math, and many other subjects with social studies.

Research Questions

1. What is a map?

2. Describe three different types of maps and explain their purposes.

3. What are some ways in which maps are used?

4. How have maps been used throughout history?

5. What are some common terms used with maps?

Web Sites

http://www.aquarius.geomar.de/omc/
This Web site is a fabulous connection for both students and teachers who are required to make a map . . . of anything. The introduction to the site explains maps and map making, and with a click of a button, students are introduced to an informational form that helps them create a computer-organized map. (S: All, T: All)

http://pittsford.monroe.edu/Schools/Jefferson/Maps&Globes/MapsGlobesFrame.html
This Web site offers basic information on maps and globes. A concept is explained and activities and quizzes pertaining to that concept are offered. A variety of maps and globes appear on this site, including the Earth, climate, time zones, water, and landforms. The site also includes a glossary so children can look up new vocabulary. (S: 3–6)

http://www.lib.utexas.edu/Libs/PCL/Map_collection/Map_collection.html
The Perry-Castaneda Library Map Collection at the University of Texas has thousands of maps from around the world. This super site is a "must-see" for any teacher presenting a map study unit to kids. (T: All)

Literature Resources

Day, Malcolm, Woodward, Kate & Steele, Philip. (1991). *Children's World Atlas*. Pleasantville, NY: Reader's Digest Association.

Brightly colored maps fill the pages of this world atlas. The text is written for children and opens with instructions on how to use an atlas. The atlas includes broad topics such as the Earth, the physical world, climate, vegetation, animals, population, land use, agriculture, minerals, industry, nations, languages, and even religion.

Knowlton, Jack. (1985). *Maps and Globes*. New York: Crowell.

In this book children are introduced to the topic of maps. The history of how maps were made and why they were needed is explained in easily understood text. After a discussion of the history of maps is a lesson about reading maps and globes.

Taylor, Barbara. (1994). *Be Your Own Map Expert*. New York: Sterling.

The detailed, realistic illustrations in this book combine with a simple, reference-style text to thoroughly explore the world of maps. The text begins with an explanation of why we have maps. It then moves on to other topics, such as what maps are, types of maps, history and evolution of maps, measurements and scales of maps, symbols on maps, longitude, latitude, time zones, compasses, grids, and how maps are made. This is a wonderful reference source for any classroom.

Activities and Projects

1. Divide the class into six groups. Each group is to use a tape measure to measure a different area outside (one group for the blacktop, one group for the parking lot, two groups to divide the playground equipment, and two groups for the sports fields). After the measurements are taken, divide the students into different groups, ensuring that each group has a member from each of the measurement groups. Assign each group member a task (recorder of measurements, art supply person, clean up person, discussion leader, etc.). When the new groups meet each student should present the measurement to the group verbally, as directed by the discussion leader. The group recorder will write down all the measurements to ensure the accuracy of the work. The group should then discuss and agree on a scale, then draw a map of the playground to scale. When the students have completed the maps, they will be hung in the entrance of the school for students, faculty, visitors, and parents to enjoy.

2. Have each student select a local landform from an envelope. The location might be a mountain range, a desert, a peninsula, or a beach. Each student should look for information on her or his area on the Internet, in the school library, and in the encyclopedia. After students record this geographical information in their journals they can use it to create a salt map of their area. Ask them to use the following recipe:

> **Salt Map**
>
> 4 cups of flour
> 1 cup of salt
> 1 1/2 cups of warm water
>
> Knead all the ingredients for about 10 minutes. The mixture should be stiff but pliable. Spread the mixture out on a cookie sheet or piece of aluminum foil, forming it into various landform areas. Brush with egg yolk mixed with 1 tablespoon of water and bake at 325 degrees for about one hour or more, depending on size, until very dry. Seal with two or three coats of polyurethane. Paint various areas with tempera paints and label.

3. Provide students with opportunities to create personal and individual maps. Some students may wish to create simple maps of their bedrooms at home. Others may want to create maps of their homes or immediate neighborhood or community. Some students may want to attempt to create specialized maps of their town, such as a map of all the shopping areas, a map of all the entertainment areas (playgrounds, theaters, etc.), or a map of all the community helpers (police, firefighters, etc.).

4. Ask students to create a large poster devoted exclusively to map legends. Have them collect several different examples of legends from a variety of maps and paste them or redraw them on the poster. They should provide explanations for each of the legends or groups of legends.

5. Provide students with opportunities to create their own three-dimensional maps of the local community or geographical area. Following is a recipe for "Edible Spreadable Clay," which can be used to construct various landforms and then be eaten when the activity is completed.

   Mix two parts peanut butter with one part honey. Add three parts dry milk (a little at a time) until a stiff mixture forms. The mixture should be thoroughly kneaded with hands. Refrigerate overnight and use the next day.

6. Have students prepare both written directions and a map to guide new students to different locations in the school. As a class, brainstorm about what places in the school would be important to locate for new students. Good ideas are the cafeteria, library, nurse's office, principal's office, and restrooms. Take a "quiet tour" of the school, and have groups of four or five students create written directions to the selected places. When back in the classroom, students should compare notes with other groups and cooperatively develop a key to follow. Have the students prepare a final written copy of the key. Using a legend, a compass rose, and a scale, students should create a map that will be both easy to read and helpful for new students. They should make copies of both the map and the written directions, which will be given to new students on their arrival.

Globes

Introduction

Simply stated, a globe is a model of the Earth. It is particularly useful for children because it helps students orient themselves to the Earth. Globes can help students distinguish between land and water areas and can also correct the common misperception that "up" on a map is north and "down" is south. A globe helps students understand that up is away from the center of the Earth and down is the reverse. With a globe, students can learn that north is toward the North Pole and south is toward the South Pole. These concepts are particularly difficult to illustrate clearly on a wall map. Globes are excellent geographic tools; however, they are unable to present lots of geographic detail. When detail is important, it's time to turn to the traditional wall map.

Research Questions

1. How is a globe similar to a map?

2. How is a globe different from a map?

3. What are the lines that go around the globe called?

4. What are the lines that go up and down called?

5. What does a globe show that a map cannot?

Web Sites

http://library.advanced.org/10157/
Geo-Globe is an interactive geography site that assists students in mastering basic concepts about maps and globes. (S: 4–6)

http://hum.amu.edu.pl/~zbzw/glob/glob1.htm
Hundreds of different projections of the world can be found on this all-inclusive and simply amazing web site. A great compliment to any study of globes this will be a classroom favorite for a variety of social studies units. (T: All)

Literature Resources

Cassidy, John. (1994). *Earthsearch: A Kid's Geography Museum in a Book*. Palo Alto, CA: Klutz Press.
This beginning book on geography takes the reader all over the world through discoveries of artifacts.

Crewe, Sabrina. (1997). *Maps and Globes*. New York: Children's Press.
This book has wonderful color photos and maps that enhance the text. These photos and accurate maps introduce the reader to maps and globes.

Knowlton, Jack. (1986). *Maps and Globes*. New York: Harper Trophy.
This book provides young readers with a brief history of map making. It also describes how globes and maps are read along with the variety of maps available.

Sweeney, Joan. (1996). *Me on the Map*. New York: Crown.
This book is about a little girl. It starts with a drawing of her in her bedroom. On the next page readers see a picture of her bedroom in her house. The little girl keeps drawing to larger scale and eventually ends up with a picture of the world.

 # Activities and Projects

1. The Globe Game: Divide the class into two teams and have them individually locate several locations on the globe, being careful not to let the other team know what places they are working on. Each student should come up with five clues to help the other team guess the location. The clues should start out general and become more specific, for example:

   Clue 1: I am in the Western Hemisphere.

   Clue 2: I am located south of the equator.

   Clue 3: I am located 70 degrees west of the Prime Meridian.

   The more clues needed, the fewer points are received for a correct answer. The teams should alternate, making sure everyone gets a turn. The team with the most points wins.

2. Ask small groups of students to log on to one of the Web sites above. Have each group prepare a booklet or brochure on the differences between maps and globes. Challenge each group to prepare their booklet for students in a grade lower than yours or for students in a grade higher than yours. What facts must be included so that other students understand these two important concepts?

3. Obtain a globe of the world. Ask students to interview their parents, grandparents, and other relatives about their countries of origin. As students obtain the necessary information, ask each one to pinpoint a country or countries on the globe by placing a pushpin into the correct location(s). Afterwards, have students engage in one or more of the following activities/answer the following questions:

   What identified country is farthest from our school?

   What two countries are farthest apart?

   Ask each student to identify a Web site related to a specific country (using Web sites cited elsewhere in this book). Using the information on that site, ask students to create a series of travel brochures for each identified country. Students can direct their brochures to adults or students.

Ask students to locate related pieces of children's literature for some or all of the geographic regions identified on the globe. Have students use the resources listed in previous chapters in this book to assemble a display of children's books related to the countries from which their relatives originated.

4. An excellent CD-ROM on maps and globes is *Our Earth* (No. U06741; National Geographic Society, P.O. Box 10597, Des Moines, IA 50340, 1-800-368-2728, cost $69.95, available for both Mac and PC). This outstanding program is designed for students in grades K–2 and offers a voyage around the planet during which they can investigate oceans, rivers, mountains, and deserts. They'll also learn map concepts such as location, symbols, and cardinal directions.

Neighborhoods

Introduction

A neighborhood is defined as a place where people live near one another. A neighborhood may be large and consist of many houses and other community buildings, or it may be small, existing within a much larger community or apart from a large urban environment. In many cases, large communities have many neighborhoods and small communities have a dearth of neighborhoods.

Most important for students to understand is that a neighborhood is a group of people and families who live in proximity to one another. That closeness implies a sharing of responsibilities, rights, and obligations. "Neighbors helping neighbors" is often the "catch phrase" of a close-knit and well-functioning neighborhood. In short, a neighborhood is much more than a group of houses in a defined area—it is a mutually supportive enclave of people who know each other and support each other.

Research Questions

1. What is a neighborhood?

2. How is a neighborhood like a community?

3. What do neighbors do for each other?

4. How large can a neighborhood be?

5. How many people live in your neighborhood?

Web Sites

http://pbs.org/rogers/

This is a PBS site dedicated to the *Mr. Rogers* television program. It allows viewers to travel through his neighborhood and visit different individuals. There are many activities for children and adults. (S: K–3, T: K–3)

http://www.eyesofachild.com/

Students can take a trip with 12 children as they guide viewers through their respective neighborhoods in New York City. (S: All)

http://www.kqed.org/tv/productions/hood/

Visit the various neighborhoods in one of the great American cities—San Francisco. Lots of details and cultural information is available on this site. (T: All)

Literature Resources

Bauer, Caroline Feller. (1987). *Midnight Snowman*. New York: Macmillan.

This is a great story about a neighborhood where snow is not a common sight. When a girl and her friend enjoy the event by building a snowman, they realize that the entire neighborhood wants to join in. The illustrations are created from watercolors, which add a snowy, blurry feeling.

Munsch, Robert. (1991). *The Fire Station*. Toronto, Canada: Annick Press.

This is a humorous story about a boy and girl whose curiosity leads them to the fire station for a tour. They didn't realize that they would be going to an actual fire, though. The book illustrates what firefighters do and presents the idea that children should not get into things they were told to stay away from.

Myers, Edward. (1995). *Forri the Baker*. New York: Dial Books for Young Readers.

This story is about the village baker, who is somewhat different from the rest of the villagers. When the village is being attacked and is desperate for help, a strange hero emerges.

Rathmann, Peggy. (1995). *Officer Buckle and Gloria*. New York: Putnam.

Officer Buckle struggles to keep the attention of students when he visits local schools with his safety tips. But one day he is given a partner and he becomes the hottest act in town. The illustrations provide a visual humor to complement the text.

Rockwell, Anne & Rockwell, Harlow. (1985). *The Emergency Room*. New York: Macmillan.

The emergency room is a scary place for most children, and this book helps to eliminate those fears. It explains what happens to a boy who has sprained his ankle and how he realizes that the emergency room is a good, helpful place. The watercolor illustrations are pleasant and simple.

Activities and Projects

1. Create a neighborhood in the school. Designate certain areas or rooms in the building as places you would find in the community. For example, the nurse's office would be the hospital, the principal's office would be the mayor's office. Then, as a class, ask students to produce a map of the make-believe neighborhood, including a key explaining the function of each place. Ask students to make a list illustrating in what ways the school is its own neighborhood.

2. Ask students to plan a day when individuals will come to the school and explain what they do for the neighborhood. The students may wish to contact the mayor, postal workers, police officers, firefighters, business owners, or citizens who have lived in the area for many years. Students should prepare a variety of questions for the visitors to answer, and then record the information obtained in their journals.

3. Ask students to design their ideal neighborhood, through drawing, poetry, a song, or building a replica out of cereal and tissue boxes. These neighborhoods should then be presented to the class accompanied by an oral explanation of the things they have included.

4. Ask students to interview several of their neighbors: What are some elements of that neighborhood that make it a special place? What kinds of changes should be made in the neighborhood to make it better? Why is it important to be neighborly? Provide opportunities for students to share the results of their interviews with all members of the class.

5. Ask students to create special "yellow pages" for neighborhood services, such as street and sidewalk cleanup, leaf raking, and block parties. Encourage students to design the directory as an abbreviated or modified version of the local yellow pages, one that could be a quick and ready resource for neighborhood leaders or citizens looking for specialized services.

6. Ask students to create a neighborhood newspaper. They should create current event articles on the local neighborhood, a series of community cartoons, a sports page, movie and play reviews and schedules, PTO meetings, etc. Students who live in the same neighborhoods can rotate assignments (sports reporter, fashion editor, etc.).

Occupations

Introduction

"What do you want to be when you grow up?" This is a universal question asked by adults of children. Often children are influenced by the occupations of their parents, but they are equally influenced by those they see on TV or in the movies. Many schools have Career Days on which various members of the community visit the school to describe and explain the jobs they hold and how they contribute to the economic stability of that community.

What is most interesting about the topic of jobs and occupations is that most people go through a variety of jobs in their lifetimes. In fact, as of this writing the average person in the United States will have more than seven jobs and five occupations during her or his lifetime. Exposing students to the variety of occupational choices there are and giving them the freedom to experience and look into those career choices may be one of the most important things we do as teachers.

Research Questions

1. What do you want to be when you grow up?

2. How do people end up with certain jobs?

3. What jobs are the most popular?

4. What is the most exciting job you can think of?

Web Sites

http://library.advanced.org/11720
Students can start thinking about occupations with the information on this Web site. It provides a step-by-step process for making career decisions and what to do about those decisions once they are made. (S: 4–6)

http://www.dol.gov
Teachers can use this site to discover the laws and regulations about holding a job (e.g., child labor laws) and share them with their students. (T: All)

http://www.whatdotheydo.com./
This is an incredible site that lists loads of occupations, their educational requirements, their descriptions, and a wealth of other information. This is an all-purpose site for any classroom. (S: 4–6)

Literature Resources

Radford, Derek. (1992). ***Bernie Drives a Truck***. Cambridge, MA: Candlewick Press.
This book describes the exterior and interior of Bernie's truck. The story goes through a checklist of precautions Bernie must complete, and everything is defined and labeled. Bernie's job is more complicated than driving a truck; it's a long day of hard work.

Rathman, Peggy. (1995). ***Officer Buckle and Gloria***. New York: Putnam.
Officer Buckle and his dog Gloria, are a safety team. The two of them have hundreds of safety tips they share with just about everyone. However, it seems that lately Gloria has been stealing the show and Officer Buckle feels all his hard work has gone unnoticed.

Ready, Dee. (1997). ***Community Helpers: Farmers***. Minneapolis, MN: Bridgestone Books.
This book describes what farmers do, wear, use, and drive; where they work; and who helps them. The end of the book contains a hands-on activity (plant and grow beans), some words to know, other book titles, and Internet sites to find more information.

Ready, Dee. (1997). ***Community Helpers: Veterinarians***. Minneapolis, MN: Bridgestone Books.
This book describes what vets do, what they wear, what tools they use, veterinary schooling, and people who help veterinarians. In the back of the book a hands-on activity is suggested (care for birds). Bibliographies and Web sites are included to provide more information on this topic.

Reeves, Diane Lindsey. (1998). ***Career Ideas: For Kids Who Like Talking***. New York: Checkmark Books.
This volume is part of a series about career ideas for kids. Each book contains tons of career possibilities based on children's specific interests, skills, and talents. These books are highly motivational but also just plain fun!

 ## Activities and Projects

1. Ask the students to create their own classified ads for the job of their choice. To begin this project, they can research different types of occupations that interest them (via Web sites and literature). Ask them to check the format of an actual classified ad. They should include salary requirements, part-time/full-time status, and a job description of their identified job. A collection of ads should be compiled to form a page of the class newspaper.

2. Ask students to write a series of letters to local business people, service personnel, civic officials, and other individuals in the town or city, inviting them to visit the classroom to describe their jobs, or they can interview the individuals using a portable tape recorder. Plan time for students to collect information from these interviews and assemble it into a "Careers" bulletin board.

3. Provide students with copies of the daily newspaper's want ads. Explain the different kinds of abbreviations used in want ads and prepare a sample want ad for classroom display. Ask students to work in groups to design want ads for various classroom jobs: What special qualifications should applicants for each job have? The student-designed ads can be posted periodically when it is time to assign students to classroom chores.

4. Ask students to discuss the elements that are necessary for being happy in one's job: What conditions must be present? What type of people should one work with? What kind of boss should one have? How long should one work each day? Have students record their responses and then compare them to the responses of their parents. What similarities or differences do they note?

5. There is a wide variety of series books by various publishers on the jobs and occupations that people have around the world (far more than what is listed above). Ask students to select books from two or more series, each book focusing on a single occupation. Encourage small groups of students to compare and contrast the information in those books: Do two books on the same occupation present the same type of information? Which book is more realistic? Which book has missing information? Plan opportunities for students to discuss any similarities and/or differences.

Community Services

Introduction

Community service plays a vital role in our cities today. For example, when there is a flood or tornado, many organizations will offer assistance to victims. Volunteer firefighters in some small towns offer the only hope for victims of fire. Through organizations like Habitat for Humanity families are given a chance to start over, and places like the YMCA/YWCA offer children a place to go after school. The American Red Cross offers various forms of assistance during natural disasters. The question then is, why do people give their time, their money, and sometimes their lives for others? People care, and they want to make their community better for everyone. They are proud of where they live, and we should be grateful that there are people who do care, because without them this world and our communities would be a poorer place.

Research Questions

1. What are some community services in your town?

2. Why do people volunteer?

3. What are some ways to volunteer in your community?

4. What are some examples of national community agencies?

5. What is the role of community agencies?

Web Sites

http://www.redcross.org/hec/index.html
This site allows students to explore the services of the American Red Cross. Pictures and maps of regions in crisis can be found here. An excellent resource to keep up on current events. (S: 4–6, T: 4–6)

http://www.habitat.org/
Habitat for Humanity works very hard to help people in need in many communities. This Web site shows how to get involved, where they build, how it works, and true stories about the new homeowners. This site is an excellent way for students to discover how organizations can help people in their own community. (S: 4–6)

http://www.voa.org/
This site allows students to explore the different ways Volunteers of America assist others, from children and their families to the elderly and homeless. It also allows students to locate the branch of this organization in their home state. (S: 4–6, T: 4–6)

http://www.fema.gov/kids/

The Federal Emergency Management Agency (FEMA), is an organization that helps those involved in natural disasters. This site contains a kid's menu, including information and safety tips to use during an earthquake, a tornado, etc. It also has personal stories from survivors of natural disasters. (S: 4–6, T: 4–6)

http://www.salvationarmyusa.org/

This site explains how the Salvation Army functions to help those in need, including services, disaster relief, current news, and how people can help. An easy way for students to explore the various ways the Salvation Army is working in their community. (S: 4–6, T: 4–6)

http://www.officialcitysites.com/

This site has lots of information related to cities and communities. Children select the country, the state, and then the city or county. Once connected to the desired community, this site features local weather, local government, entertainment, education, sports, etc. (S: 4–6, T: All)

Literature Resources

Gibbons, Gail. (1994). *Emergency*. New York: Holiday House.

This book is a great choice for young readers. It is an excellent way for children to see which emergency vehicle is used in which situation. It also contains a section on emergency equipment from the past. An ideal opportunity to incorporate history into reading.

Gray, Nigel. (1988). *A Country Far Away*. New York: Orchard Books.

This story depicts the daily life of two boys, one from the United States and one from a Third World country. Their daily lives and communities are compared and contrasted throughout the story. This is appropriate for primary grades and will help children understand that two communities can be both different and similar.

Johnson, Jean. (1986). *Police Officers: A to Z*. New York: Walker.

This book informs students about police officers while using the alphabet as a guide through their equipment and responsibilities.

Kallen, Stuart. (1997). *The Police Station*. Minneapolis, MN: Abdo and Daughters.

This book is designed to help young readers understand what happens at a police station. It explains what goes on in different areas of the police station, such as the dispatch room and the police lab.

Lewis, Barbara. (1995). *The Kid's Guide to Service Projects*. Minneapolis, MN: Free Spirit.

This book is an excellent resource on ways children can help their communities. It contains 500 different service ideas that can be applied to any community. This book is a must for anyone wanting to become more involved in the community.

Morris, Neal. (1997). *The World's Top Ten Cities*. Austin, TX: Steck-Vaughn.

This book provides a brief overview of the world's 10 most populated cities. A glossary in the back lists many useful terms and definitions.

Rathman, Peggy. (1995). *Officer Buckle and Gloria*. New York: Putnam.

This book is a very entertaining story about a police officer and his dog. It not only gives safety tips but also shows how with teamwork any job can get done.

Royston, Robert. (1985). *Your World 2000: Cities.* New York: Facts on File.
    This book discusses how cities evolve over time, how they are planned and built, and what it's like to live in a city.

 # Activities and Projects

1. If possible, students should visit a local nursing home or senior citizen center and interview residents about the "good old days": What community services do they have now that were not available when they were growing up? How has life in the local community changed in the last 50 or 75 years? What elements of the "old community" do they miss most? The results of the interviews should combined into a journal or scrapbook with photos.

2. Ask students to volunteer for various school-related activities. These could include (but are not limited to) cleaning up the playground on a regular basis, volunteering to sort and catalog books in the school library, assisting in the main office, and helping the custodial staff at the end of the school day. Plan sufficient time for students to discuss their volunteer efforts and how they affect the performance and/or maintenance of the school. Provide opportunities to discuss the impact volunteerism has on the local community.

3. Ask students to interview several individuals in the local community about the services they provide residents. Students should consult the local phone book for lists and addresses of community agencies and then make arrangements to interview personnel. Encourage students to assemble their collected information into a set of "yellow pages" for kids. What community services are geared toward kids? What services do kids need to know about?

4. Ask students to consult several of the Web sites listed in this section or to read *50 Simple Things Kids Can Do to Save the Earth* (Kansas City, KS: Andrews and McMeel, 1990) . Ask them to develop a plan of action for making the world or their local neighborhoods more beautiful. Be sure to encourage some healthy discussion about their proposals.

5. After they investigate some of the Web sites listed in this section, ask students to create a series of posters or advertisements for particular community services (especially those that are in your local town or city). What facts, figures, data, or illustrations need to be included in the advertisement/poster to stimulate people to volunteer their services or donate money? If appropriate, ask to have these posters placed in local businesses or designated agencies.

6. Divide the class into several groups. Direct each group to interview a class of community workers (health workers, paramedics, counselors, educators, political figures, etc.). Have each group construct a collage or scrapbook of their findings for display in the classroom.

Transportation

Introduction

Most communities in colonial America sprang up near bodies of water. There was a good reason for this: transportation. Water provided a way to travel. Before the advent of automobiles and trains, boats were the fastest way to carry cargo and people from one place to another. Later, roads were built to connect one community with another. Carriages, wagons, and horses used these roads as part of the extension of a community. Often roads from two or more communities would converge at a place known as a crossroads. Because roads were primarily used to transport people and goods, it was not unusual for a store or group of stores to spring up at these crossroads to provide goods and services for travelers.

Transportation is an important part of any community. It allows goods and services to be brought in from faraway and serves as a way for community goods to be transported to faraway locations. The economic vitality of a community is often dependent on the strength of its transportation system. Transportation provides a method and a means for communities to stay active and actively engaged with one another. It is both a lifeline and a conduit.

Research Questions

1. What are some different forms of transportation?

2. What form of transportation is used most in the United States?

3. What are some forms of transportation that travel on the water?

4. When were humans first able to travel through the air?

5. What form of transportation is most efficient?

Web Sites

http://www.transport-pf.or.jp/english/index.html
This is a marvelous Web site at which teachers and older students can learn all about various forms of transportation in Japan. Delightful! (S: 4–6, T: All)

http://www.allstar.fiu.edu/aero/princ1.htm
This all-inclusive site explains the principles behind flight. Intense and complete! (S: 4–6, T: 4–6)

http://www.uprr.com/uprr/ffh/photos/
Here youngsters can download an array of photographs about trains and the places they go. (S: 4–6)

http://cars.motorcities.com/
    More than 100 photos of automobiles can be downloaded from this Web site. (S: All, T: All)

http://www.helis.com/
    Just about everything—from history to warfare—can be located at this complete site on helicopters. (S: 4–6, T: 4–6).

 Literature Resources

Balkwell, Richard. (1999). *The Best Book of Trains*. New York: Kingfisher.
    This book lives up to its title and provides young readers with an array of exciting information.

Bingham, Caroline. (1999). *Big Book of Trucks*. New York: DK Publishing.
    This fun book features some of the world's most bizarre and amazing vehicles. This is a book kids will find hard to put down.

Corbett, David. (1999). *Automobiles (History Series)*. Hauppage, NY: Barrons.
    This book presents a thorough overview of the history of the car, from 1888 to the present day.

Gibbons, Gail. (1999). *Bicycle Book*. New York: Holiday House.
    Just about everything a young reader would want to know about bicycles can be found in the pages of this richly illustrated book.

Graham, Ian. (1998). *The Best Book of Spaceships*. New York: Kingfisher.
    Space travel gets a complete and thorough overview in this well-illustrated book.

Graham, Ian. (1993). *Boats, Ships, Submarines, and Other Floating Machines*. New York: Kingfisher.
    Just about every floating device ever invented or created can be found in this book.

Graham, Ian. (1999). *Built for Speed: Aircraft*. Austin, TX: Raintree/Steck-Vaughn.
    Some of the fastest aircraft in the world are profiled in this descriptive book.

 Activities and Projects

1. Provide students with several old magazines. Divide the class into three small groups and assign one of the following three topics to each group: air transportation, water transportation, and land transportation. Ask each group to go through the magazines and cut out pictures of their designated form of transportation. Ask each group to design a colorful display of various forms of transportation within their given category. Plan opportunities for students to discuss their collages: What form of transportation is most prevalent? Are there more different types of land transportation than of water transportation?

2. Invite an individual from the local community to visit your classroom. This individual can be from a local municipal bus company, taxi service, airline, cargo shipping company, etc. Provide students with an opportunity to interview the individual about her or his job and its impact on the local community or economy. Students can extend this activity by conducting a series of tape-recorded interviews throughout the community. These tapes should be reviewed and discussed in the classroom.

3. Encourage students to interview their grandparents or other adults in the community. They should ask the adults how transportation has changed during their lifetimes. Students can inquire about the most advanced or sophisticated form of transportation when the adults were children: What has changed most in the intervening years? How has transportation changed from then to the advanced forms of transportation today that can transport humans into outer space?

4. Ask students to create a transportation time line. Post a long piece of newsprint along one wall of the classroom. Ask students to consult the Web sites in this section as well as any literature resources to obtain information on significant events in transportation history. Have the students record these dates and events along the sheet of newsprint in chronological order. Students may supplement their written information with appropriate illustrations or photographs.

5. Print the word *TRANSPORTATION* vertically down an extended sheet of newsprint that has been posted on one wall of the classroom. After students have conducted sufficient research on the Web sites and literature listed in this section, ask them to brainstorm for forms of transportation beginning with each letter of the word. For example, for "T" students could list *truck, train,* and *trailer.* Write the names of those forms of transportation next to the corresponding letter of the word. Keep the sheet posted for an extended period of time so that students can add to it on a continuing basis.

Chapter 7

Communities Here and There

Urban Communities

Introduction

Urbanization is the changing of an area from a country to a city society. Before the Civil War, only about 20 percent of the population of this country lived in cities. By 1900, the number of people in urban areas had increased to 40 percent. Cities in this country grew for a number of reasons. Farming in the late 1800s was becoming increasingly difficult and people moved to the cities for the jobs they provided. Cities also served as centers of economic stability and transportation hubs and offered cultural and recreational attractions unavailable in more rural areas. The quality of life in a city, particularly at the end of the nineteenth century, could vary tremendously depending on one's economic status, race, immigrant status, or social class. Cities were areas rich in diversity.

Today, our concept of city life is different than it was 100 years ago. Means and modes of transportation have changed, buildings have soared into the sky, communication systems have revolutionized the business of a city, and the pace of life has increased. People still live in cities for a variety of reasons, just as they have for decades. The problems are more complex and the pace of life is faster, but cities remain an important part of the U.S. landscape.

Research Questions

1. Define *urbanization.*

2. What are some buildings you would find in any city?

3. What are the two main differences between urban and rural life?

4. Why do so many people live in cities?

5. Why do so many people work in cities?

6. What are some of the major problems of urban life?

Web Sites

http://r2.gsa.gov/fivept/fphome.htm
This site provides an archeological history of an urban neighborhood in New York City. It shows artifacts from the area and a visual tour of the urban community. (S: 4–6)

http://designltd.com/cats/houston/houston.htm
In this site, two cats lead you on a tour of Houston, Texas. They cover all of the major areas and provide great pictures of a large urban area. (S: All)

http://www.centrepoint.org.uk/start.asp

This United Kingdom site is about homelessness. Here one can participate in a virtual homelessness game. In the game, students are asked to make decisions about how they would survive on the streets. (S: 4–6)

http://www.nationalgeographic.com/3cities/

This is an incredible site that compares three cities: Alexandria in 1 C.E., Cordoba in 1000 C.E., and New York City in 2000 C.E. Fascinating and interactive, this site is a "must see." (S: 4–6, T: All)

http://www-geoimages.berkeley.edu/GeoImages.html

This site provides panoramic images and photographs of cities around the world. (T: All)

http://www.indo.com/distance/

At this site (one of my favorites) students can list any two cities in the world and the site will automatically calculate the distance between them. Great for geography studies. (S: All, T: All)

http://www.nationalgeographic.com/resources/ngo/maps/

Here, students can see a detailed maps from around the world. Perfect for downloading and sharing. (S: All, T: All)

 # Literature Resources

Bunting, Eve. (1994). *Smoky Night*. San Diego: Harcourt Brace.

Daniel and his mother look out their apartment window to see a city in riot. This touching story brings a human face to an urban problem.

Costa-Pace, Rosa. (1994). *The City*. New York: Chelsea House.

This book provides information about the development of the modern city and how various forms of pollution affect a metropolis.

Hill, Lee. (1999). *Get Around in the City*. Minneapolis, MN: Carolrhoda Books.

This book describes how a truck makes its way through a city during a typical workday.

Morgan, Sally. (1998). *Homes and Cities: Living for the Future*. New York: Franklin Watts.

This is a nice compare and contrast book about different types of urban environments and homes.

Ringgold, Faith. (1991). *Tar Beach*. New York: Crown.

The tar beach is actually a little girl's rooftop, where she dreams about being free to go anywhere. One night her dreams come true and she begins a soaring adventure over the city.

Sammis, Fran. (1998). *Cities and Towns*. New York: Benchmark Books.

The descriptive text, colorful maps, and varied activities help readers explore various aspects of cities and towns.

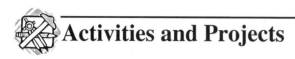

Activities and Projects

1. Ask students to list some of the major cities in the world. From that list, students should choose their favorite and plan a trip to that city for five days. Working in small groups, they should decide which tourist attractions they will visit, what areas they want their hotels to be in, and how much time will be spent at each place on their trip. Their research should use Internet searches, library work with periodicals, and/or information from local travel agencies. The students should present the acquired information in the form of a poster or a brochure.

2. Encourage students to pretend that they have just moved to a major city. Ask them to write letters to their friends in their old community telling how their lives have changed. Students should discuss the differences or similarities in the attitudes of people there, the new places to visit, and how the sizes of the buildings have changed.

3. Ask students to list the advantages and disadvantages of living in an urban area as compared to living in a suburban or rural area. List these differences on a posterboard. After making the list, ask selected small groups of students to conduct a debate on the advantages and disadvantages of urban living, suburban living, and rural living.

4. Using the overhead projector, show students a map of their state. Ask them to pinpoint urban areas, suburban areas, and rural areas. Then ask them to list the factors that make those places urban, suburban, or rural. For example, students may note that a city in their state is located near a body of water. They may see that a small town is surrounded by large expanses of ranchland. Ask students to discuss some of the factors (geographical, political, economic) that may have determined the present size of various towns, villages, or cities in their state.

5. Encourage students to put together a "world record" book about cities. They should provide information in response to the following questions:

   What is the world's oldest city?

   What is the oldest city in the United States?

   What is the world's most populous city?

   What is the most populous city in the United States?

   Which U.S. city has the most cars?

   Which city has the tallest building?

Suburban Communities

 ## Introduction

Life in suburbia changed dramatically during the second half of the twentieth century. Early suburbs were simply an extension of the city, a few houses, a few streets, and perhaps a few other buildings. Today, however, suburbia has established its own sociological niche. The typical suburban environment (if there is such a thing) is composed of large manufacturing plants, shopping malls, tract homes and housing developments, and all the traffic and pollution that are typically associated with large urban environments.

Many students live in suburban environments and go to suburban schools. It is important for students to recognize the similarities that exist between their environments and the environment of those who live in cities or out in the country. Suburbs are distinctive, but they also share characteristics with city and rural environments.

 ## Research Questions

1. What is a suburb?

2. How is a suburban community similar to an urban community?

3. How is a suburban community different from a rural community?

4. Where are the nearest suburbs to where you live?

5. What are some of the major issues facing suburbs today?

 ## Web Sites

http://enteract.com/~tomkat/county.htm
This site offers viewers an inside look at six suburban Chicago counties. Students will learn that there's more to suburbia than just a bunch of shopping malls and car dealerships. (S: 4–6, T: 4–6)

http://www.epa.gov/region5/sprawl/suburban.htm
There are many different kinds of decisions that suburban communities must make (just like urban communities) that affect quality of life. This site presents a complete overview of major problems and decisions. (T: 4–6)

http://www.nacaa.org/NDPSEC.HTM
This site presents an extensive and thorough overview of a National Dialogue on Poverty. It profiles how various types of communities (rural, suburban, and urban) are addressing this social concern. (T: 4–6)

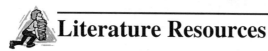

Literature Resources

Baylor, Byrd. (1983). *The Best Town in the World*. New York: Atheneum.
   This children's book allows readers to see what it is like to live in a town. Because this is the "best town in the world," everything is perfect, from eggs to chocolate cake. Children of all ages will enjoy hearing or reading this book. (Ages 9–12)

Duper, Linda Leeb. (1996). *160 Ways to Help the World: Community Service Projects for Young People*. New York: Facts on File.
   Duper presents excellent ideas on ways children can improve their communities. Step by step, readers are informed about how to get started in community service programs and follow through with them.

Fleischman, Paul. (1997). *Seedfolks*. New York: HarperCollins.
   Hoping to attract her father's spirit in a dingy town, a young Vietnamese girl plants seeds in a vacant lot in her neighborhood. Although planting the seeds for her own happiness, Kim, the Vietnamese girl, changes the life of many of her neighbors in this dim town.

Geisert, Bonnie. (1998). *Prairie Town*. New York: Walter Corraine.
   Geisert depicts relationships between people living in towns and on farms. Beautifully detailed panoramic views of town life allows reader to feel as if they are in the scene. Well detailed, this piece of literature depicts birth, celebrations, and death in a town setting, with great illustrations to enhance it.

Geisert, Bonnie. (1999). *River Town*. New York: Walter Corraine.
   A follow-up to *Prairie Town,* this book allows students to experience the four seasons in a town. Everything from a spring flood to the cracking ice in winter is depicted in this panoramic book. Beautiful illustrations allow readers to feel like they are in that scene at that moment.

Soto, Gary. (1992). *Neighborhood Odes*. New York: Harcourt Brace
   A fun book to share with children, these poems describe aspects of what it is like to live in a neighborhood. Filled with humor, sensitivity, and insight; children will gain a lot through exploring this book.

Activities and Projects

1. Have students explore *Neighborhood Odes*. Ask the students to write an ode about how they would feel about living in the suburbs. Ask them to write about one aspect of suburban community life. If more background information is needed, encourage students to check out *Seedfolks*, *River Town*, or the Web site http://www.wholeliving. com/dcsprawl/getting/html. Ask each student to illustrate their odes and post them in the hallway for others to enjoy.

2. Take the entire class on a field trip to a suburban community. Ask students to take a piece of paper along to record their observations. They should write down as much information about this community as they can, especially emphasizing the aspects that are different from and similar to their own community. Ask students to form small groups of four or five where they will share their observations. Within the group, students should construct a mural on large sheets of poster paper depicting their community and the one they visited. Display the murals around the classroom and provide time for each group to view the other groups' murals.

3. Provide materials for students to build their own suburban community. Ask them to explore literary sources such as *River Town*, *Prairie Town*, and *Seedfolks* and Web sites like http://enteract.com/~tomkat/county.htm for ideas about what to include in their suburban community. Popsicle® sticks could be electric poles with embroidery thread for power lines, empty milk cartons could be formed into houses. Allow the students enough time to complete their community. Once their community is complete, ask students to write a story about what a day in this suburban community is like. Once both parts of the project are completed, ask students to present their communities to the class and read the stories they wrote for it.

4. Conduct a class debate on whether a suburban community or the students' community is a better place to live. Divide the class in half and provide literary and Internet sources (such as the ones listed above) for each community type. Ask students to collect appropriate information. Organize a classroom debate on the advantages or disadvantages of living in one type of environment versus another.

5. Ask students to create a "Suburban Community" bulletin board. They should find pictures of suburban communities in magazines and on Internet sites, then place the pictures on the bulletin board along with adjectives that describe suburban communities. Literary sources such as *Seedfolks, Neighborhood Odes,* and *Midnight Snowman* and Internet sources such as http://enteract.com/-tomkat/county.htm and http://www.wholeliving.com/dcsprawl/getting/html will be helpful. Once the bulletin board is complete, have the students write journal entries about how they feel about their community bulletin board and how accurate they believe it is.

6. Ask students to find at least one or two books about suburban communities in their school library and/or in a public library. Have them create brochures or posters based on the literature they obtain. Their brochures or posters should include population, diversity, locations, characteristics, etc. Tell them to leave room on the brochures or posters to draw and color pictures depicting what suburban communities look like. Once the brochures and posters are completed, ask the students to present their information to the class. Display their work on a "Suburban Community" bulletin board.

Rural Communities

Introduction

Rural communities are more commonly referred to as "small town America." They usually have a small, spread out population with houses located some distance from each other. Typically, rural communities are populated by farmers or ranchers, although not always. According to the latest statistics from the Census Bureau, less than 3 percent of the population of this country lives in a rural environment.

Small towns and cities are the backbone of rural communities. Usually, less than 10,000 people inhabit these communities, and it is not unusual for everyone to know everyone else. Most of the goods and services needed by the people in these communities are provided by a host of small businesses. Not surprisingly, life in a rural community is not as fast paced as urban life. It is often reminiscent of life as it was at the beginning of the twentieth century.

Research Questions

1. What type of land generally makes up a rural community?

2. What are some occupations common to rural communities?

3. What are some activities people do in rural communities?

4. How is life in a rural community different from life in an urban community?

Web Sites

http://www.bestsmalltowns.com/
At this site students can access general information about small towns across the United States. For a more centralized search, the student can type in a specific state and access information on that particular state's small towns. (S: 4–6, T: All)

http://www.ers.usda.gov/briefing/rural
This site offers students a look at the economy and occupations of rural America. The primary focus is agriculture in rural areas and government issues that affect farmers. (T: All)

http://www.western2.com/mall/farm/
This is a detailed look at the lifestyles and activities of the farmer and the cowboy. The site illustrates multiple aspects of country life in a host of easily accessible searches. (S: 4–6, T: All)

http://www.midwestliving.com/index1.html
This site offers an overview of life in a Midwest state, from occupations to activities and recipes. Almost everything you want to know about the Midwest lifestyle and country living can be found here. (S: 4–6)

Literature Resources

Bial, Raymond. (1999). *One Room School*. New York: Houghton Mifflin.
The author presents a beautiful look at small town education through pictures he has taken of one-room schoolhouses. Go back in time and see school before computers and technology replaced the strong sense of family values and community in the classroom.

Brady, Peter. (1996). *Tractors*. Mankato, MN: Capstone Press.
This book goes into the who, what, and where of tractors. Find out about the tractor and its many uses for a farmer.

Halley, Ned. (1996). *Farm*. New York: Knopf.
This wonderfully illustrated, informative book teaches about the intricacies of a farm. Learn about the entire farm process, equipment, structures, and animals. Learn the history of farming and how it has evolved over time. See why it takes the entire family and community working together to make a farm successful.

Hirschi, Ron. (1989). *What Is a Horse?* New York: Walker.
This book looks at horses and their many qualities. The reader can learn about horses' many uses and their characteristics.

Jeffers, Susan & Wells, Rosemary. (1993). *Waiting for the Evening Sun*. New York: Dial Books for Young Readers.
Set in a small Vermont town in 1917, this book offers a wonderful view of country living and the farm. It details the story of a young boy who struggles with the idea of his older brother leaving home to travel abroad.

Motyka, Sally Mitchell. (1989). *An Ordinary Day*. New York: Simon & Schuster.
This book depicts a typical summer day of a child in a rural area. Read about the actions and interactions a child has as the child goes through the day.

Ready, Dee. (1997). *Farmers*. Mankato, MN: Capstone Press.
This book explains the who, what, and where of farm life. Readers get a brief overview of the farming experience.

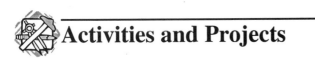

Activities and Projects

1. Ask students to interview their grandparents about what it was like when they were in school. Students should brainstorm as a class for questions to ask. Have students do a brief writeup about what they have learned and share it with the class. If practical, students may wish to conduct a series of oral interviews or produce a brief series of videotaped conversations with their grandparents. These can be kept in the classroom or donated to the school library.

2. Take the class on a walk through the community. Discuss the different things (e.g., structures, people, vegetation) that you see on your travels. What makes those things unique to the town? Could you see some of the things in your community if you lived in a rural area? Ask students to construct a Venn diagram of the city structures that would also be found in a rural community and those that might not be found in a rural community.

3. Have students read *One Room School*. Ask students to list the similarities and differences between the schools in the book and their own school. Encourage students to access the Web sites listed above and note additional similarities and differences. If they had a choice, which type of school would they prefer attending? Provide opportunities to discuss their choices.

4. Ask students to prepare a description of their local area from the perspective of an inanimate object. For example, if they live in an urban area, how would that area look from the perspective of a factory? If they live in a suburban area, how would that area look from the perspective of a stop sign? If living in a rural area, how would that area look from the perspective of a barn? After students have had an opportunity to share their perspectives, ask them to take on the imaginary role of an object in a community different from their local one and repeat this activity again.

5. Divide the class into two groups. Ask each group—using the Web sites and literature above—to create a special dictionary: One group should create a dictionary of country words and the other a dictionary of city words. Show them several examples of children's dictionaries for ideas on format or design. After the dictionaries are complete, ask the two groups to compare their lists. Are there words that appear on both lists? If so, why?

6. Country fairs mean lots of good food. Following is a recipe for some blue ribbon oatmeal muffins you and your students may enjoy preparing:

Oatmeal Muffins

1 egg	1 cup of buttermilk
1/2 cup of brown sugar	1/3 cup of shortening
1 cup of quick-cooking oats	1 cup of flour
1 teaspoon of baking powder	1 teaspoon of salt
1/2 teaspoon of baking soda	

Heat oven to 400 degrees. Grease bottoms of 12 medium muffin cups. Beat egg; stir in buttermilk, brown sugar, and shortening. Mix in remaining ingredients until flour is moistened. Batter should be lumpy. Fill cups and bake for 20 to 25 minutes. Remove from cups immediately. Spread with butter and enjoy!

Goods and Services

 ## Introduction

Goods and services are known to most as an economic concept. Goods are products or objects that are purchased and sold in stores and businesses. A service is any kind of work that is performed for another's benefit. Goods can be felt and are tangible, whereas a service may be seen but is not really touchable. Although these are abstract concepts, they can be made concrete, for example by studying people whose jobs are performing a service for the community or by examining the goods a grocery store or a farm carries and/or produces.

 ## Research Questions

1. What is a good?

2. What is a service?

3. Why is recycling a service?

4. What kinds of goods can be found at a grocery store? At a department store? At a toy store?

5. What are some services performed in your community?

 ## Web Sites

http://tqjunior.advanced.org/3901/
This Web site is a town called Econopolis; it contains a link called "Goods and Services Farm." Here students can read about what the difference is between a good and a service. This site also contains teaching resources and additional links for instructors. (S: K–3, T: K–3)

http://www.usps.gov/
This page is about the United States Postal System. At this site you can find out postal rates, locations of post offices, the history of the United States Postal System beginning with the Pony Express, and other general information. (T: All)

http://www.cyberspaceag.com/
This site is full of information about cattle farming, planting, and harvest times on a farm. There are fun crossword puzzles, lots of pictures, and stories. (T: K–3)

Literature Resources

Ahlberg, Janet & Ahlberg, Allan. (1996). *The Jolly Postman or Other People's Letters*. Boston: Little, Brown.
This book explains how the postal service works by having a postman deliver letters to fairy-tale characters. The book includes envelope pouches and letters in its pages, duplicates of the letters being sent to the various cartoon characters.

Allen, Thomas B. (1989). *On Granddaddy's Farm*. New York: Knopf.
Beautifully illustrated with chalk-on-canvas drawings, this book describes the goings-on of a farm from the point of view of a young person.

Borton, Lady & Root, Kimberly Bulcken. (1997). *Junk Pile*. New York: Philomel Books.
Jamie's dad runs a junkyard behind their home, and Jamie makes the best playthings from what others have deemed "junk." She has everything she could desire except a true friend. When she offers a gift made from scraps to a boy named Robert, she begins to find a friend in one who originally made fun of her.

Bourgeois, Paulette & Lafave, Kim. (1999). *Police Officers*. Toronto, Canada: Kids Can Press.
This book portrays friendly officers as they go about their daily duties. Children learn different aspects of police work, such as how they respond to calls to booking and legal processes.

Florian, Douglas. (1994). *A Carpenter: How We Work Series*. New York: Greenwillow Books.
This book in the How We Work Series is about the skills and jobs that a carpenter must possess and do. There are many different kinds of carpenters that create various wooden objects, and many of them are described in this book.

Florian, Douglas. (1994). *A Fisherman: How We Work Series*. New York: Greenwillow Books.
This book in the How We Work Series describes the services a fisherman provides for society, namely the food he provides.

Gibbons, Gail. (1992). *Recycle! A Handbook for Kids*. Boston: Little, Brown.
This book goes through the steps involved in recycling various kinds of materials. There are statistics in the back of the book that can provide a larger picture of the trash problem communities are facing.

Kuklin, Susan. (1999). *Fighting Fires*. New York: Aladdin Books.
Providing a behind-the-scenes look at the work and services provided by firefighters, this book tells about firefighting, from the call to the clean-up at the station. The book also provides color photographs of firefighters training and ends with fire safety tips.

Showers, Paul. (1994). *Where Does the Garbage Go?* New York: HarperCollins.
This book is very informative about what goes into our landfills and how we can reduce it by recycling.

Suen, Anastasia. (1999). *Delivery*. New York: Viking.
The book begins with the newspaper being delivered by bicycle and continues through to the gas at the pumping station being delivered by truck. Many goods are delivered everywhere around the world.

Activities and Projects

1. Lead a class discussion on the various goods and services provided in your local community. Ask youngsters to create a series of charts or graphs illustrating the different types of goods available as well as the individuals responsible for getting those goods into the hands of consumers. If practical, invite a local merchant to explain the process of getting a particular product from the manufacturer into the hands of a purchaser.

2. Conduct a survey of your students' parents. How many of them are involved in distributing goods throughout the community or across the country? How many of them are involved in service occupations? Ask pairs of students to interview selected parents about their jobs. After the interviews, encourage students to create a large wall mural listing the occupations and the responsibilities of each.

3. Share information with the class about the United States Postal System and read *The Jolly Postman* to the class. Afterwards, invite a local mail carrier to visit your classroom to discuss the duties and responsibilities of that job. Why are mail carriers essential to the community? Do they deliver goods or do they provide a service? Afterwards, your students may be interested in setting up a mail delivery system between your class and other selected classes throughout the school.

4. Share *Deliveries* with the class. Bring in lots of old magazines of every kind and ask the children to look through them and cut out any pictures that portray deliveries being made or that have been made. Children can also draw their own illustrations. After accumulating a huge pile of delivery pictures, have the children create a massive wall collage on large sheets of butcher paper.

5. Lead a class discussion about the goods and services offered in your school or in your classroom. What types of both are provided? Do teachers provide a service (instruction) or do they offer goods (materials and supplies)? What other types of goods are available in the school? What individuals are responsible for offering specific services? How is the school environment similar to a city or community environment? Ask students to construct an oversize Venn diagram on one wall of the classroom illustrating the similarities and/or differences.

Obeying Community Laws

 ## Introduction

Communities have laws to protect citizens. These laws are typically enforced by police officers. It is the duty of police officers to ensure that everyone obeys the laws of a community.

When a law has been broken, an officer may try to discover who was involved. Sometimes this may involve an arrest and the detention of an individual at the police station. A suspected lawbreaker is brought before a judge. If there is enough evidence to believe the suspect has broken the law, the individual goes to trial. A trial is a hearing at which a person is judged to be innocent or guilty. If an individual is found guilty, a fine or sentence may be imposed. This system of justice ensures that all citizens of a community are treated fairly and equally.

 ## Research Questions

1. What is the primary responsibility of the police?
2. What do judges do?
3. What is the role of lawyers?
4. Why are juries important in our judicial system?
5. Who are some law enforcement officers in your community?

 ## Web Sites

http://www.ncpc.org
This site provides access to the National Crime Prevention Council's (NCPC) Online Resource Center. It covers topics such as how to organize a neighborhood watch, general safety tips, and frequently asked questions about the NCPC. (S: All, T: All)

http://www.nhtsa.dot.gov/kids/biketour/
This site focuses on bike safety by providing students with a virtual bike tour. Throughout the tour, students can learn about proper bike equipment, reasons to wear a helmet, and how to properly navigate city traffic on a bike. (S: K–3, T: K–3)

http://www.dare-america.com/
This is the official D.A.R.E. site, an organization dedicated to keeping kids drug free by providing information about drugs. Students can find out about the organization and read poems, comments, and questions from kids. (S: K–3)

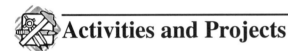

Literature Resources

Adams, Lisa. (1997). *Dealing with Lying*. New York: Rosen Publishing.
  This book deals with an issue common to children: lying. It presents valuable information and opportunities for readers to make their own decisions.

Boelts, Maribeth. (1997). *A Kids Guide to Staying Safe at Playgrounds*. New York: Rosen Publishing.
  This book deals with the issues of encountering strangers and what to do when accidents happen and provides guidelines to keep kids safe in all areas.

MacGregor, Cynthia. (1999). *What to Do If You Get Lost*. New York: Rosen Publishing.
  This book presents readers with valuable information on what to do if they should become lost. It discusses the use of 911 and how police officers can be of assistance.

Activities and Projects

1. Ask students to "produce" a public service announcement that instructs other students on how to be safe. Organize the class into groups and allow students to choose their topics. For example, one group could talk about the importance of wearing light-colored clothing when walking at night. Bring in a video camera to tape the students doing their one-minute ads. Students can bring props, organize a skit, play music, etc.

2. Invite a local police officer to talk to students about safety in their community. If appropriate, invite a lawyer or judge as well to speak to students about the judicial process, particularly in their own community. After the visits, ask students to create a "Comparison Poster" listing some of the rules or laws in the local community and corresponding rules or laws in the school community. What similarities do they notice?

3. Ask students to initiate a "Safety Committee" at school. Students can use resources such as Web sites, interviews with community leaders, and literature to educate themselves about the importance of safety and what they can do to make their town more safe. Then, ask groups of students to visit classes in grades lower than yours to "educate" students in those grades about safety in the local community.

4. To promote safety, initiate a bike helmet campaign. Ask students to read about the myths and facts about wearing a bike helmet, using selected Web sites. Then ask students to create a special bulletin board display that depicts their collected information. They can post their collected information on a schoolwide bulletin board or assemble the data into an attractive brochure to be distributed throughout the school.

5. As a class, make a list of all the safety rules inside and outside of the classroom, based on information the students have found on the Internet, in pamphlets, and in other sources. Hang the list on a bulletin board so everyone can see it in the classroom. Using that list, have a "Safety Kid of the Week." Students can nominate another student who they think exhibited an important safety rule for the week. They should write a brief paragraph describing why and how they thought that student performed a safety role and drop it in the "Safety Box" (a brightly colored shoebox or cardboard box). At the end of each week, draw a nominee at random and announce the winner.

Governing Our Nation

Introduction

The governmental system of the United States can be described as a constitutional democracy with features that reflect its European heritage and the specialized conditions of the New World. The basis of this government is to derive its powers from the consent of the governed, and these powers are subject to limitations and change. Flexibility is also a crucial element of our government. If we find fault with laws of the past, they can be changed. If we don't like how a senator is running things, we can vote for someone else. If we think an important issue has been left out, we can bring it to public attention. Our great nation is based on choice, and this right of choice is denied to no one.

Research Questions

1. Why is the Constitution an important document?

2. What does the Bill of Rights do?

3. What are the duties and responsibilities of the president?

4. What are the duties and responsibilities of a governor?

5. What are the duties and responsibilities of a senator?

6. What does the word *democracy* mean?

Web Sites

http://www.ipl.org/ref/POTUS

This site contains a brief biography of each U.S. president and shows the major accomplishments during each president's term. It describes the presidents' campaigns and the election results and contains interesting facts on each president. (T: All)

http://www.law.emory.edu/FEDERAL/usconst.html

This site breaks down the articles of the Constitution into specific sections for easy access. It is well organized and easy to navigate. This is a superior site for classroom teachers. (T: 4–6)

Literature Resources

Lubov, Andrea. (1990). *Taxes and Government Spending*. Minneapolis, MN: Lerner.

This book explains the many taxes we, as Americans, have to pay. It also shows what each tax dollar is used for. It shows how police, parks, schools, museums, and national defense are all funded through taxes.

Pascoe, Elaine. (1997). *The Right to Vote*. Brookfield, CT: Millbrook Press.

This book contains information on the right to vote and how this right has been acquired. It also shows the difference between direct and representative democracies. This book highlights the different types of elections and election campaigns.

Sandak, Cass. (1995). *Lobbying*. New York: Henry Holt.

This book shows what lobbying groups do and how they affect our lives. It shows how lobbying can increase and decrease votes. This book also explains the different public interest groups and what they do, as well as the major issues lobbyist groups deal with, such as gun control and healthcare reform.

Steen, Sandra. (1994). *Independence Hall*. New York: Dillon Press.

Independence Hall was the meeting place for one of the most famous events in U.S. history, the signing of the Constitution. This book describes the events leading up to the making of the Constitution. It also describes the struggle for independence, including the Revolutionary War.

Activities and Projects

1. After teaching the students about the topic of lobbying, ask the students to identify issues that they would like to see change. These may include school lunches and longer recess time. Divide the students into equal-sized groups, if possible, according to topic of interest. Ask the children to discuss ways they could work to change their specific topics. These may include talking with the principal or lunch providers.

2. Conducting a classroom election can be an interesting and productive exercise for understanding the different phases of an election. Allow the class to elect candidates and follow through with campaigning. After the students have been informed of each candidate's views and ways to improve their classroom, have a debate involving the rest of the class. This will allow them to ask questions as if they were representatives of the media. Then hold the election. After a candidate has been chosen, ask the students to write down why or why not they think this candidate should have been chosen.

3. After studying the Bill of Rights, ask students to review their rights as a student at school. Using the Bill of Rights as a guide, have the students revise their rights as a student. At this time, students will be able to add additional rights as they see fit. Divide the class into groups, then ask the students to construct their own Bill of Rights. After this has been completed, have the students compare their versions. Ask the students to come to an agreement and construct one Bill of Rights that the whole class can feel good about. Make sure that this Bill of Rights is constantly in effect in the classroom.

4. Divide the class into three groups: legislative, judicial, and executive. Ask each group to consult the Web sites and literature listed above and put together an informational poster or brochure containing important facts related to their assigned branch of government. Engage students in a discussion about which branch of government seems to have the most responsibilities. Provide sufficient opportunities to talk about our system of "checks and balances" and how it makes our form of government so unique.

5. Ask students to vote for two class senators to represent the class and sit in on monthly PTO meetings. Be sure the senators take the concerns, grievances, or issues of the class to each scheduled PTO meeting. The senators should report their findings to the class.

6. Designate yourself president of the class. Assemble a cabinet, choosing specific students (on a rotating basis) for cabinet positions, as follows:

Secretary of Transportation : Makes sure students get to the buses on time each day.

Secretary of Labor: Designates students for various classroom jobs.

Secretary of Treasury: Counts the lunch money each day.

Secretary of State: Shares classroom discoveries with students in other classes.

Attorney General: Ensures the rules of the classroom are adhered to by all.

Secretary of Education: Ensures that homework assignments are completed each day.

Asian Communities

Introduction

The largest city of Japan, indeed one of the largest cities in the world, is Tokyo. This capital city is over 226 square miles in size and has more than 8 million residents. An economically diverse city, it is the headquarters of several major worldwide corporations and plays a significant role in the social, political, and day-to-day life of the Japanese people. In China, the capital city of Beijing has more than 12 million residents and has long been the center of culture and politics for the entire country. A country that is fast becoming one of the most economically diverse in the world, China is still trying to deal with the constraints of a socialist government in an increasingly diverse economy. Korea is a country divided by wars and politics. North and South Korea, although separated only by a thin "line in the sand," are worlds apart in terms of economics and sociology.

Research Questions

1. What is the largest city in Korea?

2. What is the principal agricultural product of Japan?

3. How many people live in China?

4. How large is China?

5. How many islands make up the country of Japan?

Web Sites

http://library.advanced.org/26469/index2.html
Here students can access the history of China, the Cultural Revolution, cityscapes, and China's contributions to culture and society. (S: 4–6, T: 4–6)

http://www.artisandevelopers.com/web/tokyo/
This is a Web site created by two Americans who took a trip to Tokyo, Japan. Along with realistic photographs, they present many aspects of the culture, schools, transportation, senior citizens, television stations, trends, and landscape of the beautiful city. (S: All)

http://tqjunior.advanced.org/5110/
This all-inclusive site illustrates the differences and similarities between Korea and China. There's lots to discover here. (S: All, T: All)

http://www.odci.gov/cia/publications/factbook/ks.html
Facts about the government, people, economy, and geography of South Korea can be found on this complete site (S: 4–6)

http://www.lex5.k12.sc.us/ces/Japanmn.htm

At this site students can read about the history, cultures, sites, and other aspects of Japan as written by a group of fifth grade students. (S: 4–6)

http://www.supersurf.com/index.htm

At this all-inclusive site students can learn valuable information about dozens of countries around the world – including Japan. (S: 4–6)

http://www.kiku.com/qtvr/index.html

This is an impressive site that offers students QuickTime videos of selected places around Japan and China. This is a great complement to any unit. (S: 4–6)

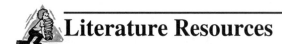# Literature Resources

Armstrong, Jennifer. (1996). *Chin Yu Min and the Ginger Cat*. New York: Random House.

Illustrated with pastels, this is the story of a widow named Chin Yu Min, who finds happiness in a mysterious ginger cat.

Chang, Margaret. (1997). *The Beggar's Magic*. New York: Margaret McElderry.

This is the story of a boy and his friends, who are fascinated by a holy beggar priest who comes to Fu Nan's village. The magic he works is fascinating as he fills an old widow's dry well with water and performs other magical feats.

Cotterell, Arthur. (1994). *Ancient China*. New York: Knopf.

This book presents Chinese history, from the earliest dynasty to the twentieth century, and the contributions China has made to the world.

Denenberg, Barry. (1999). *The Journal of Ben Uchida*. New York: Scholastic.

This book is the actual journal of Ben Uchida, a Japanese boy. He never thought he looked different, but he describes his feelings and thoughts as he realizes he does look different than the other kids.

Kent, Deborah. (1996). *Beijing*. Chicago: Children's Press.

In this book are descriptions of the physical aspects of Beijing as well as the history, social life, and customs of the capital of the People's Republic of China.

Ohmi, Ayano. (1999). *In Search of the Spirit*. New York: Morrow.

This book describes some of Japan's arts, such as Yuzen dyeing, bamboo basket weaving, Bunraku puppetmaking, ceramics, swordmaking, and Noh Theater.

Parker, Lewis J. (1994). *Dropping in on Japan*. Vero Beach, FL: Rourke Books.

Experience the natural beauty of Japan through large, beautifully realistic pictures in this book that introduces the people of Tokyo and how they live.

Activities and Projects

1. Ask students to imagine that they have a pen pal in Beijing, China, Tokyo, Japan, or Seoul, Korea. Ask them to prepare one or more letters to their imaginary friend inquiring about selected customs, traditions, or holidays. Students should use several of the Web sites and literature presented above.

2. Have students access the Web site http://www.jlnjapan.org/kidsweb and collect information about education in China and Japan. Divide the class into groups and have them construct compare and contrast lists to share with the class while you make a master list on the chalkboard.

3. Divide the class into several small groups. Ask each of three groups to assume the role of students in Korea, China, and Japan. Each of these groups will need to collect pertinent information about their lives in their "assigned" country. The other groups of students can take on the role of newspaper or television reporters preparing a story on the life of an "average" child in that particular country. Through a series of interviews, the "reporters" should collect the necessary information to assemble into a series of informative brochures.

4. Ask students to contact one or more travel agencies in your area. Have the students collect brochures or other materials that might reveal information about daily life in each of the three countries. Ask small groups of students to gather data about community or daily life in a specific country and present it to another class.

5. Following is a recipe for oriental fried rice that your students may enjoy:

Fried Rice

1 small onion, chopped
2 tablespoons of chopped green pepper
2 tablespoons of vegetable oil
2 cups of cooked rice
1 can of water chestnuts, thinly sliced
1 can of mushroom stems and pieces
2 tablespoons of soy sauce
3 eggs, beaten

Cook and stir green pepper and onion in oil in a skillet for about three minutes. Stir in rice, water chestnuts, mushrooms, and soy sauce. Cook over low heat, stirring frequently, for about five to seven minutes. Stir in eggs. Cook and stir four to five minutes longer. Makes four to five servings.

After the rice is made, hand out some chopsticks and demonstrate how to use them. Take one stick between the thumb and first finger. Trap the base of the other in the pouch of the thumb and rest the tip against the third finger. Only the upper chopstick is moved. Have students try eating the rice with chopsticks.

Australian Communities

Introduction

The culture of Australia has been shaped, and in some ways inhibited, by its isolation as an island continent. When British explorers landed on this continent they found a vast and largely empty land. Only about 300,000 aborigines lived on the continent then. Today, only about 100,000 aborigines are left in Australia.

Because the land was mostly dry, most of the earliest settlements were along the eastern coast. It was here that the cities of Melbourne, Brisbane, and Sydney were founded. Indeed, to this day, most of the major cities and towns of Australia cling to the eastern or western shoreline where the weather is temperate and there are more natural resources. Australian communities share many of the same features and characteristics of those in the United States.

Research Questions

1. What is the capital of Australia?

2. What are some of Australia's largest cities?

3. Why does most of the population live in large cities?

4. How is an Australian community similar to a U.S. community?

5. What kinds of communities do aborigines inhabit?

Web Sites

http://library.advanced.org/50055/australia.htm

This site provides information on the many areas of Australia. It covers different types of animals, geographic features, and customs of this fascinating country. It also includes many great photographs, maps, and fun facts. (S: 4–6, T: All)

http://www.ipl.org/youth/cquest/australia/australia.html

On this site, students have two tour guides—"Owl" and "Penguin." The guides travel to the different regions of Australia and give great descriptions of each. (S: K–3)

http://www.australia-online.com/

Just about anything anyone would ever want to learn about Australia can be found on this all-inclusive web site. A perfect addition to any unit! (T: All)

http://www.lex5.k12.sc.us/ces/Australia.htm

On this site students can read about the cultures, geography, people, and land of Australia as written by a group of fifth grade students. (S: 4–6)

Literature Resources

Arnold, Helen. (1996). *Australia (Postcards From)*. Austin, TX: Steck-Vaughn.

In this book, through several cleverly designed postcards, readers get a first-hand look at some of the most interesting places in this fascinating country.

Brown, Rollo. (1985). *An Aboriginal Family*. Minneapolis, MN: Lerner.

An eleven-year-old girl tells this story for children in grades 1–3. She tells about her family's life on a cattle station in Australia's Northern Territory.

Crew, Gary. (1995). *Angel's Gate*. New York: Simon & Schuster.

This book is about missing children living in the bush. Narrated by a thirteen-year-old boy, this story describes life in a small Australian community.

Darian-Smith, Kate. (1995). *The Australian Outback and Its People*. New York: Thomson Learning.

The Australian Outback is studied through its history, environment, inhabitants, and future. The impact of the Europeans on the aboriginal culture is discussed.

Drobismeisel, Jacqueline. (1997). *Australia: The Land Down Under*. New York: Benchmark Books.

This book has lots of information regarding life in Australia. Interesting facts can be found on holidays, sports, and schooling-by-radio. It focuses on the history of the continent and on aboriginal and immigrant cultures.

Hintz, Martin. (1998). *Australia*. New York: Children's Press.

This overview of Australia presents its history, natural resources, and aboriginal and immigrant cultures. It is accented with colorful photographs.

McCollum, Sean (1999). *Australia (A Ticket To)*. Minneapolis, MN: Carolrhoda Books.

This book provides young readers with snippets of information about Australia's geography, language, customs, religion, lifestyles, and culture.

Morin, Paul. (1998). *Animal Dreaming: An Aboriginal Dreamtime Story*. New York: Silver Whistle.

This book is about a creation myth originating from tribes in the Northeast Territories. Perfect for grades K–4, this story is accompanied by beautiful illustrations.

Olawsky, Lynn. (1997). *Colors of Australia*. Minneapolis, MN: Carolrhoda Books.

Filled with colorful photography and descriptive information, this book offers lots of interesting and valuable data on this island continent.

 # Activities and Projects

1. Ask students to look through literature and Internet sites for pictures of the Australian Outback. Have them create a series of "adding machine tape movies" showing the Outback's terrain, wildlife, and vegetation. Materials needed are shoeboxes, adding machine tape, pencils, and colored pencils or markers.

2. Ask the class to write to the Australian Tourist Commission or access it via the following Web site: http://www.australia.com/. Students should obtain tourist information, maps, and other free information to share with the entire class. Ask class members to assemble an informational newsletter or a video about selected sites in Australia, especially those sites that might be of most interest to U.S. students visiting there.

3. Students may enjoy a traditional Australian treat known as Damper. Here's how to prepare it:

Damper

Preheat an oven to 375 degrees. While the oven is heating, grease a large cookie sheet. Sift 2 cups of all-purpose flour, 4 teaspoons of baking powder, and 1/2 teaspoon of salt into a large mixing bowl. Add 3/4 to 1 cup of milk, 1 teaspoon of cinnamon, 1/4 cup of raisins, and 1/4 cup of sugar. Stir with a spoon until the dough is soft. Use your hands to form the dough into a large ball and place it on the cookie sheet. Bake the dough ball for 30–35 minutes, or until it sounds hollow when it is tapped on the bottom. Allow to cool, cut into pieces, serve, and enjoy.

4. Ask students to access one or more of the Web sites listed above. Using the information provided [and the data in *Australia (Postcards From)*], have students create their own series of imaginary postcards from Australia. Tell students that the class has been commissioned by the Australian Department of Tourism to create a new set of postcards that will be sold at tourist spots throughout the country. Students will need to decide on the 15–20 sites to be featured on the cards and the specific elements to be included in the illustration(s) and descriptive details on the back of each card. Arrange a collage of student's postcards on a classroom bulletin board.

European Communities

Introduction

Europe is the sixth largest continent. Its land mass covers 4 million square miles and it is home to a large number of countries. Europe is heavily populated—in 1991, Europe had an estimated population of 502 million people.

Most of the communities of Europe reflect the wonderful culture of the past while mixing it with the environment of the present. Europe is rich in history, culture, and the arts. Communities in Europe are as diverse as the people; as disparate as the multitude of languages and customs pervading this remarkable and unique part of the world. Civilizations have risen and fallen; traditions abound in a panorama of music, song, and dance; and the geography is as varied as anyplace on the globe. To say that the communities of Europe are rich in diversity is to state the obvious; to say that they are ripe for examination and discovery is to provide students with a peek into history, a glance into geography, and a look at political and cultural landmarks found nowhere else.

Research Questions

1. What are the countries of Western Europe?

2. What are the countries of Eastern Europe?

3. What are some of the important mountain ranges in this region of the world?

4. What are some important oceans or seas in this region?

5. What are some of the climatological zones in this region?

Web Sites

http://www.lib.utexas.edu/Libs/PCL/Map_collection/europe.html
This site contains an excellent online map of Europe. It shows many of the smaller countries that were once part of the Soviet Union but are now individual countries. (S: All, T: All)

http://www.mrdowling.com/708europe.html
Wow! Lots of information and tons of data fill this complete and thorough Web site. This site is ideal for all European studies. (S: 4–6, T: 4–6)

http://wfs.vub.ac.be/cis/festivals/
This host page for festivals and traditions contains ten links, one per country. Here, one can learn about the various celebrations and festivals observed in these countries. Some of them can be read in their native language as well as in English. Some of the European links are Austria, Belgium, Finland, France, Germany, Portugal, Spain, and Sweden. (S: 4–6, T: All)

http://www.visiteurope.com/Britain/Britain01.htm
 This Web site explains wonderful things about Great Britain. (S: 4–6)

http://www.visiteurope.com/France/France01.htm
 This Web site explains wonderful things about France. (S: 4–6)

http://www.visiteurope.com/Germany/Germany01.htm
 This Web site explains wonderful things about Germany. (S: 4–6)

http://www.visiteurope.com/Italy/Italy01.htm
 This Web site explains wonderful things about Italy. (S: 4–6)

Literature Resources

Arnold, Helen. (1996). *Postcards from Great Britain*. Austin, TX: Steck-Vaughn.
 This fascinating book presents some interesting facts about Great Britain. Pictures are on one side of the page, with a short note on the other side. The text explains something about the picture.

Burgan, Michael. (1999). *A True Book: England*. New York: Children's Press.
 This book offers a good physical description of England. It also recounts some history, covering rulers, invaders, business, and even sports. A good overview in a small book.

Dowswell, Paul. (1997). *The Roman Record*. London: Usborne Publishing.
 This book uses a newspaper format and is creatively written on a level that children can understand. This is an original way to help students understand Roman history. It is eye-catching, with short to medium stories to help students move through the bits of history they might have missed. The creative use of advertising helps to visualize the culture of the time.

Harris, Jacqueline L. (1998). *Science in Ancient Rome*. New York: Franklin Watts.
 Roman history is mixed and blended into this account of Roman science. Because Roman science was not actively seeking new discoveries but was patterned after discoveries made by others, the accumulation of scientific knowledge came with the interaction of other cultures through conquering and trading. The knowledge gleaned from others was improved upon and applied to improve the daily lives of Roman citizens.

Mariella, Cinzia. (1999). *Getting to Know Italy*. Lincolnwood, IL: Passport Books.
 This is like a thin encyclopedia explaining the country Italy. Although small, it contains a huge amount of information. A good book and very useful.

Pluckrose, Henry. (1998). *Picture a Country Germany*. Danbury, CT: Franklin Watts.
 In this book are some marvelous pictures of Germany's countryside, cities, and towns. It is interesting to see the Rhine River in the foreground, a small town just beyond, plowed fields in segmented layers going up a hill, and finally a castle in the background

Activities and Projects

1. After they review the Web sites, have students create a classroom bulletin board describing a European community. They should include facts about the community, its location in Europe, its festivals or traditions, buildings, and people. Ask students to contribute selected items for the bulletin board over an extended period of time.

2. Ask students to select a favorite illustration from one of the Web sites listed above. Have them download and print those scenes and create individual dioramas of their selections. They can add original drawings and use clay, construction paper, pipe cleaners, and wire to construct three-dimensional objects to place in the dioramas. Display the dioramas prominently in the classroom.

3. Share *Postcards from Great Britain.* Ask students to construct postcards about one or more European countries using the Web site http://www.geographia.com/indx03.htm. This Web site provides pertinent information, such as capital city and points of interests, on each country. Divide the class into several small groups. Ask students to select magazine pictures from old magazines that depict life in a selected European country. Have them paste their selected pictures on sheets of oaktag and cut them into postcard shapes. Encourage students to write messages on the back of each postcard about how they are enjoying an imaginary visit to that country. Students may wish to send their postcards to students in other classrooms.

4. Share *The Roman Record.* The Web site http://wfs.vub.ac.be/cis/festivals, which introduces the European festivals, is another good place to start. Inform the students that they will be creating a newspaper for the school concerning European communities. Ask selected groups to choose a European community to represent in the form of a newspaper. Each person in the group should be responsible for reporting on one aspect of the community. Each group should produce one advertisement, one section selling real estate, and two articles. This long-term project can be woven into other aspects of the study of European communities, with selected information presented in the form of a final newspaper.

5. Ask students to create a 12-month calendar, designating one month for each of 12 different European countries. After students have conducted appropriate research via the Web sites and literature listed above, they should note the celebrations and holidays of each country on the dates of its appropriate month.

African Communities

Introduction

As varied as its terrain, Africa has a plethora of different peoples, tribes, and cultures. Each is distinctive. Together, they form one of the most fascinating continents on Earth. Separately, they stand as important markers for the diversity of life in this rich and multifaceted land.

Africa is a continent of enormous contrasts—culturally, geographically, ethnically, and historically. It stretches 5,000 miles from north to south, and 4,600 miles from east to west. It is a land of tall mountain ranges, thirsty deserts, and lush forests, of steamy tropical jungles and bone-chilling mountain environments. Name a climatological zone, and chances are it can be found somewhere on this vast and amazing continent.

On this on continent alone there are many different social systems, religions, beliefs, and over 1,000 languages. The African people are a diverse population who often live together in tribes. Their lives are shared, their families are universal, and their gifts and faults are both celebrated and mourned by the tribe. It is the presence of community that is often the stability and union of the people.

Research Questions

1. What are some of the languages spoken on the continent of Africa?

2. How many different countries are there in Africa?

3. What are some of the major cities in Africa?

4. How is life in Africa different from life in North America?

5. How is the climate of Africa similar to the climate of South America?

Web Sites

http://www.africaonline.com/AfricaOnline/coverkids.html
This site, created just for children, offers an opportunity for youngsters to explore the diverse world of Africa. This Web site covers a variety of topics, including geography, history, and culture. The site contains kid-friendly maps, games, quizzes, and even a place to make a global buddy in Africa. It is a great place to interactively explore Africa. (S: 4–6)

http://library.advanced.org/16645/contents.html
Explore the cities and regions of Africa with this Web site. An interactive picture index leads students into the world of Africa. Youngsters can explore the wildlife, landscape, and people. An excellent resource to begin an investigation of Africa. (S: 4–6)

http://www.ccph.com/coea
    At this site students can meet the children of East Africa. Lots to do and lots to learn on this all-inclusive site. A fantastic resource, with loads of links, for teachers, too. (S: All, T: All)

http://www.pbs.org/wonders/
    Wonders of the African World, from PBS, is one of the most complete resources available for any classroom teacher. There's way too much to list here. Be sure to check it out! (T: All)

 # Literature Resources

Aardema, Verna. (1981). ***Bringing the Rain to Kapiti Plain***. New York: Puffin Books.
    This fictional tale of the thirsty African plains tells the story of a shepherd boy, his livestock, and their quest to restore the land. Its poetic form and descriptive pictures add to the seriousness of the topic and the beauty of the legend.

Arnott, Kathleen. (1990). ***African Myths and Legends***. New York: Oxford.
    This delightful compilation of myths and stories would be perfect for classroom read-alouds.

Ayo, Yvonne. (1995). ***Eyewitness Books: Africa***. New York: Knopf.
    With its exotic illustrations, diagrams, and real-life photos, this informative, nonfiction book is a terrific resource for anyone learning about Africa. It includes information about civilizations and building homes, religion and beliefs, and African mask-making.

Grifalconi, Ann. (1986). ***The Village of Round and Square Houses***. Boston: Little, Brown.
    One evening after dinner, a young girl's grandmother explains the origins of the village tradition of round and square houses. The women live in round houses and the men in square houses; the grandmother explains that this is the result of a volcanic eruption believed to be caused by the angered Gods.

Musgrave, Margaret. (1992). ***Ashanti to Zulu: African Traditions***. New York: Dial Books.
    Another "must have" book for the classroom, this classic collection of stories is ideally suited to any study of Africa.

Onyefulu, Ifeoma. (1993). ***A Is for Africa***. New York: Cobblehill.
    This delightful alphabetical exploration of the African culture is beautifully illustrated with photographs. Beginning with "A" for Africa and ending with "Z" for a zigzagging lane into the author's village, each letter of the alphabet highlights a different cultural aspect of life in Africa.

Onyefulu, Ifeoma. (1997). ***Chidi Only Likes Blue***. New York: Cobblehill.
    In this book the colors of Africa are seen through the eyes of a young child. Delightful!

Waterlow, Julia. (1998). ***A Family from Ethiopia***. Austin, TX: Steck-Vaughn.
    Children get a first-hand look at an Ethiopian family and their lifestyle in this book. Part of a series that stimulates fabulous compare and contrast studies in any classroom.

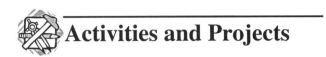

Activities and Projects

1. Ask students to consult several of the Web sites listed above to locate information on the various types of houses or dwellings that can be found throughout Africa. After students have collected sufficient information, have them create their own models of a selected house/dwelling using a variety of art materials (construction paper, pipe cleaners, glue, craft sticks, etc.). Be sure to provide an appropriate place to display these models.

2. Have students take on the role of an African woman, child, or military official. After researching titles, places in society, and values of African civilizations, students should create journals about their "characters' " lives. Offer prompts for journal expansion such as clothing, daily activities, family/social life, and forms of entertainment. If possible, have students dress the part and present several journal entries to the class.

3. Pattern and color are a key part of African tradition and belief. Have students look at pictures or pieces of African cloth, artwork, sculpture, etc., to get an understanding of the symbolism. Afterwards, have students make a decorative pattern of their own that could be used in African art design. They can make colored drawings with paint or "weave" a pattern from colored yarn or construction paper. They should include a paragraph or two explaining the meaning of the design, its function, and its symbolism to the community.

4. Students may enjoy writing a letter to a U.S. embassy in one or more African countries. The addresses of specific embassies can be obtained from the U.S. Department of State (2201 C St., NW, Washington, DC 20520). Students should decide on the type of information they would like to receive from a specific embassy (brochures, agricultural facts, type of government, etc.) before drafting their letters. As information is received, post it on a collective bulletin board; review it throughout the year.

5. Classes in many parts of Africa are typically held outdoors. Conduct a day's worth of lessons outside on the school grounds. Afterwards, ask the students to reflect on the differences between outdoor education and indoor education. How would they feel about having all their classes outdoors? What difficulties would they encounter? What modifications would have to be made in the current program?

6. Peanut soup is a very popular dish in many African countries, partly because Africa is one of the world's largest producers of peanuts. Following is a recipe you and your students may enjoy preparing and sharing:

Peanut Soup

2 celery sticks	2 carrots
2 onions	2 potatoes
2 tomatoes	4 cups of water
2 teaspoons of salt	2 bouillon cubes (any flavor)
1 teaspoon of pepper	1 cup of chunky peanut
1 cup of milk	butter
6 tablespoons of rice	2 tablespoons of brown
	sugar

Cut the vegetables into small pieces and place them in a large saucepan. Add the water, bouillon cubes, salt, and pepper and boil gently for about 20 minutes, stirring occasionally. Blend the peanut butter, milk, and brown sugar together in a mixing bowl and add to the saucepan. Stir in the rice and allow all the ingredients to simmer at a low heat for about 30 minutes. Ladle into bowls and enjoy!

South American Communities

Introduction

South America is a continent of contrasts, from large sprawling cities to dense rainforest environments. It offers a panorama of sights and sounds, people and cultures, languages and lore to be found nowhere else in the world. It is a continent ripe for discovery and rich in wonder and excitement.

For geographic purposes, South America is typically divided into two regions. The first is known as the Andean and northern countries. These countries include Ecuador, Peru, Bolivia, Chile, Colombia, Venezuela, Guyana, Suriname, and French Guyana. These countries are noted for high elevations and a widely distributed population. Spanish is the predominant language, but there is also a wide variety of Indian populations throughout this region, each with their own dialect and/or language.

The other region of South America is often known as the Silver River countries. These include Brazil, Argentina, Uruguay, and Paraguay. The major river in this part of South America is called the *Rio de la Plata,* or "River of Silver." This part of South America is also known for large expanses of treeless plains. These plains are called *pampas* and are known for huge fields of wheat, corn, and flax as well as sprawling ranches with enormous herds of cattle.

Research Questions

1. How many countries are in South America?

2. How is life in the northern countries different from life in the Silver River countries?

3. How are families different in South American communities than those in North American communities?

4. What are some of the languages spoken in South America?

5. What is the largest country in South America?

6. What is the most mountainous country in South America?

Web Sites

http://lcweb2.loc.gov/frd/cs/petoc.html
This Web site deals with society and daily life in Peru. It is mainly a site for teachers to glean information about the country and its people to develop into exciting lessons for students. (T: 4–6)

http://www.ran.org/ran/kids_action/questions.html

This is an excellent and exciting Web site for kids to learn about rainforests! Full of bright illustrations and questions most frequently asked, created by kids for kids. It also offers ways to help save the rainforest and get involved. (S: All)

http://www.embassy.org/uruguay/

Teachers can find everything they need to know at this site about Uruguay. (T: 4–6)

http://www.lonelyplanet.com/dest/sam/ecu.htm

A brief description of Ecuador and the Galapagos Islands can be found at this Web site (S: 4–6, T: 4–6).

http://www.lonelyplanet.com/dest/sam/chile.htm

At this site students and teachers can obtain information on Chile and Easter Island. (S: 4–6, T: 4–6)

http://www.mrdowling.com/712southamerica.html

This is a terrific web site that offers students and teachers valuable information and lots of insights into South America. This is a "must-have" resource for the classroom. (S: 4–6, T: 4–6)

**http://www.lib.utexas.edu/Libs/PCL/Map_collection/americas/SouthAmerica
_ref802636_1999.jpg**

This site has a full color map that can be downloaded and shared with students. (T: 4–6)

http://www.pbs.org/edens/manu/

This site is part of PBS's Living Edens series. Here, students will be able to examine one of the ancient cultures of Peru. (S: 4–6)

Literature Resources

Fredericks, Anthony D. (1996) *Exploring the Rainforest: Science Activities for Kids*. Golden, CO: Fulcrum Publishing.

In this exciting and dynamic activity book, students can examine and explore the incredible diversity of life in the rainforests of the world. The focus is on active involvement.

Haskins, Jim & Benson, Kathleen. (1996). *Count Your Way Through Brazil*. Minneapolis, MN: Carolrhoda Books.

This book can also be used as a "Math Counting" book. It has the word for each number (1–10) in English and Portuguese. On each page it explains a different aspect of Brazil, from its early history to celebrations and festivals to the country's most popular sports and foods.

Hintz, Martin. (1998). *Argentina*. New York: Children's Press.

This is a brief but thorough introduction to one of the most fascinating countries of South America.

Lyle, Garry. (1998). *Peru*. New York: Chelsea House.

A brief but thorough overview of the country of Peru is in this book.

Morrison, Marion. (1999). *Colombia*. New York: Children's Press.

This book describes the geography, history, people, industries, and culture of Colombia.

Parnell, Helga. (1997). ***Cooking the South American Way***. Minneapolis, MN: Lerner.

Lots of delicious recipes and eye-catching photography highlight this book, which should be part of any South American unit.

Pollard, Michael. (1997). ***The Amazon***. New York: Benchmark Books.

Thorough writing and plenty of photographs in this book reveal how the Amazon River was formed and the rich history of the people who live along its banks.

Torres, Leyla. (1995). ***Saturday Sancocho***. New York: Farrar, Straus & Giroux.

One Saturday afternoon, Maria Lili and her grandmother must go to the market to barter for the ingredients to make Sancocho. Children will learn about the marketplace and South American culture through their journey with Maria Lili. A recipe for the Chicken Sancocho is also provided.

Activities and Projects

1. Many people in South America live in the rainforest. Ask students to log on to the Web site http://www.ran.org/ran/kids_action/questions.html and read the book *Exploring the Rainforest: Science Activities for Kids*. Afterwards, have students develop a "plan of action" for preserving the world's rainforests. What are some of the major concerns and how can those concerns be addressed? Ask small groups of students to develop an appropriate campaign (letter writing, picketing, letters to the editor) that would bring the plight of the rainforest (particularly in South America) to the attention of legislators as well as the general population. What effects will rainforest destruction have on the lifestyles and customs of indigenous rainforest peoples?

2. As a class, ask students to think about their families. Encourage them to think about how important their families are to them. Have them use information from the Web sites listed above to describe how South Americans view "family." Make a class Venn diagram showing how students in North and South America view their families. Provide sufficient time for students to discuss any similarities and/or differences.

3. Ask students to obtain a demographic table or series of tables for selected South American countries. Using the information presented on the tables (or obtained from Web sites listed above), students should compare growth rates to determine which country is experiencing the most rapid population growth. Have students create a population map of a selected country illustrating the distribution of population within the borders of that country.

4. Divide the class into several small groups. Ask each group to select two South American countries and create a series of charts comparing their landscapes, exports, ancestries, languages, and climate. Students should obtain the necessary information from various Web sites or literature resources. Provide sufficient opportunities for students to display and discuss their findings.

5. One of the favorite dishes in many South American countries is tapioca. Tapioca is made from cassava, a starchy tuber that grows in many countries. Your students may enjoy making and eating the following:

Tapioca

In a medium-sized saucepan, whisk together 3 cups of milk, 1/3 cup of sugar, 1/4 cup of minute tapioca, 1/4 teaspoon of salt, and 2 eggs. Cover with a sheet of plastic wrap and let the mixture stand for about five minutes. Place the pan on the stove and cook over medium heat. Stir the mixture constantly until it comes to a boil. Turn off the heat immediately and stir in 1 teaspoon of vanilla. Allow to cool and thicken. Pour the cooled tapioca into several small bowls and sprinkle some cinnamon on each one. Serve and enjoy.

Central American Communities

Introduction

Central America is located between North and South America. Eight countries make up Central America: Honduras, Nicaragua, Costa Rica, Guatemala, Belize, El Salvador, Mexico, and Panama. These countries have been separate nations since 1838. The predominant language is Spanish, the language of their colonial rulers. The one exception is the country of Belize, where English is the predominant language (the country was a former British colony). In Guatemala, Indian languages predominate because most of the population is Indian, although the country's official language is Spanish. As a result of the Spanish colonial background, the Roman Catholic religion is the predominant religion in this region of the world.

Research Questions

1. How many countries are in Central America?

2. What is the largest country in Central America?

3. What is the primary language in Central America?

4. What type of climate is typical in Central America?

Web Sites

http://www.wtg-online.com/navigate/region/cam.asp
This is a great site that provides students with lots of information about eight Central American countries—Belize, Costa Rica, El Salvador, Guatemala, Honduras, Mexico, Nicaragua, and Panama. (S: 4–6, T: 4–6)

http://www.mytravelguide.com/central_america.asp?corridor=
This site offers information on the geography, climate, history, government, points of interest, holidays, and events in eight Central American countries. A valuable resource for any classroom. (S: 4–6, T: 4–6)

http://www.latinsynergy.org/def_central_travel.htm
The Central American Travel Guide offers up-to-the-minute information about travel in each of the eight Central American countries. (S: 4–6, T: All)

Literature Resources

Foran, Eileen. (1992). *Costa Rica Is My Home*. Milwaukee, WI: Garth Stevens.

This book enables the student to learn all about the country of Costa Rica by reading about eleven-year-old Evelyn Cristiana Gonzales-Hidalgo and her family. All aspects of Costa Rican lifestyles are covered. People and land are also touched on in this book.

Griffiths, John. (1985). *Let's Visit Nicaragua*. Bridge Post, CT: Burke Publishing.

This book offers a detailed look at the country of Nicaragua. The student will find information on the people, land, government, economy, activities, and just about anything else about Nicaragua.

Haynes, Tricia. (1985). *Let's Visit Honduras*. Bridge Post, CT: Burke Publishing.

This book offers a detailed look at the country of Honduras. The student will find information on the people, land, government, economy, activities, and just about anything else about Nicaragua.

Hermes, Jules. (1997). *Children of Guatemala*. Minneapolis, MN: Carolrhoda Books.

Filled with lots of photographs, this delightful book will provide young readers with some amazing information about this country.

Rau, Dana. (1999). *Panama*. New York: Children's Press.

This book has solid information on the history, geography, economics, and cultural life of Panama.

Sanders, Renfield. (1997). *El Salvador*. New York: Chelsea House.

This book surveys the history, topography, people, and culture of El Salvador, with emphasis on current economic conditions.

Staub, Frank. (1997). *Children of Belize*. Minneapolis, MN: Carolrhoda Books.

This concise photoessay focuses on a dozen youngsters and their lives in this unique and intriguing Central American country.

Winkelman, Barbara. (1999). *The Panama Canal*. New York: Children's Press.

This brief book presents a very readable account of the history of the canal that connects the Atlantic and Pacific oceans.

Activities and Projects

1. Ask students to collect newspaper articles about one or more Central American countries. Have them read the articles to locate information about the climate, animals, culture, government, or people of their selected countries. Students should record this information in journals or scrapbooks. Have students check out the information listed on some of the Web sites above to add to their knowledge about their countries. Ask youngsters to compare the information found on the Web sites with that found in newspaper accounts. Provide time to discuss any differences or similarities.

2. Ask students to color the national flag of one of the following Central American countries: Honduras, Costa Rica, El Salvador, Guatemala, Nicaragua, Belize, Mexico, or Panama. The students can use poster board and markers to create flags. Ask the students to write a paragraph about the origins of their country's flag, using literature resources or Web sites. Finally, ask the students to write a paragraph about what they think the flag means to the people of that country. Display the flags in an appropriate place.

3. Ask students to work in small groups to create collages depicting life in one Central American country. Supply each group with a collection of old magazines and ask them to cut out pictures or photographs of various scenes from a selected country. Students may also wish to download appropriate pictures from the Web sites above to include in their collages.

4. Ask students to access some of the Web sites listed above to research the powerful empires that existed in Central America. Ask small groups of students to create large time lines (on extended pieces of newsprint) on which they should record their assembled information. Be sure to post these around the classroom.

5. Ask students to investigate some of the challenges that Latin Americans have faced in the United States. These may include, but are not limited to, housing, working conditions, economic exploitation, poverty, political representation, education, and unemployment. Students should share their findings in the form of a letter or message to a state representative or U.S. senator.

Southeast Asian Communities

Introduction

Southeast Asia is the vast region of Asia situated east of the Indian subcontinent and south of China. Southeast Asia consists of the countries of Cambodia, Laos, Burma, Thailand, Vietnam, Singapore, Malaysia, Brunei, Indonesia, and the Philippines. Southeast Asia stretches 4,000 miles at its greatest extent and encompasses about 5 million square miles of land and sea, of which about 1,736,000 square miles is land. All of Southeast Asia falls within the tropical and subtropical climatic zones and receives a considerable amount of rainfall annually. It is subject to an extensive and regular monsoon weather system. Within this broad outline, Southeast Asia is perhaps the most diverse region on Earth. The number of large and small ecological niches is more than matched by a variety of economic, social, and cultural niches Southeast Asians have developed for themselves. Hundreds of ethnic groups and languages have been identified.

Research Questions

1. What is the dominant religion in Thailand?

2. What are some differences between Vietnam and the United States?

3. What is the official religion of Malaysia?

4. What are the four languages spoken in Singapore?

5. Which country in Southeast Asia has the largest port?

Web Sites

http://lcweb2.loc.gov/frd/cs/latoc.html
This site, based on the study of Laos, is a very detailed description of the country. It covers many aspects of Laos in a thorough and complete manner. (T: 4–6)

http://www.thaistudents.com
This site was constructed by Thai teachers and their students. New information about Thailand is constantly being added. This site describes the daily life of people living in the country. It contains pictures and information about the schools and festivals. (S: 4–6)

http://www2.lhric.org/pocantico/vietnam/vietnam.htm
This site contains basic information about Vietnam. It also has a list of books about Vietnam suited for children and links to applicable Web sites for further study. This is a very useful source. (S: K–3)

http://www.lib.utexas.edu/Libs/PCL/Map_collection/middle_east_and_asia/ SE_Asia_pol_95.jpg

This site has a downloadable map of the countries of Southeast Asia. (S: 4–6, T: All)

http://www.mrdowling.com/615seasia.html

This is simply a fabulous Web site that has tons of information and data about the land, people, cultures, and history of various Southeast Asian countries. Complete and thorough. (S: 4–6, T: All)

 # Literature Resources

Knowlton, Mary Lee. (1987). *Burma*. Milwaukee, WI: Gareth Stevens.

This book shows the daily routine of a young child living in Burma. It describes the everyday life of a family in Burma and the daily tasks they complete. This book contains information on the food, education, ceremonies, and even toys the children play with.

Lye, Keith. (1985). *Take a Trip to Indonesia*. New York: Franklin Watts.

This book describes the nation's cities, languages, religions, and main exports. It also contains information about Indonesia's monetary system. This book is a great way to introduce Indonesia to the younger student.

Nhoung, Huynh. (1997). *Water Buffalo Days*. New York: HarperCollins.

For a young boy growing up in the hills of Central Vietnam, the days were full of adventure. Nhuong's companion while growing up was a water buffalo. Now as an adult, Nhuong gives readers a glimpse of how he faced danger growing up in the Vietnamese jungle that was his home.

Schmidt, Jeremy. (1995). *Two Lands, One Heart*. New York: Walker.

This is the story of an American boy's journey to his mother's home in Vietnam. Vietnam's culture is described, comparing it to that of the United States.

Thomson, Ruth. (1988). *A Family in Thailand*. Minneapolis, MN: Lerner.

This book describes the life of a typical family living in Thailand. It contains a map of important areas and describes the education Thai students receive. This is an excellent book to familiarize students with life in Thailand.

Wee, Jessie. (1985). *We Live in Malaysia and Singapore*. New York: Bookwright Press.

Malaysia and Singapore are grouped together in this book because they have many similarities. This book describes the language, currency, religions, climate, government, education, agriculture, and industry of each country.

Wright, David. (1993). *Vietnam Is My Home*. Milwaukee, WI: Gareth Stevens.

This book describes the life of a Vietnamese child living in a small village with her family. It describes their home life, education, customs, and festivals.

Activities and Projects

1. Divide students into groups, assigning each group a different country in Southeast Asia. Ask students to gather information on the daily life of an average family in their assigned country. They can find this information in books and on the Web sites listed above. After obtaining this information, students should write about the daily lives of a family in their specific country. Bring the class back together and ask the students to discuss the differences and similarities between the countries.

2. Ask the students to choose a country in Southeast Asia and gather information on it, using books and various Web sites. Ask youngsters to focus on some of the important holidays and celebrations in their selected country. Have small groups of students assemble their information in the form of a newsletter or newspaper. What would be some of the headlines for a particular celebration? What types of community events might be scheduled for a national holiday? What would be some important places to visit during selected ceremonies?

3. After studying the climates of the different areas in Southeast Asia, ask the class to choose a country to study. Students should gather information about the climate of their chosen country and prepare a series of meteorological maps (similar to those found on the back page of the first section of *USA Today*). What similarities and/or differences do they note in the climate of Southeast Asia and those found throughout the United States?

4. Divide the class into pairs of students. Ask each pair to choose a major city in Southeast Asia and imagine they're going to move to this city. They should find information on what industries are located there, kinds of food they will eat, where they could have a job, and living conditions. Encourage students to use the literature resources and Web sites listed above. After sufficient information has been gathered, have each pair describe their "adopted" city in detail, with special emphasis on the features that would be most appealing to a visitor or potential immigrant.

5. *Tom Kar Gai* is a traditional dish eaten throughout Thailand. Although you may not be able to make it in your classroom, you could prepare the recipe below ahead of time and share it with your students as part of a Thai festival or at the conclusion of selected activities related to this Southeast Asian country:

> **Tom Kar Gai**
>
> In a large saucepan, mix together one 13 3/4-ounce can of chicken broth with one cup of water, 2 tablespoons of lime juice, 1 teaspoon of freshly chopped ginger, 1/4 teaspoon of salt, and 2 teaspoons of sugar. Cook over medium-high heat for about five minutes, stirring constantly. Add one 14-ounce can of coconut milk and one uncooked chicken breast that has been cut into several thin slices. Cook for an additional eight minutes, stirring frequently. After the chicken has been cooked thoroughly, pour the soup into four bowls, sprinkle a little cilantro on top of each, and serve.

Chapter **8**

Regions Near
and Far

Hemispheres

Introduction

By definition a hemisphere is one-half of a sphere. Geographically, a hemisphere is one-half of a globe. This division into halves is indicated by the use of imaginary lines—referred to as parallels and meridians. One line—known as the equator—divides the Earth into two hemispheres, the Northern and Southern Hemispheres. Another imaginary lines runs north and south halfway around the earth from the North Pole to the South Pole. This line is known as the prime meridian, and it divides the Earth into two hemispheres known as the Eastern and Western Hemispheres.

It is entirely possible for someone to be in two hemispheres at the same time. For example, we live in the United States, which is in both the Northern and Western Hemispheres. People living in Australia live in both the Southern and Eastern Hemispheres. The concepts of hemispheres assist people around the world locate specific places, whether those places are on land or water.

Research Questions

1. How many different hemispheres are there?

2. What countries would you find in the Southern Hemisphere?

3. What countries would you find in the Western Hemisphere?

4. What is the prime meridian?

5. What is the equator?

Web Sites

http://www.usgs.gov/education/learnweb/index.html
This site is a great resource for teachers. There are three sections: changing world, Earth hazards, and working with maps. Many lessons and activities are listed, including a section on how to use maps and compasses. (T: All)

http://www.rog.nmm.ac.uk/
At this all-inclusive site, teachers and students can learn about the Royal Observatory in Greenwich, which the prime meridian passes through. (S: 4–6, T: 4–6)

http://www.ontheline.org.uk/
On The Line focuses on eight countries that are all on the same meridian. This is a wonderful site filled with loads of geographical possibilities. (T: 4–6)

Literature Resources

Bramwell, Martyn. (1998). *Mapping Our World*. Minneapolis, MN: Lerner.
This is a thorough introduction to cartography and how and why humans have relied on maps for centuries.

Chambers, Catherine. (1998). *All About Maps*. New York: Franklin Watts.
This book discusses how and why we use maps and examines the many different forms that they can take.

Crewe, Sabrina. (1997). *Maps and Globes*. New York: Children's Press.
A clear design, color photos, and maps are part of this book about map design and use.

Gold, John C. (1998). *Environments of the Western Hemisphere*. New York: Twenty-First Century Books.
This book describes the physical land and environment of the Western Hemisphere. Also covered are the ways in which people adapt to and shape the environments in which they live.

Lye, Keith. (1999). *Atlas in the Round*. Philadelphia, PA: Running Press.
This is a beautifully illustrated book that takes readers on a magical tour of our planet. There's lots to see and lots to learn in the pages of this book.

Petty, Kate. (1993). *Our Globe, Our World*. Hauppage, NY: Barrons.
Harry and Ralph find out about their world by studying a road map, world map, and globe while going on a journey.

Activities and Projects

1. Provide students with opportunities to create personal and individual maps. Some students can create a simple map of their bedroom at home; others can create a map of their house, or immediate neighborhood or community. Some students can create specialized maps of their town or community, such as a map of all the shopping areas or of all the entertainment areas (playgrounds, theaters, etc.). After students have created their maps, provide time to discuss why dividing these maps into hemispheres may be inappropriate. Help students understand that a hemisphere is one-half of a globe and that their maps are flat rather than global. Talk about how other geographical concepts (latitude and longitude) may be more appropriate.

2. Ask students to create their own globes. Provide them with round balloons, newspapers torn into strips, some liquid starch, and water. Have students blow up their balloons, dip strips of newspaper into the starch, and wrap them around the balloons (two to three layers should be used). When the balloons are completely covered, allow them to dry for a day or two. When the balloons are completely dry the students should paint them with tempera paints and draw the appropriate meridians and parallels on them.

3.   Bring two oranges into the classroom. Using a permanent marker, quickly draw several countries or continents on each orange (precision is not necessary as long as students recognize that you are simply trying to simulate a globe). Use a sharp kitchen knife to cut each orange in half to create the four hemispheres (Northern and Southern on one orange; Eastern and Western on the other orange). Ask students to discuss the concept of hemispheres as they apply to the oranges. What similarities are there between an orange hemisphere and a globe hemisphere?

Parallels and Meridians

Introduction

A *parallel* is an imaginary line parallel to the equator that represents degrees of latitude. Latitudinal lines are measured north and south from the equator. Important lines of latitude include the Tropic of Cancer and the Tropic of Capricorn. A *meridian* is a circle on the Earth's surface passing through the geographical poles and any given point, or any of the lines of longitude. Longitudinal lines are measured from east or west of the prime meridian. The prime meridian is a line of longitude that cuts the Earth in half from north to south. Both longitude and latitude are measured in degrees.

Research Questions

1. What is a meridian?

2. What is a parallel?

3. What two continents are completely below the equator?

4. What are the five zones of the Earth?

5. What line of latitude is halfway between the equator and the North Pole?

6. What is the prime meridian?

7. What is the international date line?

Web Sites

http://www.indo.com/distance/
This is a neat site that students can use to find the latitude and longitude of different points. They will get the calculated distance between the two and see where they are located on a map. (S: 4–6, T: All)

Literature Resources

Knowlton, Jack. (1988). *Geography from A to Z.* New York: Crowell.
This book is a glossary of geographical terms. There are illustrations to make it easier for younger children to see exactly what the author is trying to describe. The book offers easy-to-read descriptions of different types of land formations.

Knowlton, Jack. (1985). *Maps & Globes*. New York: Crowell.

This book starts out with a brief history of mapmaking and an explanation of how to read maps and globes. Here students can also find information about different types of maps. It also shows students how to read keys on a map and how to interpret different scales.

Activities and Projects

1. Ask students to create their own globes. Provide them with round balloons, newspapers torn into strips, some liquid starch, and water. Ask students to blow up their balloons, dip strips of newspaper into the starch, and wrap them around the balloons (two to three layers should be used). When the balloons are completely covered, allow them to dry for a day or two. When the balloons are completely dry, the students should paint them with tempera paints and "decorate" them with appropriate lines of latitude and longitude.

2. Ask students to research the Web site listed above. Encourage them to go with their parents to a local travel agency to obtain brochures about foreign countries and other vacation spots. Ask students to organize this material into several categories, such as countries east of the prime meridian, countries below the 38th parallel, countries west of the international date line, or countries south of the Tropic of Cancer. Ask students to identify countries that can be placed in multiple categories.

3. Ask students to create a large poster devoted exclusively to map legends. Have them collect several examples of legends from a variety of maps and paste them or redraw them on the poster. They should provide explanations for each of the legends or groups of legends.

4. Ask students to create their own "Body Maps." Have one student lie down on a large sheet of butcher paper or newsprint. Ask other students to trace her or his outline on the paper. Afterwards, ask each student to make and cut out her or his own outline. Ask students to draw various parallels and meridians on their own body outline. Where would they draw their own "equator?" Where is their prime meridian? Where would they draw the Tropic of Capricorn and the Tropic of Cancer? After students have completed their drawings, ask them to post these "maps" around the classroom.

Latitude and Longitude

Introduction

Latitude and longitude are based on degrees used in navigation of the globe. Students should know how latitude and longitude are used to locate points on the Earth's surface. Circles that intersect make longitudinal lines, also called meridians, with both the North and South Poles, and give the directions for east and west. Latitude is measured as an angle from the equator of the Earth (0 degree) to the North Pole (90 degrees north) or to the South Pole (90 degrees south) and gives the location for places north and south. The prime meridian, the most widely used longitudinal line, is based on the Bureau International de l'Heure (BIH) Zero Meridian. This meridian is also known as the Greenwich Meridian, because it runs through the original site of the Royal Observatory, which was located at Greenwich, just outside of London, England. Longitude runs from 0 degrees at the prime meridian to 180 degrees east or west, halfway around the globe. The international date line follows the 180-degree meridian.

Research Questions

1. What is the purpose of latitude and longitude?

2. Where is 0 degree latitude and longitude located?

3. What is the definition of latitude and longitude?

4. Zero degree longitude is located in what town and country?

5. Each degree of latitude is approximately how many miles apart?

6. What happens as the degrees of longitude approach the poles?

Web Sites

http://www.lib.virginia.edu/exhibits/lewis_clark/ch5.html
This site follows Lewis and Clark, who used various methods to determine latitude and longitude. Students will learn how latitude and longitude can be determined by the position of the sun. (T: 4–6)

http://www.ncgia.ucsb.edu/education/curricula/giscc/units/u014/u014.html
This site provides a great amount of detail about latitude and longitude. Tons of information and lots of fascinating data enhance this Web site for older students. (T: 4–6)

http://www.usgs.gov/education/learnweb/index
This is a great site for teachers. Simple materials to demonstrate latitude and longitude are presented here. (T: K–3)

Literature Resources

Berger, Melvin & Berger, Gilda. (1993). *The Whole World in Your Hands*. Nashville, TN: Ideals Children's Books.

This book explains what maps are and how to use them; discusses map symbols and their meanings; and includes maps of houses, communities, cities, states, countries, and the world. Students will find that latitude and longitude have a lot to do with finding places on a map.

Ganeri, Anita. (1995). *Maps and Mapmaking*. Danbury, CT: Franklin Watts.

This is an exciting project series that combines historical facts with ideas for craft activities. Students will learn how to create their own maps. Through the activities they will learn how to create lines of latitude and longitude.

George, Lindsay B. (1999). *Around the World: Who's Been Here?* New York: Greenwillow Books.

This book describes a teacher who travels around the world viewing animals in their natural habitat and writes back to her class about her findings.

Hartman, Gail. (1991). *As the Crow Flies*. New York: Bradbury Press.

This book looks at different geographical areas from the perspectives of an eagle, rabbit, crow, horse, and gull.

Knowlton, Jack. (1985). *Maps & Globes*. New York: Crowell.

Maps & Globes offers, a brief history of mapmaking, a simple explanation of how to read maps and globes using latitude and longitude, and an introduction to the many different kinds of maps.

Morris, Scott E. (1993). *Using and Understanding Maps: How to Read a Map*. New York, Philadelphia: Chelsea House.

This very interesting book describes how to use and understand maps and apply them in the study of geography, cartography, and social studies. Students will understand using the concept of latitude and longitude to find places on a map.

Richards, Jon. (1997). *The Young People's Atlas of the World*. Brookfield, CT: Copper Beech Books.

This creative book uses maps, including a large foldout world map, to present information on the formation of the solar system, the physical features of Earth including what each marking represents on a map, weather systems, climate, etc.

Taylor, Barbara. (1993). *Maps and Mapping*. New York: Kingfisher.

There are many interesting things in this book, including an explanation of what maps are and why they are used, an introduction to symbols found on maps, and a description of how cartographers map the world. Students will also learn how to use latitude and longitude to find places on a map.

Activities and Projects

1. Have students play a game of "latitude and longitude baseball." Before the game begins, select 40–50 cities from around the world and note their latitude and longitude. Randomly assign each city a designated "rating" (e.g., single, double, triple, home run). Divide the class into two teams. Ask the first team what type of "hit" they would like—a single, double, triple, or home run. Select the card from the representative pile and read the name of the city to the team. Allow them a designated amount of time, such as three minutes, to determine the latitude and longitude of that city. If they get it right, they get the number of "bases" on the card. If they are wrong, they get an out. After three outs the other team is "up." Follow the rules of baseball and designate a certain time period for the game to end. The team with the most runs is the winner.

2. Ask the students to create a treasure map for the classroom. Mark the classroom with the following cardinal directions: north, south, east, and west. Then make grids on the floor with tape or chalk. The size of the grids depends on the size of the room available. There will be one main starting point for everybody to start from, so everybody uses the same grid. Then ask each student to locate an object in the room and write the coordinates to find the object. For example, if the grid was one inch by one inch and the student wants the treasure finder to discover a piece of chalk, she or he would give a coordinate such as 10° north (the student would walk ten grids north) and 5° east (student walks five grids east). These coordinates would lead the student to the designated item. Ask students to locate and identify several items throughout the room or gridded area.

3. Encourage students to visit Web sites to locate the coordinates for several towns or cities in their area. To find this information, students can visit www.mit.edu/geo. Ask groups of students to record the information obtained (on index cards arranged around the perimeter of an oversized wall map) and post it on a classroom bulletin board.

New England States

Introduction

Rich in history and traditions, the New England states include Maine, New Hampshire, Vermont, Massachusetts, Rhode Island, and Connecticut. The landscape in this part of the country is varied and spectacular. Small towns and isolated communities are scattered throughout this region of the country, with a few large cities such as Boston, Burlington, and Hartford situated near large bodies of water. In fact, no part New England is far from a body of water, be it the Atlantic Ocean or the numerous rivers that crisscross the land.

Research Questions

1. What are the states of New England?

2. How did New England get its name?

3. What state has the most people?

4. What is the largest city in this region?

5. What is the smallest state in this region?

Web Sites

http://www.visitmaine.com/
This is the official Web site of the Maine Office of Tourism. There's lots to discover here. (S: 4–6, T: 4–6)

http://www.nh.com/
Just about everything you would want to know about New Hampshire can be found on this site. (T: 4–6)

http://members.aol.com/frotz/
All Vermont Pages is filled with the latest information (updated frequently) on the sights and scenery of Vermont. (T: 4–6)

http://www.connecticut.com/overview
At this site youngsters can identify Connecticut's state bird, flower, and tree. They can also learn about its history and geography. (S: 4–6)

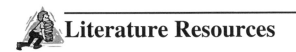

Literature Resources

Aylesworth, Thomas. (1995). *Connecticut, Massachusetts, Rhode Island*. New York: Chelsea House.

This book discusses the geographical, historical, and cultural aspects of these New England states.

Aylesworth, Thomas. (1995). *Maine, New Hampshire, Vermont*. New York: Chelsea House.

This book discusses the geographical, historical, and cultural aspects of these New England states.

Chall, Marsha Wilson. (1992). *Up North in a Cabin*. New York: Lothrop, Lee & Shepard Books.

This book is about a child who lives in a cabin on Lake Mille Lacs for the summer with her grandparents. It describes the great times she has swimming in the lake, fishing, hiking through the mountains, and spending quality time with her family.

Cooney, Barbara. (1985). *Miss Rumphius*. New York: Puffin Books.

This is a great book about a young girl named Alice growing up in Maine. Her dream is to travel around the world and live by the sea. Her grandfather tells her that she must do something to make the world more beautiful. She fulfills this dream by planting lupine flowers all over the hill near her house.

Engfer, LeeAnne. (1991). *Maine*. Minneapolis, MN: Lerner.

This informational book about Maine provides pictures and factual information about famous people from Maine as well as the population and climate.

Kent, Deborah. (1999). *Maine (America the Beautiful)*. New York: Children's Press.

This is a delightful introduction to Maine, with loads of information and colorful photos.

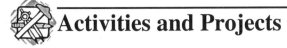

Activities and Projects

1. Divide the class into several pairs of students. Ask each pair to select one of the New England states and prepare an informational brochure about that state. Students should consult the Web sites and literature listed above. They could also visit a local travel agency to obtain pertinent information in the form of travel brochures. Ask students to assemble their brochures for display in the school library. Students can set up a "travel agency" in the classroom to provide students and teachers throughout the school with information about (and travel plans for) these states.

2. A popular recipe in many parts of the country (and especially in New England) is shortcake. This recipe has been around since colonial times and has been served in homes across the country. You and your students may enjoy making this delicious (and historical) treat:

Shortcake

2 cups of flour
1 1/2 teaspoons of baking powder
1/2 teaspoon of salt
2 tablespoons of shortening
3/4 cup of milk
3 tablespoons of sugar

Combine all the dry ingredients (with the exception of 1 tablespoon of sugar) in a medium-sized mixing bowl. Slowly cut in the shortening and then add the milk. Grease an 8-inch square baking pan with shortening. Pour in the dough and distribute it evenly throughout the pan. Sprinkle the surface with 1 tablespoon of sugar. Place in an oven (at 375 degrees) for 20 minutes. Allow to cool and cut into squares. Enjoy!

3. Students can take a virtual tour of the New England Aquarium at http://www.neaq.org to learn about the ocean life in and around the waters of New England. This interactive site will provide youngsters with an "inside look" at the workings of an aquarium while familiarizing them with native fauna.

4. Ask students to create a bulletin board display of the sights and sounds of a New England fishing village. Magazine pictures or photographs brought from home can be posted on the bulletin board in various categories. Students may wish to add their own original illustrations, too.

5. Ask students to keep a logbook or chart on the weather patterns or climate of New England. They should consult weather maps or specific Web sites (http://www. usatoday.com or http://www.weatheronline.com) to construct their maps.

Middle Atlantic States

Introduction

The Middle Atlantic states encompass an area of enormous diversity, both geographically and politically. This region is rich in historical traditions, an array of landforms from sweeping plateaus, gracious seaside vistas, and arching mountain tops. It is an amalgam of heritage, economic variance, climatological extremes, and a cultural affluence that may not be found in any other region of the country. From the ruralness of Pennsylvania, to the seaside communities sprinkled along the eastern shore of Maryland, to the snow-capped mountains of New York, this is a land of color and contrast, of people and persistence.

The Middle Atlantic states are comprised the states of New York, New Jersey, Pennsylvania, Delaware, and Maryland. Bordered by the Atlantic Ocean on the east and the Great Lakes on the west, this part of the country has an amazing variety of cities, towns, villages, and hamlets sprinkled across its disparate and dissimilar landscape. A popular area for tourists and visitors, there is much to discover and much to learn about this unique section of America.

Research Questions

1. What states make up the Middle Atlantic states?

2. What are some of the most well-known tourist attractions in the Middle Atlantic states?

3. What is the largest state in this area?

4. What is the most populous city in this region?

5. Why is Pennsylvania called the "Keystone State?"

6. Why is Delaware called the "First State?"

Web Sites

http://www.state.de.us/kidspage/welcome.html
At this site students can access links to facts about Delaware, take a tour of the governor's mansion, and read articles about outdoor attractions. (S: 4–6)

http://www.mec.state.md.us/
This site contains many links to different Maryland sites. Deals with everything from contacting the Maryland government to historical attractions. (T: 4–6)

http://www.state.nj.us

This site contains information on New Jersey's state government departments and agencies, the legislature, the judiciary, and the congressional delegation, as well as news releases and some of the governor's major speeches. Also contains pictures from around the state. (T: 4–6)

http://www.state.pa.us

The first page has links to sites such as the visitor's guide and a history of Pennsylvania. Includes links to information about environmental issues, the new license plates, and a kid's page. (T: 4–6)

http://www.dos.state.ny.us/kidsroom/nysfacts/factmenu.html

At this site students can obtain tons of information about New York, including attractions, historical sites, facts, and history (S: All, T: All)

 # Literature Resources

Balcer, Bernadette. (1989). *Philadelphia*. Minneapolis, MN: Dillon Press.

Featuring the Liberty Bell, Independence Hall, and the Franklin Institute (among other sites), this book offers young readers an inside look at the "City of Brotherly Love."

Bartoletti, Susan. (1996). *Growing up in Coal Country*. New York: Houghton Mifflin.

This is a fascinating book about the immigrants who lived and worked in the coal mining regions of Pennsylvania. Filled with dynamic photographs, this book is a valuable reference about early Pennsylvania life.

Fradin, Dennis. (1995). *From Sea to Shining Sea: Delaware*. New York: Children's Press.

This book covers the history, geography, agriculture, trivia, and famous people of Delaware.

Fradin, Dennis. (1993). *From Sea to Shining Sea: New Jersey*. New York: Children's Press.

This book covers the history, geography, agriculture, trivia, and famous people of New Jersey, the "Garden State."

Howard, Elizabeth. (1991). *Aunt Flossie's Hats (and Crab Cakes Later)*. New York: Clarion.

Two sisters visit their Great Great Aunt Flossie every Sunday afternoon. This book offers a magical journey through the streets, history, and sites of Baltimore.

Jakobsen, Kathy. (1993). *My New York*. Boston: Little, Brown.

All the important sites and attractions of New York City are included in this brief overview.

Johnson, Stephen. (1999). *City by Numbers*. New York: Viking.

With an imaginative touch and striking photography, this book leads readers through the streets of New York in search of various numbers. A delightful book!

Munroe, Roxie. (1987). *The Inside-Outside Book of Washington, DC*. New York: Dutton.

In this book a variety of illustrations and sparse text provides readers with a thorough overview of our nation's capital.

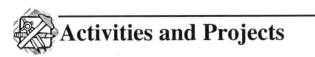**Activities and Projects**

1. Divide the class into several groups. Ask students to compose a tour through this region of the country. Ask them to imagine that they are tour directors and have been commissioned by a group of people from another part of the country. Their mission is to see as much of the Middle Atlantic states as they can in a two-week time period. Encourage students to select important sites, historical attractions, and landmarks that could be visited on a two-week car trip. Students should access information from the Web sites and literature above to design their journeys. Provide opportunities for various groups to share and compare their trips.

2. Share a recent copy of *USA Today* with your class. Divide the class into several groups and ask students to create a regional newspaper of the Middle Atlantic states using the same format as *USA Today*. Students should focus on the people of this region, its culture, sports teams, climate, or other selected topics. Two or three students in each group can be responsible for gathering relevant facts about this region and contributing articles for the whole class newspaper.

3. Ask students to select one or more famous Americans from the Middle Atlantic states. They should consult Web sites and library resources and present a compendium of biographical information to the class. These data can be assembled into a large classroom notebook or a special bulletin board display.

4. Each of the Middle Atlantic states has its own flag. Ask students to access information via Web sites and library resources on the elements included on each state flag and why they were placed on those flags. Then ask students to imagine that they have been commissioned to completely redesign the flags for these states. Divide the class into several groups, assigning one state flag to each group. Have students create a new flag for their assigned state that accurately represents its history, features, landmarks, or traditions. Provide opportunities for students to share their new flags.

5. Ask individual students or small groups of students to select a state in this region, then write a Haiku poem about that state. Tell your students that a Haiku is a short, unrhymed, three-line poem about nature. The first line names the subject, and the third line tells about a change or movement of the subject. In addition, the first and third lines each have five syllables and the second line has seven syllables. Following is an example:

Majestic mountains
Sweeping land beyond the sun
A marriage of forms.

Southern States

 ## Introduction

The southern United States is a region of enormous diversity and panoramic landscapes. It stretches from Maryland in the northeast to Florida in the south to Texas in the west. It is rich in history and overflowing with culture and traditions. Geographically it encompasses the Coastal Plain, the Appalachian Mountains, the Piedmonts, the Ozark Plateau, the Chesapeake Bay, the Mississippi River, the Ohio River, and the Tennessee Valley.

 ## Research Questions

1. What are the 11 states that make up the southern part of the United States?

2. Who were some of the earliest explorers in the southern states?

3. What are some of the plants native to southern states?

4. What are some of the distinct geographical features of the southern states?

5. If you could visit any state, which state would you visit, and why?

 ## Web Sites

http://dhr.dos.state.fl.us/kids/
This student-friendly site provides information about people in Florida from 12,000 years ago to the present. People of all cultures are included in this site. Children can discover the state flags, emblems, symbols, historical facts, famous people, and lots more. (S: All)

http://www.gatewayno.com/history/emblems.html
This site depicts the state emblems and symbols of Louisiana. The state bird, flower, dog, tree, and seal are each shown in a color picture with a brief explanation of their significance. (T: All)

http://www.lib.utexas.edu/Libs/PCL/Maps_Collection/mississippi.html
The Perry-Castaneda Library Maps Collection provides many maps on Mississippi. Teachers can print out state maps, city maps, historical maps, and national park maps. (T: 4–6)

http://www.visitmississippi.org
This student-friendly site provides pictures and links to various topics in Mississippi. The site also includes a historical background of the state and some recreational activities tourists can participate in. (S: 4–6)

http://www.Lsjunction.com/

The Lone Star Junction can be used as a history resource for both Texans and "foreigners" in Texas. This site provides information about people, places, documents, and events of early Texas. The site also has the state symbols and emblems readily available. (S: 4–6)

http://www.lone-star.net/mall/main-areas/txtrails.htm

Learn all about Texas at this site. Teachers can research information about the Texas state flag, the Texas Revolution, the Mexican War, the state forests and national parks, and famous Texans. The daily weather in Texas is also available at this site. (T: 4–6)

http://www.state.tx.us/

This informative site about the state of Texas is a valuable resource for citizens, visitors, businesspeople, and government employees who are trying to learn more about the state of Texas. (T: 4–6)

http://www.state.sc.us/

Students can learn lots of information about South Carolina at this informative site. (S: 4–6, T: All)

http://www.secretary.state.nc.us/kidspg/homepage.asp

The Kid's Page for North Carolina provides up-to-the-minute information about the Tar Heel State. (S: 4–6)

http://www.euronet.nl/users/koert/

At this site viewers can take a virtual tour of several southeastern states. Lots of photos. (S: 4–6)

 # Literature Resources

Branch, Muriel Miller. (1998). *Juneteenth-Freedom Day*. New York: Cobblehill.

Juneteenth is the grandfather of all holidays for black Texans. From its exciting beginning on June 19, 1865, when the slaves in Texas reacted joyously to the news of the Emancipation Proclamation, the holiday has spread nationwide.

Bryant, Jennifer. (1992). *Marjory Stoneman Douglas: Voice of the Everglades*. New York: Twenty-First Century Books.

This book traces the life of a woman who fought to preserve the Florida Everglades against misuse and development. Douglas is still known as the "Grandmother of the Glades."

Calhoun, Mary. (1997). *Flood*. New York: Morrow.

This story is set during the terrible Midwest floods of 1993, and tells the tale of a family's struggle to protect their home from the flooding Mississippi River.

Carlson, Nancy L. (1993). *A Visit to Grandma's*. New York: Puffin Pictures.

A Visit to Grandma's is about a family who visits their grandmother at Thanksgiving. However, the grandmother has changed from a farm girl into a new grandma. Grandma is very different than she used to be now that she has moved to Florida.

Cech, John. (1994). *Diango*. New York: Simon & Schuster.

This is a Florida tale about a famous fiddler who inspired the animals to dance. It takes place in the Cyprus swamp, where the fiddler's music mesmerizes the backwater critters.

Cherry, Lynne. (1999). *The Armadillo from Amarillo*. New York: Voyager Picture Book.

The book tells the tale of an armadillo that sets off on an adventure to learn where in the world he is. He must leave his home in San Antonio and travel north. When he reaches Amarillo, he meets a golden eagle and with her help he discovers where he lives.

Coleman, Evelyn. (1998). *The Riches of Oseola McCarty*. San Diego: Harcourt Brace.

This is a biography of Oseola McCarty, a hard-working washer woman, who never received any formal education. She dedicated a portion of her life savings to the University of Southern Mississippi for scholarships for needy students.

George, Jean Craighead. (1997). *Everglades*. New York: HarperCollins.

The story about an exploration of a unique ecosystem, the Everglades. Everglades tells the story of its original creation as a blue-green sea to its evolution as a miraculous river, the home to egrets, orchids, and alligators.

Harper, Craig. (1998). *Prairie Dog Pioneers*. New York: Scholastic.

This is the story of one of the first families to settle on the Texas side of the Red River. The family moves so they can own their own land. A relationship is built and grows between a father and daughter throughout the story.

Hiscock, Bruce. (1997). *The Big Rivers: The Missouri, the Mississippi, and the Ohio*. New York: Atheneum.

This book focuses on the history of flooding along the mighty Midwest rivers, and more recently the flood of 1993. It includes an explanation of the causes of the disaster, the role of the river basin, and why the dams and levees failed.

Konigsburg, E. L. (1999). *T-Shirts, T-Shirts, Coat, and Suit*. New York: Hyperion.

While spending the summer in Florida, a young girl discovers that her aunt's job is being threatened by competitors wearing inappropriate clothing. Freedom of expression becomes a vital and important issue in this book.

McDonald, Megan. (1997). *Beezy*. Danbury, CT: Orchard Books.

Beezy is about a young girl who visits her grandmother in Florida. While she is visiting a hurricane hits the shore. Beezy and her friends do not fear the storm; instead they have fun throughout the storm.

Mendel, Lydia. (1993). *All Dressed up and Nowhere to Go*. San Diego: Harcourt Brace.

This is a story about a boy named David, who is visiting his grandparents in Florida for Christmas. He hopes to build a great jolly snowman for these grandparents, but he encounters a few problems.

Mikaelson, Ben. (1996). *Stranded*. New York: Hyperion.

This novel tells the story of a young girl's determination to do the right thing and to prove herself to her peers and her family. Several events change her life forever.

Mitchell, Margaret King. (1998). *Granddaddy's Gift*. New York: Troll Associates.

This book is about a man in the South trying to exercise the right to vote. The story is told by a young girl who learns first-hand about racism in the segregated South. Through this man's struggle, the girl learns the value of education.

Rice, James. (1991). *Cajun Alphabet*. New York: Pelican.
   This alphabet book introduces the Cajun vocabulary and the Cajun culture in Louisiana. A friendly alligator is your tour guide through the full-color lessons.

Stevenson, James. (1995). *The Worst Goes South*. New York: Greenwillow Books.
   This story tells the tale of a town preparing for its annual Harvest Festival. The "worst person in the world" takes off to get away from the hype and finds himself down in Florida.

Turner, Robyn. (1996). *Texas Traditions: The Culture of the Lone State*. New York: Sierra Book Club.
   This is an introduction to the state of Texas. It explores the different traditions and rich history that have shaped the culture of the Lone Star State. Historical pictures, paintings of famous people, and hundreds of facts fill the pages of this book.

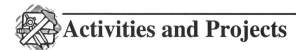

Activities and Projects

1. Divide the class into several small groups. Ask each group to plan a two-week trip to one or more southern states. Students should access information from the Web sites and literature listed above. Ask each group to share their completed project with the rest of the class or with another class at your grade level.

2. Using the Web site http://www.lone-star.net/mall/main-area/txtrails.html, have the students keep a running record of the weather in the state of Texas. Keep the record for two weeks. Have the students compare the weather in Texas to the weather in your state. How is the weather similar and different? Have the students create charts comparing the two states.

3. Ask individual students to pick a southern state and identify its state flag, tree, bird, song, dog, and slogan using reference materials in the library and the Internet. Students should create posters with a collage of pictures or drawings. Provide opportunities for students to share their products with another class.

4. Have students create clay models of the southern state of their choice. Using the Web site, students should identify important cities in the state, any significant landforms, famous tourist attractions, and any other information they find interesting. Have students log onto http://www.lib.utexas.edu/Libs/PCL/Map-Collection.com for information and maps about the southern state of their choice.

5. Read *Cajun Alphabet* to the class or have them or log onto http://www.floridajuice.com/florida/citrus/kids/index.htm. Ask students to create a menu or a food guide for a tourist visiting a southern state. What would be on the menu? How would the food be served? Is the food spicy or mild? Provide opportunities for the students to share their menus with the class. After the projects are completed, have the class choose a recipe they would like to make in class. If possible, prepare the recipe and share it with the entire class.

6. Ask students to make a list of the major landforms and bodies of water in the South, using the resources listed above. Have students describe and explain each one and where it is located. Small groups of students can create murals or posters illustrating each body of water or landform.

Midwestern States

Introduction

A land of quiet beauty, sweeping vistas and seemingly endless stretches of farmland, richness and grandeur unlike any other—that's the Midwest. Often referred to as the heartland of America, this section of the country was a powerful magnet for immigrants from Europe and the large cities of the east during the 1800s. Immigrants from Germany, England, Scandinavia, Ireland, and Russia established farms in the Midwest during the mid-1800s. Many of these farms were begun under the Homestead Act of 1862, which gave free land to U.S. citizens as well as those who intended to become citizens.

The Midwest is crisscrossed by vast and powerful rivers, fertile soil, and an array of cities both large and small. Bordered on the north by the Great Lakes and on the south by the mighty (and often unpredictable) Ohio River, the Midwest includes the states of Ohio, Indiana, Illinois, Michigan, and Wisconsin. It's a land shaped by the movement of glaciers as well as by the blood and sweat of early pioneers who recognized its potential.

Research Questions

1. What states make up the Midwest?

2. Why is this part of the country referred to as the "Midwest?"

3. What is the most populous state in this region?

4. What is the largest city?

5. How has farm life in this region changed over the last 100 years?

Web Sites

http://www.midwestliving.com/index1.html
This site offers an overview of life in the Midwest, including occupations, activities, and recipes. Loads of valuable information can be found here. (S: 4–6, T: All)

http://www.lib.utexas.edu/Libs/PCL/Map_collection/ohio.html
At this site teachers and students can download loads of maps most cities and geographic features in Ohio. (S: 4–6, T: All)

http://www.lib.utexas.edu/Libs/PCL/Map_collection/indiana.html
Lots of maps about every aspect of Indiana can be found on this site. (S: 4–6, T: All)

http://www.state.il.us/kids/default.htm

Discover Illinois will provide students with lots of great information about the sixth most populous state in the country. (S: All, T: All)

http://isd.ingham.k12.mi.us/~99mich/

Michigan, My Michigan is an online project for students that presents tons of information and lots of exciting data, collected for kids by kids. (S: All, T: All)

http://www.state.wi.us/

Just about everything one would want to know about Wisconsin can be found on this Web site. (S: 4–6, T: 4–6)

Literature Resources

Aylesworth, Thomas. (1990). *Chicago*. Brookfield, CT: Blackbirch.

This book describes the city of Chicago, its history, and its people. There are a map, a city directory, and lots of fascinating information.

Aylesworth, Thomas. (1995). *Eastern Great Lakes: Indiana, Michigan, Ohio*. New York: Chelsea House.

This book discusses the geographical, historical, and cultural aspects of Ohio, Indiana, and Michigan.

Blashfield, Jean. (1998). *Wisconsin (America the Beautiful)*. New York: Children's Press.

This book introduces the geography, history, government, economy, industry, culture, historic sites, and famous people of Wisconsin.

Bunting, Eve. (1995). *Dandelions*. New York: Harcourt Brace.

This book is about a young girl, Zoe, and her family, who travel across the Great Plains to start a new life. Zoe sees that her Papa is eager and her Mama is sad, both to leave their old lives and start new ones.

Fradin, Dennis. (1991). *Illinois: From Sea to Shining Sea*. New York: Children's Press.

This is an introduction to the history, geography, important people, and interesting sites of Illinois. A good overview of the "Land of Lincoln."

Fradin, Dennis. (1993). *Ohio: From Sea to Shining Sea*. New York: Children's Press.

This book presents young readers with an overview of Ohio, including its geography, industries, notable sights, and famous people of the "Buckeye State."

Wills, Charles. (1996). *A Historical Album of Michigan*. Brookfield, CT: Millbrook Press.

This is a thorough overview of the history of Michigan, including lots of fascinating facts and information.

Activities and Projects

1. Ask your students to log on to http://www.epals.com and locate one or more schools in the Midwest with which they can establish a pen pal relationship. Ask students to collect as much information as possible about the specific area in which their e-pals live, including historical sites, industry, economy, attractions, famous people, lifestyle, etc. Provide opportunities for students to share the information collected from their pen pals on a regular basis.

2. Divide the class into several groups and ask each group to plan a trip from Connecticut to Ohio in the 1800s. Ask each group to put together a list of supplies and equipment they would need on their journey. What would be some essential items? What would be some desirable but nonessential items? Encourage students to compare their lists and post them on the bulletin board for class discussion.

3. If possible, obtain a copy of the CD-ROM "The Midwest" (Catalog No. U86051, Mac/Windows) from the National Geographic Society (P.O. Box 10597, Des Moines, IA 50340; 1-800-368-2728, cost $59.95). This outstanding piece of software examines the geography, economy, and culture of this scenic and bountiful region of the country. Fabulous photography and descriptive information make this a perfect classroom supplement.

4. Of necessity, the food of the early immigrants to this part of the country was quite simple, requiring a minimum of ingredients. Following is a recipe for apple fritters you may enjoy making with the help of your students:

> **Apple Fritters**
>
> 1 1/2 cups of flour   2/3 cup of milk
> 1 egg, well beaten   2 apples, cut in thin slices
> pinch of salt   powdered sugar (optional)
> 2 level teaspoons of baking powder
>
> Sift together the flour, baking powder, and salt. Add the egg and milk, then the sliced apples. Drop by teaspoonfuls into a deep pan with 1/2 inch of hot cooking oil in it (the oil should be hot enough to brown a piece of white bread). Cook until brown. Drain the fritters on paper towels and sprinkle with powdered sugar. (**Note**: The use of hot oil requires extreme caution.)

5. If a video camera is available, ask students to put together a video travelogue through the Midwest. After students have had an opportunity to access the Web sites and literature above, ask them to form small groups (one for each state) and write and produce an imaginary travelogue throughout this region. Photographs or student-drawn illustrations can serve as a backdrop for selected sites, with accompanying narration. Provide sufficient opportunities for students to review and evaluate the videos.

Plains States

Introduction

The plains states—North Dakota, South Dakota, Nebraska, Kansas, Minnesota, Iowa, and Missouri. Because they are so far away from the moderating effects of a large body of water, these states experience extremes of winter and summer weather. It can be very hot during the summer months, and six months later bitterly cold, with temperatures falling well below 0 degrees.

This part of the United States has two distinct areas. The lowland Central Plains are known for their rich farmlands and abundant rainfall. The Great Plains, rising gradually from the Mississippi River to the foothills of the Rocky Mountains, are actually a high plateau. Less rain falls at the higher altitudes and farms must be irrigated. The "flatness" of this region of the country is due in large measure to the fact that this area was an enormous inland sea millions of years ago. In fact, some of the best specimens of prehistoric life are typically found in this region.

Research Questions

1. What is a plains state?

2. Where are the plains states located?

3. What are the names of the plain states?

4. What are some tourist attractions of the plains states?

5. What are the main agricultural products of the plains states?

Web Sites

http://www.wheatmania.com/
This site is about wheat in Kansas. It covers a history of wheat, how it is produced, and the progress of wheat. This site also has a link to fun activities for students. (S: K–3)

http://www.state.nd.us/
This site includes everything about North Dakota. It has links to history, agencies, tourism, employment, etc. It also has information about local and state government. Students are also given places to contact for more information. (S: 4–6)

http://deckernet.com/minn/
This site has just about everything anyone would want to know about Minnesota. Tons of data and loads of pictures highlight the site. (S: 4–6, T: All)

http://www.feist.com/~okpaws/kansas.html

All About Kansas will provide students and teachers with a wealth of information about this plains state, from its history to current events. (S: 4–6, T: All)

http://www.lib.utexas.edu/Libs/PCL/Map_collection/iowa.html

At this site teachers can obtain maps of famous sites and important cities throughout Iowa. A great classroom resource. (T: 4–6)

Literature Resources

Aylesworth, Thomas G. & Aylesworth, Virginia L. (1996). *The Great Plains*. New York: Chelsea House.

Everything you wanted to know about the Great Plains is in this wonderful little book. It covers everything from the states, to the climate, places to visit, events, and history of each state. To better illustrate the great plains are maps, fact spreads, and other illustrated material that highlights these aspects.

Fradin, Dennis B. (1980). *Iowa in Words and Pictures*. Chicago: Children's Press.

That Iowa was named after the Ioway Indians will not be the only interesting fact the reader will gain from this book. From the Ice Ages to the 1980s, this book covers the land, people, explorers, and industries of this beautiful plains state.

Fradin, Dennis Brindell & Fradin, Judith Bloom. (1995). *From Sea to Shining Sea, South Dakota*. Chicago: Children's Press.

Children will get a good look at South Dakota's land, tourist attractions, history and much, much more in this well-laid-out book. Students will feel like they are in the state.

Goble, Paul. (1989). *Beyond the Ridge*. New York: Bradbury Press.

Goble's portrayal of a lush natural world, along with his deep understanding of the Plains Indians, culture lures the reader into this book. He brings to life the world of a tribe of Indians living on the plains.

Steptoe, John. (1984). *The Story of Jumping Mouse*. New York: Lothrop, Lee & Shepard Books.

Steptoe brings to life the legend of a mouse that goes to a far-off land where no mouse goes hungry. In this great adventure the mouse encounters many obstacles as he selflessly gives his senses to other animals that live in the Great Plains.

Williams, David. (1993). *Grandma Essie's Covered Wagon*. New York: Knopf.

Beautifully illustrated, this book brings to life a covered wagon ride from Missouri to Kansas and back to Missouri while Grandma Essie searches for a better life. Not only is this book exciting to read, it also goes into detail about the Great Plains.

Activities and Projects

1. Ask students to write letters to tourist attractions and/or visitor bureaus in the plains states asking for brochures and literature about that area. Some places for children to write to are:

Sioux Falls Convention and Visitors Bureau
200 N. Phillips Ave., Suite 102
Sioux Falls, SD 57104

Iowa Convention and Visitors Bureau Association
8345 University Ave., Suite F-1
Des Moines, IA 50325

Also encourage students to check out American Automobile Association tour books. Once the children have received information on some of the tourist attractions, ask them to make a presentation of the information. The presentations may be brochures, a video, a poster, etc.

2. Ask students to log onto the Web site www.epals.com and obtain a pen pal from one of the plains states. Students should share important information about their state or community and request the same type of information from their pen pals. This mutual exchange of information will assist students who do not live in that part of the country in understanding the geography and lifestyles of the people who do live there. Most important, it can help eliminate any misconceptions or misperceptions students may have about life in the plains states.

3. Ask students to recreate the classroom into a selected plains state. Using information obtained from the Web sites and literature above, small groups of students can decorate the room so that it resembles a large cyclorama of the Central or Great Plains. Post large sheets of newsprint on the walls and ask students to decorate them with wheatfields or large expanses of corn. Selected plains cities (Bismarck, Pierre, Omaha, Dodge City, Minneapolis, Dubuque, or Springfield) can also be illustrated on these oversized murals. After students have turned the classroom into one or more plains state, ask other classrooms to tour it with your students as the tour guides.

4. Ask students to use the books and Internet sites listed above to obtain some information about the characteristics of plains states. Divide the class into groups of two or three and have them use this information to create a plain states game. If they choose to, they could recreate a game currently on the market, such as Jeopardy®.

5. Ask students to check an almanac for the yearly rainfall for your area, then locate several cities in the Central or Great Plains and find the normal annual precipitation there. Have them compare the rainfall in several cities with the rainfall in your city, plotting that information on a large chart. Ask students to note any similarities or differences. Students may wish to obtain additional information about regional weather patterns from the following Web sites:

http://www.princeton.edu/Webweather/ww.html
http://www.weatheronline.com
http://www.wunderground.com
http://www.accuweather.com/weatherf/index_corp

Southwestern States

Introduction

The wide-open spaces of the American Southwest are like no other area of the country. Crisscrossed by deep canyons, flat-topped hills, and towering rock sculptures, the Southwest is a land of contrasts, beauty, and mystery. The harshness of its climate has led to some interesting adaptations by the flora and fauna that live there. Cacti have developed specialized leaves, lizards and snakes typically come out at night when the temperature is cooler, and mammals such as prairie dogs burrow deep underground to escape the unrelenting sun.

The states of the Southwest include Arizona, New Mexico, Texas (which is so large that it is sometimes classified as both a southern and southwestern state), and Oklahoma. The area is vast and often communities are geographically distant, but it is rich in culture, history, and tradition.

Research Questions

1. What kinds of plants grow in the Southwest?

2. What is the largest city in the Southwest?

2. In what state is the Grand Canyon?

3. How large is Texas?

4. Why is New Mexico called "The Land of Enchantment?"

5. What are some major resources of this region?

Web Sites

http://www.swanet.org
This site includes links to all the states of the southwestern part of the country. Each link covers details about state history, archeology, crafts of the area, and Native Americans residing in the state. (T: 4–6)

http://gosouthwest.about.com/travel/
This Web site provides links to the following states: Arizona, Nevada, Utah, and New Mexico. Included in the linked sites are facts about the history of the Southwest, traditional foods and cooking in the Southwest, natives of the Southwest area, and landmark sites (e.g., the Grand Canyon, other national parks). (T: 4–6)

http://www.arizonaguide.com
This site provides students with an overview of Arizona geography as well as information about its flora and fauna. (S: 4–6, T: All)

142

http://www.state.nm.us
Students will be able to access a wide range of factual information about New Mexico on this site. Be sure to check out "New Mexico Fun Facts." (S: 4–6, T: All)

http://www.hud.gov/local/okl/oklacomm.html
This is a good site for links about many of Oklahoma's cities and towns. (S: 4–6, T: 4–6)

http://www.texas-best.com
Students will find lists of Texas best animals, foods, and plants at this site. They can also learn about the life of a cowboy. (S: 4–6, T: 4–6)

 # Literature Resources

Aylesworth, Thomas G. & Aylesworth, Virginia A. (1992). *The Southwest*. New York: Chelsea House.
This book is focused on the southwestern states of Texas, Colorado, and New Mexico. Each section of the book provides information on the state seal, flag and motto, capitals, nicknames and flowers, etc. Each section also describes state industries, governments, and agriculture.

Filbin, Dan. (1991). *Arizona*. Minneapolis, MN: Lerner.
Included in this book are details about living and working in Arizona, a time line, famous Arizonians, and a picture tour of the state.

Fradin, Judith Bloom & Fradin, Dennis Brindell. (1993). *New Mexico*. Chicago: Children's Press.
This book provides many details about the state, including its nickname, the climate, the wildlife, and many famous New Mexicans. Some history is given, and some facts about New Mexico today are included.

Heinrichs, Ann. (1999). *Texas (America the Beautiful)*. New York: Children's Press.
This book is an introduction to the history and geography of the second largest state in the union.

Reedy, Jerry. (1998). *Oklahoma (America the Beautiful)*. New York: Children's Press.
This book introduces this central state, which has been a "dust bowl," Indian Territory, oil rich, and a promised land to settlers.

Thompson, Kathleen. (1996). *Arizona (Portrait of America)*. Austin, TX: Steck-Vaughn
The history, economy, culture, and future of Arizona are presented in the pages of this book.

Thompson, Kathleen. (1996). *Texas (Portrait of America)*. Austin, TX: Steck-Vaughn.
History, geography, culture, and important cities fill the pages of this book.

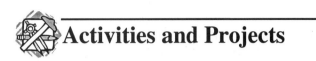 **Activities and Projects**

1. Students may enjoy creating their own desert terrarium. The following directions will help them design a fully functioning terrarium:

    a. Fill the bottom of a large glass container with a layer of coarse sand or gravel. Combine one part fine sand with two parts of potting soil and spread this over the top of the first layer.

    b. Sprinkle this lightly with water.

    c. Place several varieties of cactus in the terrarium (it might be a good idea to wear gloves). Most nurseries carry cacti, or they can be ordered through the mail from selected seed companies and mail order nursery houses.

    d. When planting the cacti be sure that the roots are covered completely by the sandy mixture.

    e. You and your students may decide to place several desert animals such as lizards or horned toads in the terrarium. Be sure the animals have a sufficient quantity of food and water.

    f. The desert terrarium can be left in the sun and does not need a glass cover. It should, however, be lightly sprinkled with water about once a week.

2. Ask students to write to one or more of the following national parks and request information about the flora and fauna that inhabit those special regions. When the brochures, flyers, leaflets, and descriptive information arrive, ask students to assemble them into an attractive display in the classroom or a school display case.

        Death Valley National Park
        P.O. Box 579
        Death Valley, CA 92328

        Joshua Tree National Park
        74485 National Park Dr.
        Twentynine Palms, CA 92277

        Great Basin National Park
        Baker, NV 89311

        Big Bend National Park
        Big Bend, TX 79834

3. If possible, have students visit a local gardening center or nursery. Ask them to purchase a cactus plant (these are typically very inexpensive). Ask them to carefully observe their respective cactus. What shape is it? Does the shape change as it grows? What do the needles look like? Students should observe cactus features with a magnifying lens and record their observations in a "Desert Journal."

4. Students can keep up-to-date on the latest events, discoveries, and news about life in the deserts of the United States by accessing the Web site of *Desert USA Magazine* (http://www.desertusa.com). Here they can learn about the lives of the flora and fauna that inhabit U.S. deserts. They may wish to gather selected information together in the form of descriptive brochures or pamphlets for the classroom library.

5. Deserts are often described as areas in which less than ten inches of rain falls per year. Ask students to compare the amount of rain that falls in their part of the country with the amount of rain that falls in parts of the Sonoran Desert (approximately one to three inches per year). The following activity will help them accurately measure rainfall in their area.

   The following instrument will help students accumulate rainfall data over an extended period of time—a week, a month, or a year:

   Materials:

   > a tall jar (an olive jar works best)
   > a ruler
   > a felt tip pen
   > a funnel

   a. Use a ruler and a felt tip pen to mark off quarter-inch intervals up the side of the olive jar.

   b. Place a funnel in the jar and put the jar outside in a secure location. (The funnel will help collect the rainwater as well as prevent some evaporation from taking place.)

   c. Ask students to use a chart or graph to record the amount of rain your area gets in a week or in a month. Encourage them to keep an ongoing record.

   d. Have students compare their findings with those reported in the local newspaper.

	MY TOWN/CITY	THE DESERT
One Day	_____	_____
One Week	_____	_____
One Month	_____	_____
One Year	_____	_____

Mountain States

Introduction

The mountain states have spectacular scenery, incredible mountain ranges, and unbelievable vistas. Ever since the early pioneers traveled across this area and sent back tales about the landscape, people have been mesmerized by this region. It is crossed by the vast Rocky Mountain range, created over a period of millions of years. Its major resources include oil, natural gas, timber, minerals, water power, and wildlife.

The states of Colorado, Utah, Nevada, Wyoming, Idaho, and Montana make up this unique portion of our country. Sparsely populated, they are meccas for tourists and travelers from around the world. They are rich in history and geography and totally unlike any other region of the country.

Research Questions

1. What mountain state has the largest population?

2. What is the largest city in this region?

3. What state has the highest overall elevation?

4. In what state does the Colorado River begin?

5. What is the Continental Divide?

Web Sites

http://www.denver.org/visitors/kids.asp

This Web site, created especially for children, reveals interesting facts about the state of Colorado, including information about Colorado's history, geography, and fun attractions and activities. (S: 4–6)

http://www.state.id.us/

This Web site reveals lots of current information about Idaho. Teachers and students alike can use it to learn more about Idaho's environment, arts, culture, natural resources, and much more. (S: 3–6, T: 3–6)

http://montanakids.com/home.htm

This Montana Web site was created just for kids. Students can use it to learn interesting information about Montana wildlife, national parks, and cool places to visit! Games and activities will surely keep student interest high when they visit this site. (S: All)

http://fwp.state.mt.us/kids/kids.htm

This Web site is filled with information for students who are curious to learn more about Montana. Students can find information about Montana wildlife, parks, news, and much more! (S: All)

http://www.state.wy.us/kids/html

This is an excellent Web site for students to visit! They can explore various areas of Wyoming while learning more about Wyoming wildlife, school kids, news, and much more. (S: All)

# Literature Resources

Bledsoe, Sara. (1993). *Colorado*. Minneapolis, MN: Lerner.

This book, filled with wonderful photographs, takes readers on a trip around Colorado, describing its history, geography, people, and environmental conditions.

Bunting, Eve & Moser, Barry. (1997). *On Call Back Mountain*. New York: Blue Sky Press.

This fictional book tells the story of two brothers and a friend living at the foot of Call Back Mountain. The moving story and beautiful illustrations help readers to appreciate life on a mountain.

Fradin, Dennis Brindell. (1993). *Colorado*. Chicago: Children's Press.

This book will surely interest young readers with its beautiful photographs and interesting facts about the Centennial State. Included in this book is information about famous Coloradans and a "Did You Know?" section.

Fradin, Dennis Brindell. (1995). *Idaho*. Chicago: Children's Press.

This book reveals detailed information on the history, geography, and people of Idaho. It is filled with beautiful photography.

Fradin, Dennis Brindell & Fradin, Judith Bloom. (1994). *Wyoming*. Chicago: Children's Press.

This book introduces Wyoming, the "Equality State," through brilliant photography and detailed information about the state's history, geography, and people.

Gerrard, Roy. (1996). *Wagons West!* New York: Farrar, Straus & Giroux.

This fictional storybook reveals the story of Buckskin Dan and his pioneers as they embark on a wild journey on the Oregon Trail. Readers learn of troubles encountered while crossing the Rocky Mountains.

LaDoux, Rita C. (1991). *Montana*. Minneapolis, MN: Lerner.

This book takes the reader on a trip around the state of Montana, introducing the state's history, geography, people, industries, and other highlights, with photographs on nearly every page. Readers can learn a lot about this beautiful Rocky Mountain state.

Pelta, Kathy. (1994). *Idaho*. Minneapolis, MN: Lerner.

This book introduces the reader to the mountainous region of Idaho. The reader will be enticed by the colorful photographs, maps, and vivid illustrations.

Activities and Projects

1. After they read suggested literature and acquire information from various Web sites about the Rocky Mountain states, ask students to create a picture map of their favorite state using pictures from old magazines. Display the picture maps around the classroom and encourage students to share and discuss their creations with classmates.

2. Using Internet and literature resources, students should create a chart or graph on the elevations of the highest mountain peaks in the Rocky Mountains. Students can create a bar graph that illustrates the comparative elevations. Which state has the most mountains over 14,000 feet in elevation?

3. Divide the class into several small groups and assign one of the mountain states to each group. Encourage each group to imagine that they are doing a "fly-over" of their region. They should check out one or more of the Web sites and literature listed above for necessary information. Ask each group to share details about the geography and vegetation they see on their "fly-overs." After students have had opportunities to share appropriate information, ask each group to create a mural or poster of the important sites in their designated state.

4. Have students use an encyclopedia or selected Web sites to create a report on the Lewis and Clark Expedition of 1804–1806. Students should pay particular attention to the contributions Lewis and Clark made to the accurate mapping of this part of the country, the scientific understanding of the flora and fauna of the West, and the development of trade routes and trails. Students can also create a series of fictitious diaries that would have been maintained by members of the Lewis and Clark party.

5. Ask students to select three or four different locations in the mountain states that they would enjoy visiting. Ask them to imagine that they are vacationing in those locations. Encourage each student to write a series of postcard messages to send from each place—messages that accurately sum up the sights and sounds of each location. Students may wish to post these messages around a large wall map of the mountain states.

Pacific States

Introduction

California, Oregon, Washington, Alaska, and Hawaii—the states of dreams, of travelers and tourists from around the world, of wide panoramas and photographic majesty, of enormous cities and small isolated villages, and of passion and promise as well as grandeur and glory. Perhaps a more varied collection of individual states cannot be found in any other region of the country; they are as diverse in their geography as any group of states could be. They represent all the major climatic zones in the world, from desert to alpine. They include the state with the largest population and the state with the fewest people per square mile. They include the state with one of the world's most active volcanoes as well as the rainiest state in the country.

This is a land of discovery, from the early Polynesians who crossed the vast expanses of the Pacific Ocean to land on the "island-below-the-star" (Hawaii), to the pioneers who braved weather and geography to blaze a trail to the West Coast, to the thousands of immigrants who wished to leave the snow and frigid temperatures of the East for the warmth and sunshine of California—this region is ripe for discovery and adventure.

Research Questions

1. What is the largest state in the country?

2. What is the most populous state in the country?

3. Why are so many volcanoes located in this part of the country?

4. Why does this part of the country have so many earthquakes?

5. Why does Washington have so much rain?

6. What is the largest city in Oregon?

Web Sites

http://www.bestofhawaii.com
This site has loads of tourist information about Hawaii. There's lots to see and lots to appreciate on this site. (S: 4–6, T: All)

http://www.hshawaii.com
This is the home page of the Hawaiian State Vacation Planner. Students can select one of four islands and create an imaginary itinerary for a future visit. (S: 4–6, T: All)

http://www.ca.gov/s/

At this site students can learn about the government of California as well as discover information about natural resources. (S: 4–6)

http://tqd.advanced.org/3615/

At this site students can access information about the people and history of California's Spanish missions. (S: 4–6, T: All)

http://www.scecdc.scec.org/eqsocal.html

Students can search this site for a map of the fault lines of southern California. They can also read about individual earthquakes. (S: 4–6, T: All)

http://www.isu.edu/~trinmich/Oregontrail.html

Students can learn all about the Oregon Trail from this site. They'll learn about the dangers and hardships faced by the early pioneers. (S: 4–6)

http://www.sos.state.or.us/

At this site students will learn about the origin of Oregon's name, the state bird, state insect, and state nut, as well as other facts about this state. (S: 4–6, T: 4–6)

http://www.wa.gov/features/kids.htm

This Web site provides students with valuable information about Washington's symbols, state song, important buildings, and other details. (S: 4–6, T: 4–6)

http://www.alaskasbest.com/facts.htm

This site has an extensive list of fun facts about Alaska and serves as an excellent introduction to the state. (S: 4–6, T: 4–6)

Literature Resources

Fradin, Dennis. (1995). *Oregon (From Sea to Shining Sea)*. New York: Children's Press.
Lots of information about the culture, economy, geography, and government of Oregon can be found in this book.

Fradin, Dennis. (1997). *Washington (From Sea to Shining Sea)*. New York: Children's Press.
Lots of information about the culture, economy, geography, and government of Washington can be found in this book.

Heinrichs, Ann. (1998). *California (America the Beautiful)*. New York: Children's Press.
This book introduces readers to the beautiful, diverse, and wealthy state of California.

Moss, Marissa. (1998). *Rachel's Journey*. New York: Scholastic.
Rachel is traveling west with her family from her home in Illinois to Sacramento. She records the sights and sounds of the trip in this compelling book.

Munoz, Pam. (1997). *California Here We Come!* Watertown, MA: Charlesbridge.
This book is filled with miscellaneous facts about different regions of California.

Rumford, James. (1998). *The Island-Below-the-Star*. Boston: Houghton Mifflin.
A magical tale with rich, dynamic illustrations, this book tells the story of five brothers and their journey across the Pacific Ocean in search of the islands of Hawaii.

Shepherd, Donna. (1999). *Alaska (America the Beautiful)*. New York: Children's Press.
      Included in this book is information on the geography, history, economy, government, and culture of Alaska.

Siebert, Diane. (1996). *Sierra*. New York: Harper Trophy.
      The author describes the beauty of the Sierra Nevada, along with giving factual information in a lyrical poem. This is an awesome book!

Silverman, Jerry (1998). ***Singing Our Way West: Songs and Stories of America's Westward Expansion***. Brookfield, CT: Millbrook Press.
      This delightful book contains a host of songs sung by the early pioneers in the West. A delightful addition to any unit or lesson.

Siy, Alexandra. (1991). *Hawaiian Islands*. New York: Dillon.
      This is an all-inclusive look at our fiftieth state, including its geography, culture, traditions, and incredible scenery.

Stein, Richard. (1989). *Oregon (America the Beautiful)*. New York: Children's Press.
      Information on the geography, history, government, economy, industry, and culture of Oregon is presented in these pages.

Stein, Richard. (1991). *Washington (America the Beautiful)*. New York: Children's Press.
      This is an introduction to the geography, history, economy, people, and interesting sites of the "Evergreen State."

Thompson, Kathleen. (1996). *Alaska (Portrait of America)*. Austin, TX: Steck-Vaughn.
      This book offers details about the history, economy, culture, and future of Alaska.

Thompson, Kathleen. (1996). *California (Portrait of America)* Austin, TX: Steck-Vaughn.
      In this book students will read about the history, economy, cu. lture, and future of California.

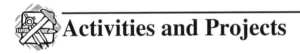

Activities and Projects

1. Divide the class into five small groups. Ask each group to select a separate state and create an abbreviated book outlining its geography, culture, tourist attractions, and history (students may want to pattern their book on one or more of the books listed above). Encourage students to gear their respective books to students in a grade lower than yours, senior citizens, or any other specific audience. After checking out some of the Web sites listed above, students should also include the following information in their books:

     When the state officially became a state

     What the state's motto is

     The state symbols

     The population of the state

     A section on culture

A section on weather

Pictures of the landscape

Tourist attractions

A brief history

Famous people from that state

2. Divide the class into five groups and assign each group one of the five states. Ask students to imagine they are on the travel and tourism board for their state and they have been asked to design a brochure or public relations campaign to attract new tourists. Provide extended opportunities for students to create their promotional materials and share them with other groups. After students have developed some plans, ask them to access the tourist pages of each state's official Web site to compare their information with "official" resources.

3. Ask students to write to the Hawaii Visitors Bureau (2270 Kalakaua Ave., Suite 801, Honolulu, HI 96815) to obtain information and brochures about the state. Students should also contact a local travel agency for posters, brochures, and travel information.

4. Following is a traditional Hawaiian recipe for Macadamia-Coconut Bread that will have your students begging for more:

Macadamia-Coconut Bread

2 cups of all-purpose flour
1 1/2 cups of shredded coconut
1/2 cup of chopped macadamia nuts
1/2 cup of sugar
2 teaspoons of baking powder
1 teaspoon of salt
1 teaspoon of ground allspice
1 teaspoon of ground nutmeg
1 teaspoon of ground cloves
2 eggs, beaten
1/2 cup of coconut milk (fresh or canned), unsweetened
1/2 cup of melted butter

(continued)

Macadamia-Coconut Bread

Preheat the oven to 350 degrees. In a large mixing bowl combine the flour, coconut, nuts, sugar, baking powder, salt, allspice, nutmeg, and cloves. In a separate bowl, whisk together the eggs, coconut milk, and butter. Fold the liquid ingredients into the dry ingredients. Blend thoroughly.

Pour the mixture into a lightly greased 9-by-5-inch loaf pan. Bake for 45 to 50 minutes, until a toothpick inserted in the center comes out clean. Place the bread on a rack and allow to cool slightly before eating.

5. Ask students to create individual or group mobiles about the Pacific states. On the first level of each mobile, ask students to record pertinent facts. On the second level, students should hang names of tourist spots and attractions from throughout the state. On the third level, names and descriptions of selected animals from the state should be recorded. Be sure to display these around the classroom.

6. Ask students to contact the Alaska Tourism Marketing Council (http://www.travelalaska.com) to obtain relevant information including maps, brochures, pamphlets, and other printed materials about the state. Ask students to set up an attractive display or information center on Alaska.

Chapter 9

History of Our Country

Columbus and the New World

Introduction

Trade between Europe and the Indies was an important part of the economic well-being of many countries during the fifteenth century. Unfortunately, the trade routes, although well established, took many months to traverse. Not only was the journey long, it was also dangerous. Merchants frequently risked their lives at the hands of robbers or the unpredictability of the high seas. Many people believed that there had to be a faster and easier way to get between Europe and the Far East.

One of those individuals was Christopher Columbus, an Italian mapmaker and sailor. Columbus also believed that the Earth was round, instead of flat as others believed. Not knowing that North and South America even existed, he thought that by sailing west across the Atlantic Ocean he would find a quicker route to the Indies and all the treasures that they held. After many failures and many years Columbus was finally able to convince Queen Isabella and King Ferdinand of Spain to give him three ships, the *Niña*, the *Pinta*, and the *Santa Maria*. Columbus set out from Spain on August 3, 1492, and the rest, as they say, is history.

Research Questions

1. When did Columbus make his voyage to the Americas?

2. Who funded his trip? Why was he rejected so many times previously?

3. What are some misconceptions about Columbus and his discovery of our continent?

4. Where did Columbus first believe he landed, and where did he really end up?

5. Why is Columbus recognized as being one of the greatest explorers?

Web Sites

http://www.mariner.org/age/columbus.html
The Mariner's Museum supplies this Web site that contains quality information about the explorations of Christopher Columbus. It begins at the very start of his life and finishes with his death. (S: 4–6, T: 4–6)

http://www.surfnetkids.com/columbus.htm
This site provides basic information about Christopher Columbus and references where one can find more information about the man and his travels. (S: 4–6)

http://metalab.unc.edu/expo/1492.exhibit/intro.html
An exhibit of the Library of Congress in Washington, D.C., has provided this site on Christopher Columbus and his travels. (T: 4–6)

http://marauder.millersv.edu/~columbus/data/art/LAUFER02.ART

This site provides some of the myths and facts about Columbus. There's lots of interesting information here that will dispel some of the common misperceptions about this explorer. (S: 4–6, T: 4–6)

http://metalab.unc.edu/expo/1492.exhibit/c-Columbus/columbus.html

This site offers interesting information on Columbus: Man and Myth. The site is filled with many facts and some interesting and unknown background information about Christopher Columbus. (S: 4–6, T: 4–6)

http://www.indians.org/welker/columbu1.htm

This site is a portal to several articles and writings that paint a different picture of Columbus. Many of the features concern Columbus and Native Americans. These articles are sure to generate a lot of discussion and controversy in the classroom. (S: 4–6, T: 4–6)

Literature Resources

Adler, David A. (1991). *A Picture Book of Christopher Columbus*. New York: Holiday House.
This book explains the life and voyages of Christopher Columbus in an easy-to-read style. The last page lists important dates, including birth, death, and voyages.

Brenner, Barbara. (1991). *If You Were There in 1492: Everyday Life in the Time of Columbus*. New York: Simon & Schuster.
This book allows the reader to be in Columbus's shoes by painting a complete picture of what life was like in those days. What happened after 1492 is also explained.

Sis, Peter. (1991). *Follow the Dream: The Story of Christopher Columbus*. New York: Random House.
Imagine a boy who lives at a time when many people still think the world is flat. Imagine him dreaming about faraway people and places he has only read about. This book takes the reader into the fifteenth century, providing an artist's interpretation of the Columbus voyages of discovery.

Activities and Projects

1. Ask small groups of students to select one of Columbus's four voyages. Using a variety of Web sites and children's literature, each group should create an imaginary logbook that Columbus (or one of his sailors) might have carried on the voyage. What notes or observations would go into the log? What things were sighted during the trip? What types of people did they meet during their various landfalls? Ask groups to discuss their respective voyages with each other.

2. Provide selected students with a map of the Atlantic Ocean. Give each of the students a different colored length of yarn and have each one plot the course of each of Columbus's voyages. This can be done by gluing a length of yarn to the map along the route taken during a specific voyage. After the four routes have been identified, be sure to post the map on a wall of the classroom.

3. Ask students to write a sailor's diary entry for October 10, 1492, the day before land was sighted on Columbus's first voyage. Other students should write a speech Columbus might have made to his crew to prevent them from being discouraged.

4. Ask students to determine the total number of miles sailed on each of Columbus's four voyages. Using the Web sites listed above, students can calculate the number of days each voyage took and the distance the ships traveled during that time. Post this information on a chart or graph for display in the classroom.

5. A food staple of early sailors was an item known as hardtack. Simply put, it was nothing more than hardened bread. Its advantage was that it could be stored for long periods of time—for example, during the course of an extended sea voyage. Your students may enjoy making this version of hardtack:

Hardtack

Mix 3 cups of flour and 2 teaspoons of salt in a large mixing bowl. Add 1 cup of water and work with your hands to blend thoroughly. Knead the dough, adding a little more flour if the mixture becomes sticky. Turn it out onto a floured board. Roll the dough into a rectangle about 1/2 inch thick. Use a very sharp knife to cut the dough into 3-inch squares. Use the tongs of a fork to punch approximately 20 holes through each of the squares. Bake these at 375 degrees for about 25 minutes or until they are brown. Allow to cool and then store them in an airtight container.

English Explorations of North America

Introduction

The Age of Exploration was a fast-paced race against time and rest of Europe. At first, curiosity drove countries such as England, Spain, and Italy to sail throughout the world, exploring and claiming new lands. However, once valuable commodities (like spices and precious metals) were discovered, the race sped up. England and Spain feuded with one another over land. As a result, enormous expeditions and vast sums of money were spent to discover and claim new lands. England, with its naval superiority, sought to expand its empire. Henry Hudson, John Cabot, and others set their sails for distant lands, both to explore and to conquer. It was a race of honor, of pride, and of enormous sacrifices—but the riches that awaited were worth it.

Research Questions

1. What were the major reasons for exploration during the 1500s?

2. Who were some of the most significant English explorers?

3. Do you feel that "Age of Exploration" was an appropriate title for the 1500 and 1600s? Is exploration still occurring today? Why or why not?

4. Why were spices so important?

5. What tools or devices were used by the explorers to find their way around the world?

Web Sites

http://www.lib.virginia.edu/exhibits/lewis_clark/ch4-26.html
This Web site is devoted to George Vancouver, an explorer from England who made his mark by circumnavigating the world under Captain James Cook and then continuing on to explore the American northwest coast alone. (S: 4–6, T: 4–6)

http://www.mariner.org/age/menu.html
This site focuses on English explorers such as John Cabot, Francis Drake, and Henry Hudson. The site notes each explorer's conquests, background information, and accomplishments. General vocabulary, time lines, and activities for students and teachers are also included. (S: 4–6, T: 4–6)

http://www.hudsonriver.com/halfmoonpress/stories/hudson.htm
This site provides a detailed explanation of how Henry Hudson began exploring the globe in search of spices for the Dutch East India Company. It includes the trials and tribulations he encountered (such as a difficult crew), how they were dealt with, and Hudson's tragic ending. (S: 4–6, T: 4–6)

 # Literature Resources

Asimov, Isaac. (1991). *Henry Hudson*. Milwaukee, WI: Gareth Stevens.
This book focuses on Henry Hudson's life. It tells of his voyages through the Arctic, Hudson River, and Hudson Bay. The book also describes what life was like during the 1600s on land and at sea. Colorful pictures and maps are paired with the text to give the reader a complete look at Henry Hudson.

Fritz, Jean. (1994). *Around the World in a Hundred Years: From Henry the Navigator to Magellan*. New York: Putnam.
Beginning with explorers of the fifteenth century, the author weaves magical tales of adventure and discoveries in this captivating book. Ideal for any classroom.

Malam, John. (1999). *John Cabot*. Minneapolis, MN: Carolrhoda Books.
Part of a series, this book conveys some of the discoveries and explorations of one of England's most well-known adventurers.

Morriss, Roger. (1998). *Captain Cook and His Explorations of the Pacific*. New York: Barrons.
This book describes the background and discoveries of Captain James Cook. A time line sets his discoveries against the backdrop of Britain's rivalry with France and Spain.

 # Activities and Projects

1. Host an Exploration Jeopardy® game. The main theme is English exploration, so all the questions will deal with that topic. As a class, come up with specific topics for the questions. You should create the final questions and assemble a Jeopardy® board resembling a picture of the globe. The different countries/regions explored around the world should be removable pieces that have questions to go with them. Have the students compete in teams to answer the questions. If they answer correctly, post the country of their choice on the Jeopardy® globe and make a mark signifying that the country has been "claimed" by that team. Whichever team can claim the most territory by answering questions wins the game.

2. Ask students to write an imaginary letter to Queen Elizabeth I requesting permission to explore a certain area of the world. Students should use atlases, almanacs, the Internet, and encyclopedias to make their choices. They must include specific reasons about why they want to travel to that region/country, the route they will take by boat, and the items they will need from the Queen.

3. Hang up a drawing/picture of a cross section of a boat that would have been used by one of the English explorers (can be found on the Internet). The cross section should be the center of the bulletin board. Label each room in the boat with the appropriate name. As a class, draw in the objects that belong in each room (food, water, beds, etc.) and what the purpose of each object is. Then have students create their own boat cross sections. They should make an illustration with an explanation of what each room is, its function, and the objects contained in that room. Allow each student to explain her or his boat and then hang them around the large boat on the board.

4. Ask students to find their way around the school using a compass. Show the students how to use a compass, then organize the class into groups of three and give each group a compass, piece of paper, and pen or pencil. Prior to the activity, decide different routes for the groups to take around the school (or playground). Rather than tell each group which hallways to go down and rooms to pass, just give them directions such as "go northwest for three steps and then head north for five steps." The students must follow the directions and write down the path they ended up taking by identifying the hallways they walked down and landmarks they passed.

Spanish Explorations of North America

Introduction

Spain sought to colonize the New World for two main reasons: They wanted to spread Christianity across the world and they wanted the riches (gold and silver) that they believed could be found this new territory. For these reasons, Spain began many colonies throughout the New World, including the islands of the Caribbean, the southern and western parts of North America, and extensive territories throughout Central and South America. Many of these early explorers were spurred by tales of vast cities of gold or by legends of eternal fountains of youth. Whatever their impetus, Spanish explorers left an indelible mark on the landscape and culture of this part of the world.

Although there were many different Spanish explorers during the first half of the sixteenth century, some of the most notable were Ponce de Leon, Cortes, Narvaez, Cabeza de Vaca, de Soto, Coronado, Cabrillo, and Menendez de Aviles. These men set up colonies and claimed land that now includes portions of the states of Florida, Texas, Kansas, New Mexico, Arizona, California, and Colorado. Many of the towns and cities in these states have Spanish names, reflecting their heritage and history.

Research Questions

1. Who were some Spanish explorers? Why did they come to America?

2. What are some things the explorers brought with them?

3. Why did the explorers leave Spain?

4. What are some early tools used for navigation?

5. What was the first city established in Florida?

Web Sites

http://www.umich.edu/~proflame/texts/mirror/conflict.html
This site describes Hernan Cortes's expedition to Mexico and provides selected biographical information. (T: 4–6)

http://www.desertusa.com/mag98/sep/papr/coronado.html
This Web site describes the life and journeys of Coronado. (S: 4–6, T: 4–6)

http://www.win.tue.nl/~engels/discovery/cabrillo.html
This site is a brief biography of Juan Cabrillo and his discoveries along the California coast. (S: 4–6, T: 4–6)

http://marauder.millersv.edu/~columbus/data/art/LAUFER02.ART

This site provides some of the myths and facts about Columbus. There's lots of interesting information here that will dispel some of the common misperceptions about this explorer. (S: 4–6, T: 4–6)

http://metalab.unc.edu/expo/1492.exhibit/c-Columbus/columbus.html

This site offers interesting information on Columbus: Man and Myth. The site is filled with many facts and some interesting and unknown background information about Christopher Columbus. (S: 4–6, T: 4–6)

 # Literature Resources

Anderson, Dale. (1993). *Explorers Who Found New Worlds*. Austin, TX: Steck-Vaughn.

Descriptions of a diverse array of explorers from Columbus to Lewis and Clark are accompanied by maps, portraits, sketches, and photographs.

Greenway, Shirley. (1998). *Exploration of North America*. Hauppage, NY: Barrons.

This magazine-style book presents the explorations of many early explorers, including several Spanish ones.

Jacobs, William (1994). *Coronado: A Dreamer in Golden Armor*. New York: Franklin Watts.

This is an overview of the life and times of this great Spanish explorer. Filled with lots of facts and delightful information, this is an ideal classroom book.

Ross, Stewart. (1996). *Conquerors and Explorers*. Brookfield, CT: Copper Beech Books.

This is an colorful and captivating introduction to some of the world's great explorers, including many Spanish ones.

Sis, Peter. (1993). *Voyages to the New World*. New York: Thomson Learning.

This is an excellent book of exploration and encounters. It describes the times in which the explorers lived and the myths believed about the sea at those times. It also tells of Columbus's voyages, his navigational tools, and daily life on a ship.

Wilber, C. Keith. (1996). *Early Explorers of North America*. Old Saybrook, CT: Globe Pequot.

This is a complete and thorough examination of the lives of some of the most well-known explorers of the North American continent.

 # Activities and Projects

1.   What would you bring if you set off to explore a new land? After students have had an opportunity to collect pertinent information from the Web sites and literature listed above, ask them to form several small groups. Have each group put together a list of essential supplies and materials for an imaginary voyage to the New World in the early 1500s. After groups have had sufficient time to assemble their lists, provide opportunities for all to compare and contrast their respective lists.

2.   When the Spanish explored North America, they brought along with them many new things and took back to Europe many new things. Some of the things that the Spanish brought to America were cattle, horses, sheep, pigs, sugarcane, and diseases. What

would life have been like if they had never discovered America? Ask students to write a story about what their lives would be like if the Spanish had never come to America. Students should access various Web sites and library resources prior to drafting their stories.

3. Have students participate in a readers theater presentation of one of the most well-known explorers to sail for the country of Spain—Christopher Columbus. The following script is taken from *American History Through Readers Theatre,* by Anthony D. Fredericks (Englewood, CO: Teacher Ideas Press, 2000). Ask four students to take on the roles of the four characters in this script and read aloud (there is no need to memorize any dialogue) their parts.

Columbus Pleads His Case

STAGING: The narrator can sit on a stool or stand at a lectern on the side of the staging area. Columbus should be standing or can move back and forth across the staging area. The other two characters can sit on stools or chairs side by side.

```
                    Queen Isabella      King Ferdinand
                         X                   X

           Columbus
              X

  Narrator
     X
```

NARRATOR: It is Spring 1492. For seven years Christopher Columbus has been pleading with King Ferdinand and Queen Isabella of Spain for men and ships to search for a new sea route to the West Indies. He is frustrated because he cannot convince Spain's rulers that the route would bring them riches and their country fame.

ISABELLA: Christopher, for seven years you have been telling us about this new route to the West Indies. Why should we invest our money and men in something that everyone says can't be done?

COLUMBUS: (frustrated) But, dear Queen, it can be done! Even some of the most renowned men of science agree that the world cannot be flat—it must be round. Look at the work of Juan Carlos, who keeps describing the "disappearing horizon"—a horizon that is never reached, but keeps moving away from the traveler. Surely that must be a sign that the Earth is round, not flat.

FERDINAND: You are quite passionate about your views. That is all well and good. But, you have asked us for vast sums to finance this voyage into the unknown . . . a voyage across an ocean no one has ever sailed. What will we gain?

COLUMBUS: (somewhat excited) Great riches! New lands! New territories! Spices, silk, wealth, and untold fortunes!

ISABELLA: (indignantly) You sound like a prophet—promising much, but delivering little.

COLUMBUS: (contrite) Trust me, my queen. If I discover this new route by sailing west across the Atlantic Ocean your coffers will be filled with gold. Your cabinets will be filled with the finest spices. Your palace will be trimmed with silks and treasures from distant lands and faraway ports. And your place in history shall be assured.

ISABELLA: (insistent) Yes, that all sounds well and fine. But you have been promising us these things for many years. Why should we trust you now?

COLUMBUS: Because the time is ripe. Because Prince Henry of Portugal is funding some of the finest sailors of Europe to search out and establish these sea routes. He knows, as do you, that the Italian cities of Rome and Venice and Naples control the overland routes to the Indies. (faster) He knows that those routes are hard and dangerous and that a sea route is the only way to obtain the riches he covets. He knows that time is important. So too, does he wish to have all the glory and all the riches for himself. (louder and louder) What then of Spain's place in history? Will Spain be second-rate? Will Spain not prosper from the riches that await in distant lands? (more passionate) Will Spain defer to Prince Henry? Will Spain's armada and navy be constrained to the European continent? Does Spain not wish to rule the waves, rule the sea, rule the world?

FERDINAND: You are, indeed, most fervent in your belief.

COLUMBUS: (somewhat subdued) I am, your majesty. There is much to discover across the sea—much to bring back to Spain, her people, and most certainly, her noble rulers.

ISABELLA: What if we give you the men and ships you seek. Where will you go?

COLUMBUS: I will sail west—into the setting sun.

ISABELLA: Is that not dangerous? Are there not monsters awaiting errant sailors?

COLUMBUS: I believe not, your highness. I believe that there is but a small ocean to sail across. I believe that the Indies lie just over the horizon.

FERDINAND: And how long will this voyage of discovery take you?

COLUMBUS: We shall take but a handful of days. And we shall return with the spices and riches you desire. And, also, we shall return with the glory that is rightfully Spain's and no one else's.

ISABELLA: But we wish much more than just riches and spices. It is the lands you would discover that we also wish. We would give you the authority to claim for Spain any non-Christian lands you might reach. We wish to promote the spread of Christianity throughout the world and the lands you would discover would be converted for the glory of the church.

FERDINAND: Our legacy should be a legacy of Christianity and it is through our religion that we rightfully and properly would secure new land.

ISABELLA: I believe that your passion has sufficiently swayed me, Christopher. I therefore command you to take charge of our three finest ships and begin your voyage without delay. Go with the knowledge that you are carrying the glory of Spain and the glory of Christianity with you. And, for every land that you discover I shall make you governor. Go wisely, Christopher, and discover what you will.

COLUMBUS: (head bowed) I fervently thank you, my queen. You shall not be disappointed. I shall carry the flag of Spain with honor and set it upon the soil of the new land—claiming it once and for all for the greatest country on Earth.

NARRATOR: Soon after, Christopher Columbus left the court of King Ferdinand and Queen Isabella to begin his preparations for the epic voyage. He and his crew, on the three vessels—the Nina, the Pinta, and the Santa Maria—sailed from Spain on August 3, 1492. Two months later, on October 10, 1492 a tiny island (now called Watlings Island), in what is now the Bahamas, was sighted by one of Columbus's men—a sailor named Rodrigo de Triana. Confident that he was in the Indies, Columbus called the people he met Indians.

For several months, Columbus and his crew sailed throughout the islands of what is now Cuba and Hispanola. The ships eventually returned to Spain—without the riches and spices he had promised Isabella and Ferdinand. Yet, Columbus thought he would find them on future trips. He made three additional trips to the New World—constantly seeking the elusive route to the West Indies. When he died on May 20, 1506, he still believed that he had, in fact, reached the shores of Asia—even though he never discovered the riches he had promised.

Possible Extensions

1. Ask students to rewrite part of the script using one of the following possibilities:

    a. The king and queen refuse Columbus's request.

    b. The king agrees, the queen does not.

    c. The queen agrees, the king does not.

2. Ask students to discuss why "Columbus Day" is celebrated in this country even though Columbus never (in his four voyages to the New World) set foot on what is now the United States.

3. Ask students to create a readers theatre script centering on the events that took place on October 10, 1492.

4. Ask students to investigate early marine maps. Discuss the symbols and creatures depicted on those maps. How are the illustrations on early sea maps different from the ones in use today.

5. Students may enjoy gathering information and data on Columbus's voyages on the following Web site: http://www.mariner.org/age/columbus.html

6.   Your students may be interested in reading one or more of the following book selections:

   a.   *Christopher Columbus and the Discovery of the New World* by Carole Gallagher (New York: Chelsea House, 2000).

   b.   *Columbus and the Renaissance Explorers* by Colin Hynson (Hauppage, NY: Barron's, 1998).

   c.   *Follow the Dream* by Peter Sis (New York: Drangonfly, 1996).

   d.   *Where Do You Think You're Going, Christopher Columbus?* by Jean Fritz (New York: Paper Star, 1997).

New England Colonies

 Introduction

Rarely do we stop to reflect on how far our nation has advanced since the seventeenth century. In this time period, separatist Puritans, better known as Pilgrims, came to the Americas from England in pursuit of religious freedom. Many of us take for granted our religious beliefs, and we don't stop to realize that without this heroic group of settlers we may all have had to follow the preaching of Catholicism. Not only did the Pilgrims bring us religious freedom, they also brought skills such as planting crops, building, trading, etc. Massachusetts, Rhode Island, Connecticut, and New Hampshire were the first colonies founded by these Pilgrims. In 1620, the Pilgrims boarded the *Mayflower,* landed at Plymouth Rock, and began their search for a new life. Today we remember these brave people who left England and celebrate their achievements every year in November when we sit down with our families for Thanksgiving dinner.

 Research Questions

1. What are the names of the New England colonies?

2. Which colony was the largest?

3. Why did people leave England and come to America?

4. What were the people who founded the New England colonies called?

5. Who greeted the colonists when they got to the New World? Did these people and the colonists remain friends? Why or why not?

 Web Sites

www.pbs.org/ktca/liberty/chronicle/diversity-phyllisw.html
This site includes information about the diversity in the colonies. A lot of information is presented about the Scotch-Irish, Scots, English, and Germans, but the focus is on the African Americans. It has accounts of their life in the colonies. African Americans are often forgotten in the curriculum of the colonial period, and this site is a great way to include them. (T: 4–6)

http://www.esd.k12.ca.us/Cadwallader/Room%2020/Colonies/Main.html
Your students will definitely want to check out this site about the New England colonies (and Middle and Southern colonies) created by a class of fifth grade students. (S: 4–6)

Literature Resources

Barrett, Tracy. (1995). *Growing up in Colonial America*. Brookfield, CT: Millbrook Press.

Daily chores, routines, leisure time, and religious and social attitudes are depicted in this book. It shows how children of colonial America lived and what roles they had to play. Readers will also learn how children were raised and what they were taught in New England and in the South.

Bunting, Eve. (1990). *How Many Days to America? A Thanksgiving Story*. New York: Clarion Books.

Bunting brilliantly depicts the struggle for freedom of a family forced to leave their Caribbean Island. They set sail in a small fishing boat for America, and when they arrive, they see it is a special day in more ways then one. Terms such as *emigrant, refugee, freedom,* and *Thanksgiving* will also become clearer to students, and they will gain a greater appreciation for their freedom by reading this book.

Egger-Bovet, Howard & Smith-Baranzini, Marlene. (1996). *U.S. Kids History: Book of the American Colonies*. New York: Little, Brown.

After reading this book, children will understand why Europeans settled in America. They will see the growth of the colonies and the reactions to the newcomers of the people already living in the New World. This book covers the New England colonies from the beginning to statehood.

Howarth, Sarah. (1994). *Colonial People*. Brookfield, CT: Millbrook Press.

This is an ideal book for children to discover the people of colonial America. It covers everyday lives of colonial people through quotations and illustrations of the time. Best of all, this book covers people of all status, so the reader gets a good idea of what people had to go through.

Howarth, Sarah. (1994). *Colonial Places*. Brookfield, CT: Millbrook Press.

Sarah Howarth takes her readers to different places of the colonial period. She depicts social life, travel, and customs of the people and introduces the reader to various places in the New England colonies such as the Governor's House, the tobacco field, and even the street. Each of these places played an important role in the colonial times, and Howarth explains what their roles were.

Reische, Diana. (1989). *Founding the American Colonies*. New York: Franklin Watts.

This book tells what it was like discovering the original thirteen colonies. The author brilliantly describes the founding, problems faced, and social and economic survival of the colonies. A must-read book for children studying the American colonies; it will answer almost all of their questions.

Wroble, Lisa. (1997). *Kids in Colonial Times*. New York: PowerKids Press.

This well-illustrated book brilliantly covers colonial times. The reader will learn about the New World, the first colonies, clothing worn, and food eaten. Children will be able to distinguish the differences between how people lived in colonial times and how we live today.

Activities and Projects

1. Ask children to explore the Internet sites and *Colonial People* to learn more about people who lived in the New England colonies. Ask students to choose one fictitious person from colonial times and discover as much as they can about that person, including information about clothing, social status, activities, family life, etc. Have the students present their people to the rest of the class in a skit, diorama, poster, etc.

2. Ask the students to turn your classroom into a colonial classroom. Students should check out some Internet sites like http://guest.btinternet.com/-mark.furnival/ darkage.htm and read literary sources such as *Colonial Places, U.S. Kids History: Book of the American Colonies* so they can add as much detail as possible. Provide horn books and colored construction paper for a fireplace and bring in quills for the children to write with. Choose a day for the class to live and dress like the colonial children did.

3. Ask students to create a newspaper from one of the New England colonies. Students should work in groups of four or five, making sure that each person has a specific part to work on. The newspaper should include a weather report, late-breaking news, and any other information or articles the students wish to include. Have students use the Web sites and literary sources available for the late-breaking news topic specific to that colony, and ask students to create pictures unique to that colony. A possible topic for the newspaper would be the first Thanksgiving feast. A reference for that topic is http://members.aol.com/calebj/mayflower.html.

4. Ask students to divide into groups of two to create a board game about the New England colonies. They should include a map showing where each colony is located, information about the food colonists ate, how colonists traveled, why the colonists came to the New World, and anything else the students would like to include. Tell the students that the information they need for the game can be found on the Internet sites and in children's books. Sources to check out are the Internet site http://www.geocities. com/SiliconValley/Way/9301/HistoryDay.html and literary sources such as *U.S. Kids History: Book of the American Colonies,* which will be provided in the classroom. After everyone's game is completed, allow time for each group to present their game to the class and explain how to play, along with time for the students to play each other's games.

5. Ask the students to imagine that tomorrow when they wake up they will have been transported back in time and will be part of one of the New England colonies. Have them students create a book describing every aspect of their day in colonial times, from the minute they wake up to nightfall when they return to bed. Allow time for the children to browse through books such as *Colonial People, Colonial Places,* and *Growing up in Colonial America,* and through various Internet sites to get an idea of what daily activities may occur while they are in the New England colonies. Ask students to type up their pages and add colorful illustrations. After the books are completed, place them on a shelf for students to refer to and enjoy throughout the rest of the unit.

6. Ask students to help you redecorate the classroom to resemble one of the New England colonies. Have them vote on what colony they want their classroom to be. After a decision has been reached, provide specific children's literature and Web sites for the students to use to find information pertaining to that colony. Each student should take on a different role. Then ask them to create their play. They may choose to use any props they wish and make backdrops out of old sheets or large sheets of construction paper. Provide time for play rehearsal and costume rehearsal a few times before the day of the performance arrives. Invite other classes to come see the class play.

7. Re-create the first Thanksgiving feast in your classroom. Ask students to find out what foods were eaten, who was there, who prepared the meal, and what occurred during the meal. Information can be found in their textbooks or in the above-mentioned Web sites and literary sources, including *How Many Days to America? A Thanksgiving Story* and at http://members.aol.com/calebj/mayflower.html.

Middle and Southern Colonies

Introduction

The middle colonies of Pennsylvania, New York, New Jersey, and Delaware shared many common characteristics. Primary was the fact that the colonists in this region depended heavily on farming for their livelihood. This contrasted with the New England colonies, whose rocky, mostly untillable soil was not conducive to farming. Farmers in the middle colonies raised crops such as wheat, corn, rye, and barley. As a result, these colonies were often referred to as the "breadbasket colonies." Not only was this area rich in agricultural products, it was also a center for pottery, furniture, and glassware. Unlike New England, most of the settlers of this region came from a variety of European, countries including England, France, Scotland, Sweden, and Germany.

The southern colonies were comprised of what are now known as the states of Maryland, Virginia, North and South Carolina, and Georgia. This area of the country was distinguished by rich and fertile agricultural farmlands—more than was the case in the middle or New England colonies. The area is dominated by a wide coastal plain and a warm climate, both ideal for farming. Cotton and tobacco were the crops of choice and were typically grown on large plantations worked by slaves. Rice was also grown in this region and was a major export to Europe. The southern colonies were highly dependent on the land and the slaves who worked that land.

Research Questions

1. What are the states of the middle colonies?

2. What are the states of the southern colonies?

3. What did these two regions have in common?

4. On what was the economy of the South based?

5. From which country did most slaves originate?

6. What was the major agricultural export to Europe during the early 1700s?

Web Sites

http://kidinfo.com/American_History/Colonization_Mid_Colonies.html
This site presents the history of each of the four middle colonies and includes information on people, religions, and natives of the middle colonies. (S: 4–6)

http://www.kidinfo.com/American_History/Colonization_S_Colonies.html
This site presents the history of important people and slavery in the southern colonies. It also supplies links to other sites with information about the colonies. (S: 4–6)

Literature Resources

Haskins, James. (1999). *Bound for America*. New York: Lothrop, Lee & Shepard Books.
   This is a very descriptive and informative review of the slave trade that provided the southern colonies with most of their workers.

Ichord, Loretta. (1998). *Hasty Pudding, Johnnycakes, and Other Good Stuff: Cooking in Colonial America*. Brookfield, CT: Millbrook Press.
   This is a potpourri of delicious recipes for students to explore at home or in the classroom.

Activities and Projects

1.   Following are two recipes for food eaten in the middle and southern colonies that students will enjoy preparing (and certainly eating). Both Hasty Pudding and Johnnycakes were quite popular during colonial times.

Johnnycakes

Beat 1 egg in a medium-sized bowl. Stir in 2 cups of oatmeal, 3/4 teaspoon of salt, and 1 1/2 cups of whole milk. Drop the mixture by teaspoons onto a well-greased and very hot frying pan. Fry each cake until it is brown on both sides. Serve hot with butter and powdered sugar.

Hasty Pudding

Into the top of a double boiler put 2 cups of water. Put some additional water in the bottom of the double boiler and bring to a boil over medium heat. Stir in 1/3 cup of cornmeal and 1/2 teaspoon of salt. Cook the mixture until it is thick (approximately 1 hour), stirring occasionally. Spoon into several small bowls and pour maple syrup or molasses over the top.

2. Students can create their own colonial candles using the following directions:

> Melt some paraffin over a double boiler. Take some small (half-pint) milk cartons and punch a small hole in the bottom of each. Thread a piece of wicking (available at hobby stores) through each hole and tie a knot in the end, or attach a paper clip to the end of the wick for weight and center the clip in the bottom of an unpunched carton. Place a pencil on the top of each carton and wrap the loose end of the wick around the pencil, making sure the wick is centered in the carton. Slowly pour melted wax into each carton (for color, crayon shavings may be added before pouring). Allow to solidify and tear the milk carton away from the outside of each candle.

3. Invite a local furniture maker into your classroom to describe the differences between furniture created during colonial times and furniture built today. You may be able to borrow a piece of antique furniture from the parents or grandparents of one of the students for display purposes.

4. Obtain a large sheet of newsprint. Ask each student to stand between the sheet and an overhead projector. Turn on the projector and ask each individual to remain still. Trace the outline of each student's silhouette on the newsprint. Create several silhouettes and ask students to illustrate or color them as though they were representative of colonial children. Students should create a "conversation balloon" (similar to those used in comic strips) with a quote or saying on it that would be representative of something a colonial child might say. Be sure to post the silhouettes and their quotes throughout the classroom.

The Revolutionary War

Introduction

The American colonies were prosperous and England needed a source of income to pay off the financial debt of the wars they had been fighting in Europe. England realized that its citizens were heavily taxed and decided to tax the colonies as well. The colonies, which had no say in the English government, asserted that they wanted representation before taxation.

The American Revolution was a war between the American colonies and England. Originally the colonies did not want to separate from England. They only wanted to protect their interests and be represented in the English Parliament. When England would not tolerate such an idea the colonies responded with minor rebellions. Each rebellion intensified feelings of dissatisfaction with the ruling country, finally giving birth to the idea of attempting to gain independence. Thus, the American Revolution was born.

Research Questions

1. What two countries fought in the American Revolution?

2. Why did the English Parliament tax the American colonies?

3. What phrase became a battle cry for the colonists?

4. Why is Valley Forge important?

5. What was the role of women during the Revolutionary War?

Web Sites

http://www.wpi.edu/Academics/Depts/MilSci/BTSI/abs_bostea.html
This Web site provides students with a description of the Boston Tea Party. (S: 4–6)

http://www.wpi.edu/lAcademics/Depts/MilSci/BTSI/abs_coer.html
This site explains the various Acts imposed on the colonies by England after the Boston Tea Party. (S: 4–6)

http://www.ilt.columbia.edu/k12/history/aha/timeline.html
This page is full of links to people, events, and documents that provide students with valuable information about the Revolutionary War. (T: 4–6)

http://www.earlyamerica.com/earlyamerica/index.html
This site is full of great links to (but not limited to):

The Declaration of Independence
The Constitution
The Bill of Rights
Maps
A gallery of early American portraits (S: 4–6)

http://www.ilt.columbia.edu/k12/history/aha/ARMain.html

This is a great site. It contains a map of early America showing the various battles fought during the Revolution. If students click on a battle title, it shows them an enlargement of the area and gives more information. (S: 4–6)

http://www.earlyamerica.com/earlyamerica/freedom/doi/index.html

This is a wonderful site that re-creates the mood of the times when the Declaration of Independence was signed and announced. (S: 4–6)

http://www.earlyamerica.com/earlyamerica/freedom/doi/text.html

At this site students will be able to read the full text of the Declaration of Independence. (S: 4–6)

http://www.contemplator.com/america/

At this site students can listen to songs of the revolutionary period in American History. They'll also be able to hear songs from other periods in our nation's history as well. A *super site* for any history unit! (S: All, T: All)

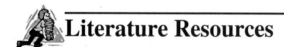

Literature Resources

Brenner, Barbara. (1994). *If You Were There in 1776*. New York: Simon & Schuster.
Different aspects of the colonies in 1776 are discussed, including such things as farms and cities, arts and crafts, rebels, Indians, and slaves.

Heilbroner, Joan. (1989). *Meet George Washington*. New York: Random House.
This is a good, short chapter book for students to read. It begins by narrating George Washington's boyhood, then goes on to his adulthood. It explains his role in the French and Indian War, the American Revolution, and as the first president of the United States.

Moss, Marissa. (1999). *The Story of a Colonial Girl: Emma's Journal*. San Diego: Silver Whistle.
This is a diary of a ten-year-old girl living with her aunt in Boston. The time is just before the American Revolution. It describes the torment people felt when trying to decide where their loyalties lay (with England or with the colonies). It also depicts a young girl becoming a spy for the colonies.

Sakurai, Gail. (1997). *Cornerstones of Freedom: Paul Revere*. New York: Children's Press.
This is an excellent account of the famous ride of Paul Revere. It describes the Boston Tea Party, messages and other political acts associated with Paul Revere, and personal facts about Paul Revere's life.

Stein, Conrad R. (1996). *Cornerstones of Freedom: The Boston Tea Party*. New York: Children's Press.
This is an excellent account of the Boston Tea Party and the events that led up to it. It depicts the anger the colonists felt toward England. This one act began a chain of events that led the colonists to fight for their (and our) independence.

Stein, Conrad. R. (1994). *Cornerstones of Freedom: Valley Forge*. New York: Children's Press.
    This is a chilling account of the events at the camp at Valley Forge. This is where General Washington and his army camped for the winter of 1777. Included are several quotes from soldiers, doctors, and other sources describing the conditions there.

 # Activities and Projects

1. Read *The Story of a Colonial Girl: Emma's Journal* and *If You Were There in 1776* to the class. Ask the children to choose a character from that time that they would like to characterize Ask students to maintain (for approximately one month) a diary of a character's life. Students should select an actual person or create a fictionalized individual. Provide opportunities for students to share events in their person's life through regular readings or classroom sharing.

2. Have the children review the Web sites http://www.wpi.edu/Academics/Depts/MilSci/ BTSI/abs_bostea.html, http://www.ilt.columbia.edu/k12/history/aha/timeline.html, http://www.contemplator.com/history.revwomen.html, and any others they find on Revolutionary War heroes. Instruct the children to pretend they are a Revolutionary War hero who has not been recognized for her or his contribution to the Revolution. (Explain that many people were not recognized for their efforts in the war.) Now they are to be recognized. Students should write a paragraph on their person's accomplishments and draw each person. Mount the portraits on a large sheet of construction paper, with the descriptive paragraph below the picture. Hang these pictures in the classroom.

3. Ask students to access some of the Web sites listed above. Have them gather as much information as possible about one of the following acts: Sugar Act, Stamp Act, Townsend Act, or Intolerable Act. Ask selected students to take on the role of a colonist and make an impassioned speech to other colonists opposing one of those acts.

4. Ask students to obtain a copy of Henry Wadsworth Longfellow's poem "Paul Revere's Ride." Have class members develop the poem into a choral reading or readers theater script. (For examples of readers theater, see *Frantic Frogs and Other Frankly Fractured Folktales for Readers Theatre*, by Anthony D. Fredericks, Englewood, CO: Teacher Ideas Press, 1993.) Students can present the poem to another class or videotape it and donate it to the school library.

5. Corn bread was popular during Revolutionary War times. You and your students may enjoy making corn bread in much the same way as the people in New England did during the war years. Following is a recipe:

> ### Corn Bread
>
> Boil 3 cups of water and stir in 1 cup of cornmeal grits. Simmer until all the water is absorbed. Allow to cool and turn onto a work surface that has been floured with a cup of fine cornmeal flour. Work the mixture into 2 round flat cakes. Bake on a greased cookie sheet at 400 degrees for about 45 minutes. Cut into pieces and serve.

The Declaration of Independence

Introduction

To pay England's debts, colonists were being forced to pay taxes without any representation in the English Parliament (taxation without representation). Some of the laws imposing these taxes were the Stamp Act, which was used to help England pay for the French and Indian War, and the Townsend Acts, which placed a tax on paper, glass, and lead. To enforce the taxes, England sent troops to the colonies. The American colonists boycotted the taxes and formed protest groups such as the Sons of Liberty.

These protests, along with other events, precipitated the Revolutionary War. In May 1775 the Second Continental Congress drafted a letter to King George III asking him to repeal the laws they believed were unjust. The king refused to accept the letter. The colonists then decided to declare their freedom from England's control and support. Drafted primarily by Thomas Jefferson, the Declaration of Independence contained three main points:

1. It listed 27 wrongs done to the colonists by King George.

2. It explained how the new nation would be governed.

3. It formally declared war against England.

The Continental Congress voted to approve the Declaration of Independence on July 4, 1776, a date often referred to as our country's birthday.

Research Questions

1. Name the five men appointed by the Continental Congress to make a draft of the declaration.

2. Who was assigned to write the original draft?

3. What was the purpose of the Declaration of Independence?

4. What were the two passages in Jefferson's first draft that were rejected by the Congress?

5. What was the first newspaper to print the Declaration of Independence, and who printed the first copy?

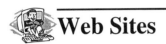

Web Sites

http://www.ourconstitution.com/DecIndep.html

This site offers a great deal of information on the Declaration of Independence. Students can read the original document just by clicking on an icon. (S: All)

http://www.indwes.edu/Faculty/bcupp/Constitution/Freedom/doi/index.html

This site outlines what was going on during the time of signing the Declaration of Independence. There is also a picture of the Declaration of Independence as it originally appeared in the Pennsylvania Packet when it was issued. (S: All)

http://www.pbs.org/ktca/liberty/chronicle/declaration.html

This is one of the most interesting sites on the Web about the Declaration of Independence. Students can enjoy a game that involves them creating their own American Revolution. This site also offers different perspectives on the Revolution from the British Army, other countries, and the colonists. (S: All)

http://www.nara.gov/exhall/charters/declaration/decmain.html

This Web site includes the history and interpretation of the Declaration of Independence. There is also an image of the Declaration taken from the engraving made by printer William J. Stone in 1823. Students can see the document as it looked in colonial times. (S: All)

Literature Resources

Brenner, Barbara. (1994). *If You Were There in 1776*. New York: Macmillan.

This interesting book demonstrates how the concepts and principles expressed in the Declaration of Independence were drawn from the experience of living in America in the late eighteenth century, with emphasis on how children lived on a New England farm, a Southern plantation, and the frontier.

Sabin, Francene. (1986). *Young Thomas Jefferson*. Mahwah, NJ: Troll Associates.

This book details the life of Thomas Jefferson. It includes the drafting of the Declaration of Independence and his election as the third president of the United States.

Schleifer, Jay. (1992). *Our Declaration of Independence*. Brookfield, CT: Millbrook Press.

A history of the Declaration of Independence, this book describes the events leading up to it, the key players in its drafting, the actual writing, and its adoption.

Van Leeuwen, Jean. (1997). *A Fourth of July on the Plains*. New York: Dial.

Young Jesse and his family are with a wagon train traveling from Indiana to Oregon when they stop to celebrate the Fourth of July. Jesse is too young to go hunting with the men, so he comes up with his own contribution to the festivities.

Activities and Projects

1. Ask students to draft a Declaration of Independence for their class. Tell them to imagine that they want to rebel against the school and its leaders. What kinds of rights do they want? What do they want to say to the king (building principal)? What are the wrongs they believe the king has committed? How will their new "nation" be governed? Allow adequate time for students to discuss the pros and cons of their Declaration of Independence.

2. Ask students to create birthday announcements for the United States. They should include information such as "mother" (England), where the "birth" took place, and when it happened. If possible, bring in several examples of birth announcement for students to study and copy.

3. Ask students to create and develop a fictitious newspaper for July 5, 1776. What would the headlines say? What events would be featured on the front page? What would be some advertisements that might be placed in the newspaper?

4. Ask students to work in pairs to write imaginary letters from the future (today's date) to a child in 1776. What types of questions might be asked? What kinds of events could be shared? What would today's child want to know about a child of 1776? What would a child of 1776 want to know about a child today? Provide sufficient opportunities for students to discuss and share their ideas.

5. Ask students to plan for the first birthday party of the country. Small groups of students can make up invitations for the celebration. Who would be invited? Who would be excluded? How would the event be celebrated?

6. Ask several students to pose as reporters for a fictitious newspaper (*The Colonial Tribune*). Have other students take on the roles of selected figures who met during the Second Continental Congress. Ask the reporters to interview the historical figures to get their perspectives on the events happening around them. Students can invite a reporter from the local newspaper to visit the class and share some interviewing techniques prior to this project.

The Constitution

Introduction

After the Revolutionary War, it was found that the Articles of Confederation had several weaknesses. They did not provide for an executive branch or for a central system of courts. They did not give the central government the power to set taxes or enforce treaties. In essence, Congress had no way of forcing states to obey the laws it passed. To rectify these deficiencies, a constitutional convention was called in May 1787 in Philadelphia. Fifty-five men, including George Washington, Benjamin Franklin, James Madison, Alexander Hamilton, and Patrick Henry, attended.

Out of that convention came the Constitution. Although the new government took office in March 1789, it wasn't until May 1790 that the final state, Rhode Island, ratified the Constitution. The Constitution is based on four principles:

1. federalism (a division of powers among national, state, and local branches)

2. the separation of powers (three branches of government—executive, legislative, and judicial)

3. the rights of individuals (the Bill of Rights or the first ten amendments to the Constitution)

4. the adaptability of the Constitution to meet the needs of the times (the amendment process, the right of government to stretch its powers, and the federal government's implied powers).

Research Questions

1. Where was the Constitution created?

2. Name several of the men who signed the Constitution.

3. How is the Constitution useful to us in today's society?

4. What are the parts of the Constitution?

5. Do other countries have a constitution? If so, how are their constitutions similar to and different from ours?

 # Web Sites

http://www.earlyamerica.com/earlyamerica/freedom/index.html

This site contains an exact-sized reproduction of the first public printing of the United States Constitution as it appeared in the September 19, 1787, issue of the Pennsylvania Packet. The site also has a running banner of what happened on this day in early America. (S: 4–6, T: 4–6)

http://www.nara.gov/exhall/charters/constsitution/confath.html

Students can log onto this site to take a journey back to the year 1787. Fifty-five delegates attended the constitutional convention sessions, but only thirty-nine actually signed the Constitution. This site provides a short biography of each of the founding fathers who were delegates to the constitutional convention. (S: 4–6)

http://www.nara.gov/exhall/lcharters/constitution/conmain.html

This site presents a simplified version of how and why the Constitution was written and ratified. It also contains a copy of the original version for students to view and compare with the simplified version. Students can read a transcription of the complete text of the Constitution and also view an image of James Madison, who played a leading role in the ratification process. (S: 4–6)

 # Literature Resources

Fritz, Jean. (1998). *Shh! We're Writing the Constitution*. New York: Harcourt Brace.

This book is about the Constitution, who participated in developing it, and when and where it was created. The book describes how the Constitution came to be written and ratified.

Johnson, Linda Carlson. (1994). *Our Constitution (I Know America)*. New York: Millbrook Press.

The author describes the sets of rules for our government that was created for our country to follow in the past, the present, and the future.

Levy, Elizabeth. (1996). *If You Were There When They Signed the Constitution*. New York: Paper Star.

This book is designed in a question and answer format. Readers are taken behind the locked doors of the Philadelphia State House during the constitutional convention to see how and why the Constitution was written.

Maestro, Giulio. (1997). *A More Perfect Union: The Story of Our Constitution*. New York: Lothrop, Lee & Shepard Books.

This is the story of the 55 men who created the Constitution in 1787. The men helped to give the new government a foundation that has held firm and solid ever since.

Quiri, Patricia Ryon. (1998). *The Constitution: A True Book*. Danbury, CT: Children's Press.

The author presents historical facts and information about the creation and ratification of the Constitution in this book targeted to four- to eight-year-old readers.

Spier, Peter. (1991). *We the People: The Constitution of the United States of America*. Indianapolis, IN: Doubleday Books.

We the People is full of historical information about the creation of the Constitution. Colorful illustrations create scenes of past and present America while the author tells the story of the writing and ratification of the Constitution.

 # Activities and Projects

1. Read to the class the preamble to the Constitution, which can be found at http://www.law.emory.edu/FEDERAL/unconst.html. Break up the class into small groups of four or five students. Ask each group to write a preamble for the class. Students should use the preamble to the Constitution as a guide. Ask students to discuss what they feel would be important to include in the preamble

2. Break up the class into small groups of three or four people. The groups should choose a delegate who participated in the signing of the Constitution. Information about the delegates can be found at www.nara.gov/exhall/charters/constitution/confath.com. Ask students to write a skit about their delegate at the constitutional convention. Ask each student to promote an issue that was mentioned in the Constitution. Issues can be found in *Our Constitution*. Have the class perform their skits for another classroom or at an "open house" for parents.

3. After reading *Shh! We're Writing the Constitution* to the class, ask students to describe, in their own words, how the Constitution was written and ratified. Have students write their own constitution for the classroom. The students should create posters about their constitution and hang them throughout the classroom.

4. Read *If You Were There When They Signed the Constitution* and *A More Perfect Union: The Story of Our Constitution* to the class. Then divide the class into three groups. Ask each group to randomly choose a topic about the Constitution. For example, three topics could be the delegates, why the Constitution was written, and the location of the constitutional convention. Have each group create a bulletin board display about their topic. Post the displays and ask students to share them with the members of other classes.

5. Ask students to construct a classroom "Bill of Rights." What laws or regulations would they like to have in terms of classroom behavior, teacher responsibilities, and individual rights? How does their Bill of Rights compare to the one in the U.S. Constitution?

Westward Movement

 ## Introduction

Americans have always had the urge to move. By 1800 nearly a million Americans were living west of the Appalachian Mountains. Although roads were few, the rivers of the Midwest were important highways for the pioneers of the early 1800s.

The reasons for this westward shift were many. Some people wanted to leave the crowded conditions of eastern cities and others sought good, cheap land in the West. Many people, who had been slaves or indentured servants in the East, saw the westward migration as an opportunity for freedom and a new life. Whatever the reason, vast hordes of people picked up their belongings and braved extremities of weather and enormous obstacles to venture across an unknown land.

Some pioneers moved west by boat; others went by raft or flatboat along the Ohio and Mississippi Rivers. Several opted for mule or wagon trains along the National Road. As the pioneers moved west, so did the frontier (an imaginary line dividing the pioneer settlements from the areas where the Indians lived). By 1870, all but a few regions of the Great Plains had been settled. By the early 1890s, the frontier had ceased to exist in the United States.

 ## Research Questions

1. What was the purpose of the Oregon Trail?

2. What types of goods would you most commonly find at a trading post along the Oregon Trail?

3. How did scouts contribute to the westward movement?

4. What were some roles of women?

5. What incentives did pioneers have to move west?

 ## Web Sites

http://tqjunior.advanced.org/6400/
This site is full of vivid pictures and easy-to-read information about the first pioneers who traveled to the new frontier. This page tells the story of the pioneers and their adventures along the Oregon Trail and the Natchez Trace. (S: 4–6)

http://endoftheoregontrail.org/
This Web site tells the history of the Oregon Trail. It can be a great learning tool for students and a resource for teachers also. The site includes a variety of colorful maps; with easy-to-locate areas detailed in graphic relief and charts of elevation. (S: All, T: All)

http://www.pbs.org/wgbh/aia/part4/4narr4.html

This is a great site to serve as a teacher's guide to westward movement. It contains a glossary of many notable people and places. The site also acts as a valuable resource for quick introductions to various curriculum topics. (T: All)

 # Literature Resources

Bentley, Judith. (1995). *Brides, Midwives, and Widows*. New York: Twenty-First Century Books.

This book presents the history of Oregon country from a woman's perspective. How women contributed to the settling of the West is the focus of this book. Maps, photographs, and charts are included.

Freedman, Russell. (1990). *Children of the Wild West*. New York: Clarion Books.

This book illustrates, through text and magnificent photographs, what life was like for Indian and pioneer children growing up in the old West. What the young people of the late nineteenth century did, how they lived, and what it was like are discussed.

Leeuwen, Jean Van. (1996). *Bound for Oregon*. New York: Puffin.

This novel is a nine-year-old girl's story of her family's adventures on the Oregon Trail. Readers will appreciate Mary Ellen's feelings of homesickness, courage, sadness, and hope.

Sandler, Martin W. (1999). *Pioneers*. New York: Harper Trophy.

In this book the journey westward is brought alive by diary entries, songs, and lithographs. Told in the present tense, the narratives can really pull students into the setting.

Schlissel. Andrea D. (1995). *Black Frontiers: A History of African-American Heroes in the Old West*. New York: Simon & Schuster.

The contributions of African American people to the settling of the western frontier are explored in this book through text and photographs. Mountain men, homesteaders, scouts, soldiers, and cowboys are focused on.

 # Activities and Projects

1. Your class may enjoy participating in an "Oregon Trail Simulation." Divide the class into groups of five. Each group is a family setting out on a journey westward. On a piece of paper each group should make a list of what they will pack in their covered wagon. In "Round One" each group selects a card containing a problem that the pioneers would have dealt with (shortage of food, crossing a flooded river, a disease, etc.). Students should decide how they will handle their problem using what they packed. In "Round Two" each wagon has the opportunity to trade their goods at a trading post along the trail. After trading, each group should decide if they can survive the journey.

2. Have students write a daily diary, playing the part of a woman living on the frontier. Ask students to check out information on the Web sites and literature listed above. What special types of challenges would a woman have had in crossing the country? How is travel for a woman today different than for a woman traveling across country in the early part of the nineteenth century?

3. Provide small groups of students with the opportunity to create salt maps of the states over which the Oregon Trail passed. The following recipe is simple and fast:

> **Salt Map**
> Mix together 4 cups of flour, 1 cup of salt, and 1 1/2 cups of warm water in a medium bowl. Pour out onto a table and knead for about 10 minutes. The mixture should be stiff yet pliable. Spread the mixture out on a large sheet of aluminum foil, forming it into a designated state. Brush with egg yolk mixed with 1 tablespoon of water and bake at 325 degrees until very dry, approximately 1 hour. After it cools, seal with two or three coats of polyurethane. Ask students to paint the various areas with a variety of tempera paints and label mountains, cities, bodies of water and other geographical features.

Provide opportunities for students to discuss the various landforms on their salt maps and the difficulties the pioneers would have had in crossing those areas of the country.

4. Have students design and create a shoebox diorama of a wagon train, a section of the Rocky Mountains, or a settlement in the West. The diorama can contain a variety of materials, including pipe cleaners, construction paper, artifacts, and/or toy people. Provide opportunities for students to display their dioramas in the classroom.

5. Ask students to write letters to students in another class as though your students were traveling across the country in the 1800s. Encourage each student to describe the adventures encountered on the journey from east to west. Encourage students from the other class to respond to those letters.

6. When traveling across the country one needs to eat. Following is a fun-to-make and fun-to-eat treat that travelers (including the early pioneers) have been using for years—granola. Provide your students with an opportunity to create this wholesome snack.

> **Granola**
> Mix the following ingredients together in a medium bowl: 1/2 cup of wheat germ, 1/2 cup of coconut, 1 teaspoon of salt, 1/2 cup of raisins, 2 tablespoons of sunflower seeds, and 1/2 cup of nuts. Melt 4 teaspoons of butter in a pan and brown 4 cups of oatmeal. Add the oatmeal, 1/2 teaspoon of vanilla, and 1/2 cup of honey to the dry food and mix thoroughly. Toast the granola on a cookie sheet in the oven at 250 degrees until brown.

Ask students to figure out how the quantities in this recipe will need to be adjusted to make sure everyone has an adequate serving. How much granola would need to be prepared for a four- to six-month journey by wagon train across the country?

Slavery

Introduction

Slavery can be described as the act of owning another individual and subjecting that person to forced labor. Slaves, black individuals from Africa, were usually treated inhumanely in the United States. They were usually bought and sold by white people.

From 1800 to 1860 most slaves worked on cotton plantations in the South. Some slaves worked in the homes of white slaveholders while others took on skilled jobs such as carpentry, butchering, and blacksmithing. Most slaves, however, were involved in some aspect of agriculture—planting, raising, and harvesting crops.

Slaves were considered property and as such they had few rights and privileges. They rarely got paid for the work they did, they had no freedom, and they could not travel without their owner's permission. Most important, slaves could not vote, could not own property, and could not go to school. Suffice it to say, slaves faced many hardships and their lives were not easy. But they often found comfort in the strength of their families and the communities they established on the plantations of the South.

Research Questions

1. What took place during the slave trade?

2. What was it like when the slaves first came to America?

3. Was it possible for a black man to enlist in the army?

4. What was the Underground Railroad?

5. Why was slavery so important to the people in the South?

6. Who were the abolitionists?

Web Sites

http://www.afroam.org/history/slavery/main.html
This site tells about the slave trade. There's lots of detail about how the Africans came over to the Americas. The site provides information on what life was like for the slaves when they were in the United States. (T: 4–6)

http://www.pbs.org/wgbh/aia/home.html
This Web site is broken down into four areas: "The Terrible Transformation," "The Revolution," "Brotherly Love," and "Judgment Day." Each of these sections has a teacher guide that will allow the teacher to share information about slavery. (T: All)

http://jhunix.hcf.jhu.edu/~plarson/smuseum/welcome.htm
    The Museum of African Slavery is an all-inclusive Web site offering teachers an array of information and resources related to slavery in the United States. (T: 4–6)

 # Literature Resources

Adler, David A. (1993). *A Picture Book of Frederick Douglass*. New York: Holiday House.
    This is a biography about an escaped slave who became an orator, writer, and leader in the abolitionist movement in the late 1800s. This book will help students understand the activities of black leaders during the time of slavery.

Benson, K. & Haskins, J. (1999). *Bound for America: The Forced Migration of Africans to the New World*. New York: Lothrop, Lee & Shepard Books.
    This book illustrates the idea of slavery as it was seen in the earlier centuries. The book describes the racial issues between the whites and the people of African descent.

Burns, Bree. (1992). *Harriet Tubman and the Fight Against Slavery*. Philadelphia, PA: Chelsea House.
    This book describes the work of Harriet Tubman, from being a slave to her work on the Underground Railroad. This book will help students understand the importance of the Underground Railroad.

McLoone, Margo. (1997). *Harriet Tubman*. Mankato, MN: Capstone Press.
    This book tells the story of the courageous woman who led many slaves to freedom. This will help students understand that not only men were important in the efforts to escape from slavery.

 # Activities and Projects

1. Divide students into several small groups. Ask each group to log onto one or more of the Web sites listed above. Have each group develop a list of ways slaves could resist, rebel, and escape slavery. Ask them to start with the simplest form of resistance and end up with the Underground Railroad. After groups have collected sufficient information, ask them to share their respective lists.

2. After students have had an opportunity to obtain the necessary information from the Web sites listed above, ask them to write about one day in the life of a slave. Have students take on the persona of a slave and comment on the slave's chores, food eaten, conversations with other slaves, and free-time activities. Ask students to post and share their stories or diary entries.

3. Divide the class into two groups and have them debate the issue of slavery. Material for the debate can be obtained from the Web sites and literature listed above. Ask one group to present reasons why the slaves should not be freed (Southern viewpoint). Ask the other group to give reasons why the slaves should be freed (Northern viewpoint). Provide each group with an opportunity to respond to the other group's reasons.

4. During the years before the Civil War, large numbers of black slaves tried to make their way to the free northern states and Canada. They traveled along an imaginary route known as the Underground Railway. Because they didn't have signposts or maps to guide them, the runaway slaves often relied on the stars to point them in the right direction. A simple song popular at that time—"Follow the Drinking Gourd"—contained helpful clues for a successful journey. Here's how it went:

When the sun comes back
And the first quail calls
Follow the Drinking Gourd.
For the old man is a-waiting for to carry you to freedom
If you follow the drinking gourd.

The riverbank makes a very good road.
The dead trees will show you the way.
Left foot, peg foot, traveling on,
Follow the Drinking Gourd.

The river ends between two hills
Follow the Drinking Gourd.
There's another river on the other side
Follow the Drinking Gourd.

When the great big river meets the little river
Follow the Drinking Gourd.
For the old man is a-waiting for to carry you to freedom
If you follow the Drinking Gourd.

This song has several clever hints hidden in its lyrics to help the slaves find their way north. For example, the Drinking Gourd is the Big Dipper; which, of course, helped to locate the North Star. The first verse: "When the sun comes back and the first quail calls" is code for spring, which was the best time of the year to travel north. The "river that ends between two hills" in the third verse is the Tombigbee River in Mississippi. The "great big river" is the Ohio River. With these "directions" slaves were able to flee from the South up north and eventually into Canada.

Ask students to select a cloudless, moonless night and go somewhere away from the bright lights of a city. Instruct them to face the north (using a compass) and look up. They'll see a pattern of seven stars, four of which form the "bowl" of the Big Dipper and three of which form the handle. Once they've sighted the Big Dipper, they should draw an imaginary line from the top outermost star in the bowl. That line will take them to a star on the handle end of the Little Dipper constellation. This star is one of the most famous in the sky—the North Star or Polaris.

The Civil War

Introduction

After Abraham Lincoln won the presidency in 1860, the country began to move slowly toward war. Various southern states, led by South Carolina, voted to leave the Union, or *secede*. By February 1861 seven states had withdrawn from the Union to form their own nation. They called themselves the Confederate States of America and chose Jefferson Davis of Mississippi as their president. Eventually four more states would join the Confederacy. The states that remained were called the Union.

On April 12, 1861, the Confederacy fired on Fort Sumter, a Union fort in Charleston, South Carolina. This was the beginning of a bloody war that lasted for four years. Interestingly, most people thought that the war would be over quickly. Heroes were made, cities were demolished, generals were promoted, and thousands of men, women, and children were killed during the bloodiest years of this country's history. Initially, the South won most of the battles, but in the end the North's resources, manpower, food supplies, and transportation proved to be too much for the Confederacy. Finally, on April 9, 1865, General Robert E. Lee surrendered to General Ulysses S. Grant at Appomattox Courthouse, Virginia, and the war was over. Just five days later President Lincoln was assassinated in Washington, D.C.

Research Questions

1. How long did the Civil war last?

2. How did President Lincoln's role affect the war?

3. What was the most decisive battle of the Civil War?

4. What is the importance of the Gettysburg Battlefield?

5. How many people were killed during the Civil War?

Web Sites

http://www.civil-war.net/
This Web site provides students with photographs, descriptions of battles, and diaries of officers as well as information on other subjects related to the Civil War. (S: 4–6, T: 4–6)

http://sunset.utk.edu/civil-war/aboutcwarhp.html
This page provides resources about the Civil War. It includes several links and valuable information. (S: 4–6)

http://scarlett.libs.uga.edu/darchive/hargrett/maps/civil.html
Rare Civil War maps from the University of Georgia are located on this site. (T: 4–6)

http://www.americancivilwar.com/women/women.html
This sight offers glimpses into the lives of women during the Civil War. (T: 4–6)

http://www.germantown.k12.il.us/html/CivilWar.html
Lots of notes, facts, and information on various campaigns are found on this Web site. (T: 4–6)

http://rs6.loc.gov/ammem/cwphome.html
At this site teachers and students can access a wide variety of Civil War photographs taken under the supervision of Matthew Brady. (S: 4–6, T: 4–6)

 # Literature Resources

Alphin, Elaine Marie. (1991). *The Ghost Cadet.* New York: Henry Holt.
A 12-year-old boy, in Virginia visiting the grandmother he has never met, meets the ghost of a Virginia Military Institute cadet who was killed in the battle of New Market in 1864.

Beatty, Patricia. (1992). *Who Comes with Cannons?* New York: Morrow Junior Books.
In 1861 12-year-old Truth, a Quaker girl from Indiana, is staying with relatives who run a North Carolina station of the Underground Railroad.

Brenner, Barbara. (1977). *Wagon Wheels.* New York: Harper & Row.
Shortly after the Civil War a black family travels to Kansas to take advantage of the free land offered through the Homestead Act.

Brewer, Paul. (1999). *American Civil War.* Austin, TX: Steck-Vaughn.
Color maps, historical reproductions, and black-and-white photographs supplement this introduction to the Civil War.

Bunting, Eve. (1996). *The Blue and the Gray.* New York: Scholastic.
As a black boy and his white friend watch the construction of a house that will make them neighbors on the site of a Civil War battlefield, they agree that their homes are monuments to that war.

Dolan, Edward. (1997). *American Civil War: A House Divided.* Brookfield, CT: Millbrook Press.
An expansive and colorful look at the Civil War, this book presents the causes, the major battles, and the final results of this epic conflict.

Egger-Bovet, Howard. (1998). *Book of the American Civil War.* Boston: Little, Brown.
This book provides detailed look at the Civil War. It is filled with amazing facts and incredible details to capture any young reader.

Moore, Kay. (1994). *If You Lived at the Time of the Civil War.* New York: Scholastic.
This book describes conditions for the civilians in both the North and South during and immediately after the war.

Sandler, Martin. (1996). *Civil War.* New York: HarperCollins.
This book is a brief text that includes a thumbnail survey of the Civil War, with an emphasis on individual subjects such as young soldiers and African American troops.

Segal, Justin. (1997). *Civil War Almanac*. Los Angeles: Lowell House.
   This is a detailed explanation of some of the major battles and conflicts of the war.

 # Activities and Projects

1. Ask students to post a large strip of adding machine tape along the walls of the classroom. Using information gathered from the Web sites and library resources listed above, small groups of students should record significant events of the Civil War along the strip in chronological order. They should post important battles in one color of ink, significant political events in another color of ink, and world historical events in a third color. Provide opportunities for students to discuss the relationships and timeframes between and among all these events.

2. If possible, take black-and-white photographs of each student in the room. After they are developed, post each photograph on a "Civil War" bulletin board. Encourage students to imagine they are soldiers fighting far from home in the Civil War. Ask each student to compose one or more imaginary letters home to family members. Letters should detail some of the battles or conflicts the soldiers fought in, the sights and sounds of the war, or the villages and towns where the fighting took place. Allow students sufficient opportunities to post and discuss their letters.

3. A favorite dessert during the Civil War era was sponge cake. You and your students may enjoy making this traditional and easy-to-prepare recipe:

> ### Sponge Cake
>
> In a medium bowl, beat 6 egg whites until they are stiff. Beat in 1/4 teaspoon of salt. In a small bowl beat the six egg yolks. Slowly add 2 cups of sugar to the egg yolks, beating constantly. Continue beating until the mixture is very thick. Gently fold the yolk mixture into the egg whites. Then fold in 2 1/4 cups of all-purpose flour. Grease and flour a 9-inch tube pan and spoon the batter into the pan. Place the pan in a pre-heated oven set at 375 degrees and bake for approximately 1 hour or until a knife blade stuck in the middle comes out clean. Allow to cool, then serve.

4. An excellent CD-ROM on the Civil War is available from the National Geographic Society (P.O. Box 10597, Des Moines, IA 50340; 1-800-368-2728). Entitled *A House Divided* and *A People at War* (Catalog No. U82084), this outstanding software allows students to trace the bloody conflict between North and South from its origins to the final surrender at Appomattox. Students will be able to examine contributing factors, including slavery, westward expansion, and states' rights. Additionally, they'll learn how slavery was abolished and the Union was preserved.

The Industrial Revolution

Introduction

The Industrial Revolution encompassed a broad expanse of years, from approximately the early 1700s to the late 1800s. It had its genesis in England, where English society was moving from an agrarian economy to one based more on manufacturing. Up until that time, manufacturing had primarily been a home-based business. After the Industrial Revolution, factories did most of the manufacturing.

The Industrial Revolution reached the shores of the United States in the late 1700s with the invention of the spinning machine. This spinning machine became the foundation for the development and financing of a cotton mill in Pawtucket, Rhode Island. This mill was the first cotton factory in the United States, and it was powered by water from nearby falls. Eventually other capitalists saw the wisdom of a factory-based economy, and by 1840 the United States had more than 1,200 clothing mills. As more and more factories were built, people moved from the farms into the cities to find jobs. Indeed, many of the cities along the eastern seaboard were created as a result of the Industrial Revolution. As cities grew, so did the local economy, a factor that had a profound impact on the economy of a state and the country as a whole.

Research Questions

1. How did Europe and the United States differ in the things they produced?

2. Why were railroads so important?

3. What was the most important machine of the Industrial Revolution?

4. Why was water power such an important commodity?

5. What types of factories sprang up in the United States during the early 1800s?

Web Sites

http://tqjunior.advanced.org/4132/index.html
   This Industrial Revolution site starts with a table of contents. Students can find general information and play games that have to do with the Industrial Revolution. There are also areas where the students can link to more specific Web sites to find more detailed information, like specific inventions. (S: 4–6)

http://www.darex.com/indurevo.htm
   This site focuses on the two countries who did the most to initiate the Industrial Revolution—England and the United States. (T: 4–6)

http://members.tripod.com/xu_chen/indusrevolt/
   Lots of "inside" information about the Industrial Revolution can be found on this site. (T: 4–6)

http://members.aol.com/mhirotsu/kevin/trip2.html
   "A Trip to the Past" has lots of data and a plethora of information about many aspects of the Industrial Revolution. (T: 4–6)

Literature Resources

Clare, John. (1994). *Industrial Revolution*. New York: Harcourt Brace.
   The Industrial Revolution was a time when even the landscape of America was changing, from railroad tracks to suspension bridges. Transportation of items from one place to another became increasingly easier.

Ingpen, Robert. (1995). *The Industrial Revolution*. New York: Chelsea House.
   This thorough and complete review of the Industrial Revolution chronicles its "pluses" and "minuses."

Wilkinson, Philip & Dineen, Jacqueline. (1995). *The Early Inventions*. New York: Chelsea House.
   For centuries people have come up with ideas that have made the world an easier place to live. Amazing inventions have changed the world dramatically. The period of the Industrial Revolution was a time when it seemed that everyone was inventing something. Some of those inventions are discussed in this book.

Activities and Projects

1.   Ask students to think of a new invention that they would like to have. Encourage them to think of the most productive way(s) to sell their product. Ask them to try to sell their products to the other students in their class. They should discuss factors in place during the Industrial Revolution that may have made it difficult to sell or advertise manufactured goods. What challenges did the early industrialists face? How are those challenges similar to or different from the challenges faced by merchants today? Discuss the impact of e-commerce and whether it could be designated as the second Industrial Revolution.

2.   Ask students to select an invention that they really like and use various Web sites or library resources to learn as much about it as they can. Have them create a brochure or advertisement for their invention that would inspire others to purchase it. What advantages should be highlighted in their "advertising" material? What links can they make between their invention and progress or profit for potential purchasers? Provide sufficient time to discuss these implications.

3.   Ask students to interview various merchants in your local community or town. What are some of the challenges they must meet to ensure that goods in their store arrive from their suppliers and eventually get into the hands of buyers? How are the merchants meeting those challenges? Have students construct modified time lines for selected merchants, each depicting the route a manufactured item takes from its creation until the time it is purchased by a consumer. These "time lines" should be posted throughout the classroom.

4. Have students access selected Web sites containing information on various machines and inventions of the Industrial Revolution. Ask students to build simple models of the first spinning machine, cotton gin, reaper, or steel plow using diagrams and/or illustrations available on various Web sites. Provide opportunities for students to display their "inventions" throughout the classroom.

5. Students may enjoy making simple looms. Provide each student with a 6-by-8-inch piece of scrapwood. Along each 6-inch end they should hammer six nails, evenly spaced. Ask students to use string or twine and wrap it tightly between the nails (these vertical threads are called the *warp*). Then have them use colorful yarn, ribbon, or fabric strips and weave over and under the warp threads (the horizontal threads are called the *woof*). Tell students to tighten each row with a comb or fork. The loose ends can be tied off or tucked into the fabric. The finished products can be displayed in an appropriate display area. Ask students to discuss the amount of time they needed to construct their looms and how that may have affected the final production of their "products." Can students make any comparisons with conditions that may have existed prior to the Industrial Revolution?

World War I

Introduction

   The genesis of World War I lay in the competition among European countries for power in Europe and for colonies overseas. In the 1880s Germany sought to protect herself from her old enemies France and Russia by joining with Austria-Hungary and Italy in a Treaty of Alliance. In 1902 England and France formed an Entente and were later joined by Russia. Various other nations took sides for their own protection. By 1914, all that was needed was a spark to set off the explosive situation.

   The spark was the assassination of Archduke Ferdinand, next in line to rule Austria-Hungary, in June 1914. He was riding through Sarajevo, a part of Austria-Hungary, when he was shot and killed by a young Serbian. Austria-Hungary blamed Serbia for the murders and declared war on Serbia. Soon the Alliance countries and their allies were pitted against the Triple Entente and its allies, and all of Europe was at war.

   The United States felt that the war was strictly a European conflict and wanted to stay out of it. Although the United States provided supplies to Allies (England, France, etc.), it attempted to maintain an official position of neutrality. On May 7, 1915, that changed, when the Germans sank the British passenger ship *Lusitania*. Over 1,000 people, including 128 Americans, lost their lives. Soon after, President Wilson asked Congress to declare war on Germany.

Research Questions

   1. What were the causes of World War I?

   2. What countries were the Central Powers?

   3. What countries were on the Allied side?

   4. What is trench warfare?

   5. Why did the United States join the war?

   6. How long did World War I last?

Web Sites

http://www.worldwar1.com/
   This site contains information about the people, places, and events of World War I. It provides information about trench warfare, weapons, documents, artwork, maps, and time lines. Also covered at this site are events prior to and after the war. (T: 4–6)

http://www.mrdowling.com/706wars.html

This site provides a basic understanding of World War I and why it happened. It has a link to information on the various political alliances, which were major contributing factors to the outbreak of war. This site makes a complicated event into an event that students can understand. (S: 4–6)

http://campus.northpark.edu/history/WebChron/World/WWI.html

This site is a time line of World War I. It starts off with events that led up to the war and ends with the aftermath of the war. The user can click on every event on the time line and read an article about it. Because the events are in chronological order they are easier for the reader to understand. (S: 4–6)

Literature Resources

Clare, John D. (1993). *First World War*. New York: Gulliver Books.

With bright, colorful pictures, this book describes almost every aspect of World War I. It covers everything from who was in the war, to the first moves, to what trench warfare and air raids were like, to women in the war. At the end of the book is an explanation of how we know so much about this war.

Cooper, Michael L. (1997). *Hell Fighters: African American Soldiers in World War I*. New York: Lodestar Books.

This book on the Great War describes what it was like for African Americans in the military. These men not only fought for their country in a brutal war but also fought against racism. A wonderful book about World War I, the hardships encountered, and racism. A great book to share with children.

Dolan, Edward F. (1996). *America in World War I*. Brookfield, CT: Millbrook Press.

This book includes a vast amount of information about World War I. Everything is covered, from the events that led to its outbreak to what led Germany to surrender. Although very thorough, this book is definitely useful for children.

Foreman, Michael. (1993). *War Game*. Boston: Little, Brown.

Three British boys are curious about the war and see all the bulletins and people cheering those who sign up for the war. Curious, the boys too sign up to fight in the war, then realize that reality isn't as glorious as the posters made it look. Foreman presents a moving story of the soldiers who lived and died, and how, one Christmas Day, they broke all the rules and played a game of soccer between the trenches and the barbed wire.

Houston, Gloria McLendon. (1988). *The Year of the Perfect Christmas Tree*. New York: Dial Books for Young Readers.

While their father is at war, Ruthie and her mother are responsible for getting the "perfect Christmas tree." Full-color illustrations help depict the poor family's struggles to provide the church with this perfect Christmas tree.

Rabin, Stanton. (1994). *Casey over There*. New York: Harcourt Brace.

This full-color book presents letters written by brothers to each other while one is fighting in the Great War. When Aubrey, the seven-year-old brother, doesn't hear back from Casey, his brother in the war, he writes a letter to Uncle Sam.

Wells, Rosemary. (1996). *The Language of the Doves*. New York: Dial.

This beautifully illustrated book goes back in time as a grandfather tells his granddaughter about how he cared for doves who carried secret messages through enemy fire; one in particular still remains alive in his memory. This is a wonderful book about grandparents, World War I, doves, Italy, and death. A must-read book for the classroom.

Wells, Rosemary. (1997). *Waiting for the Evening Star*. New York: Puffin.

Wells beautifully depicts the life of two brothers before World War I. Berty watches things being prepared to ship to Boston while listening to his brother Luke's dreams. All of this soon ends with Luke leaving for the Navy and Berty wishing on a star for his brother's safety.

 # Activities and Projects

1. Ask students to ask a war veteran to visit your class (it isn't necessary to have a WWI veteran visit). Contact your local veteran's association or VA hospital to obtain a list of potential speakers. Ask the speaker to talk about some of the happenings she or he experienced during the war and what she or he remembers most. Plan sufficient opportunities for youngsters to quiz the speaker. Afterwards, students should compare and contrast the events of WWI (via the Web sites and literature above) with those recalled by the visitor.

2. Through class discussion and the books and Web sites listed above, students should have an idea about life during World War I. Ask students to imagine they are fighting in the war. Have them write a daily journal of their life during the war. Students should indicate where they are located, where they are from, how they feel, etc. Provide opportunities for students to share their "memories" with each other. What similarities do they note?

3. Ask students to pretend they are awaiting President Woodrow Wilson's decision on whether the United States will enter the war. Have them write a letter to President Wilson opposing or supporting entry into the war. They should include facts to support their position. Students can locate information about the pre-war period at Internet sites such as http://montanakids.com/home.htm and http://www.worlddwarI.com and literary sources like *First World War* and *Waiting for the Evening Star*.

4. Divide the class into two groups. One group should design a map of the world before World War I on a bulletin board. The second group should design another bulletin board with a map of the world after World War I. These maps will allow students to see changes resulting from the war. Students can locate maps in textbooks, Web sites, etc. for guidance.

5. Ask students to create a newscast of an important event of World War I (e.g., United States enters war). Students should include several reporters, eyewitnesses, or leaders from major countries involved in the war in their broadcast. They can obtain information for their reports from literary sources such as *First World War, Hell Fighters African American Soldiers in World War I, War Game* and from Web sites such as http://campus.northpark.edu/history/WebChron/World/WWI.html and http://www.mrdowling.com/706wars.html. After the students have rehearsed their roles, videotape the broadcast and hook it up through the school's televisions so every class in the building will have the opportunity to observe the class's newscast. If possible, a few students can make a commercial so the classes will know when to "tune in."

The Great Depression

 ## Introduction

The 1930s are often referred to as the time of the Great Depression. After the stock market crash in 1929, many people who had bought stocks lost their entire investments. Businesses failed throughout the country and the world, putting millions of people out of work. Many lost their homes and cars because they could not repay their bank loans. When people could not repay their loans, many banks had to close because they did not have enough money to cover their depositors accounts.

By 1933, more than 12 million people were out of work in the United States. Others were only able to work a few hours a week. Many cities set up soup kitchens and bread lines to keep people from starving. People were evicted from their apartments and homes and were forced to sleep on the sidewalks or in parks. It was a time of despair and poverty. Although various governmental programs were established to assist people, the Great Depression lasted for more than a decade. It wasn't until 1941 that total recovery was achieved. By then, another war was looming on the horizon, a war that was to have enormous repercussions for all Americans.

 ## Research Questions

1. What major changes occurred in society during the Great Depression?

2. Why was this time period called the Great Depression?

3. How did the Great Depression begin?

4. How did the Great Depression come to a conclusion?

5. What was the New Deal?

6. What was "Hooverville?"

7. What was the "Dust Bowl?"

 ## Web Sites

http://www.ncsa.uiuc.edu/edu/ea/d300/ams/Depression/GreatDepression/html
This Web site starts out by offering a very general overview of the Depression, accompanied by a picture from the Dust Bowl. It provides links to information and pictures about the Dust Bowl, New Deal, and other topics of this time period. It also offers suggested readings. At the very bottom are more links to important topics in history that could be valuable for other lessons. (T: 4–6)

Literature Resources

Antle, Nancy. (1993). *Hard Times*. New York: Penguin.

Hard Times is a beautifully written book about Charlie, a fifth grader, who grows up in Oklahoma during the Depression Era. When a drought hits his family's farm, they are forced to migrate to California in search of a better life.

Burch, Robert. (1980). *Ida Early Comes over the Mountain*. New York: Viking.

After the death of their mother, the Sutton children are left with their aunt as caregiver in Georgia during the Great Depression. Fortunately, when the new housekeeper, Ida Early, shows up to replace Aunt Ernestine, life gets a little easier for the children during an otherwise tough time.

Myers, Anna. (1992). *Red-Dirt Jessie*. New York: Walker.

Red-Dirt Jessie is a story told from the perspective of a 12-year-old girl named Jessie in Oklahoma during the Depression. Tragedy strikes her family when her younger sister dies and her father has a nervous breakdown. Jessie hopes to heal her father's pain by attempting to tame Ring, a wild dog.

Norrell, Robert J. (1993). *We Want Jobs*. New York: Steck-Vaughn.

Based on an interview with John Waskowitz, this story tells of the struggle he and his family go through to survive during the Great Depression. After Waskowitz loses his job at the local steel mill, he witnesses up-close the power of the Depression. This story allows the reader to experience what it meant to be unemployed and homeless.

Ross, Stewart. (1998). *The Great Depression: Causes and Consequences*. Austin, TX: Steck-Vaughn.

This book is a thorough and compelling description of the Depression. It presents the causes and consequences of the Depression on both a national scale and a personal one. A great introduction to this period in American history.

Activities and Projects

1. If possible, obtain an audio recording of songs or stories from the Great Depression. (Many large book stores such as Barnes & Noble® and Borders® as well as online stores such as Amazon.com® have a variety of audiotapes for sale.) Play various selections for your students. What do they notice about the lyrics of the songs? What types of information seem to predominate in the recordings of the time? Based on these recordings, what will people a hundred years from now think about people living during the Great Depression? Provide plenty of opportunities for students to share their perceptions and insights about this time in American history.

2. Make a list of household items (cloths, toys, furniture, etc.) and their prices during the Depression. Students can interview relatives, visit stores, read magazines, surf the Internet, etc., to come up with the prices today for the same objects. As a class, present these current prices and use "play money" to demonstrate how much an item cost during the Depression and how much the same item costs now. Subtract the two numbers to find the difference. Ask students why they think prices have changed.

3. If possible, invite someone who lived through the Great Depression to visit your class-room. Encourage the visitor to share some of the sights and sounds of that time. After the visit, ask students to discuss how their lives would be different if they had lived during the Depression. What things would they have had to give up? What things would they have been unable to do?

4. Ask students to create a series of history cards (similar to baseball cards) about some of the events surrounding the Great Depression. Students can access information via the Web sites and literature listed above to create their cards. Using 4-by-6-inch index cards, students should design illustrations for the upper half of each card. On the bot-tom half of each card students should record selected facts about the event or person portrayed.

5. After students have obtained sufficient information from the Web sites above, ask small groups to create a series of original newspaper articles about an event—real or imaginary—that took place during the Depression. Encourage students to assemble their articles into a classroom newspaper for publication and distribution throughout the school.

World War II

Introduction

During the late 1930s Germany began to assert itself again, taking over territories, annexing countries, and arming itself with one of the most powerful war machines seen during the twentieth century. In September 1939 Germany invaded Poland and war was officially declared. During the war, most of continental Europe was invaded and occupied. Austria, Czechoslovakia, Albania, Poland, Finland, Denmark, Norway, Belgium, the Netherlands, Luxembourg, France, Lithuania, Latvia, Estonia, Romania, Bulgaria, Hungary, Greece, Yugoslavia, the U.S.S.R., and later Germany and Italy were all swept up in the fighting and fury of World War II.

Not surprisingly, most of these countries suffered enormous devastation and destruction. Many Americans once again felt that the war was a European conflict. That changed, however, when the Japanese, who had signed a pact with Germany in 1940, attacked the Pacific Fleet at Pearl Harbor on December 7, 1941. War was declared the next day and the United States became involved in one of the bloodiest and costliest conflicts of the century.

The war raged across the Pacific and throughout Europe. Territories were taken, lost, and reclaimed again and again. Finally Germany surrendered on May 7, 1945. It wasn't until August 15, after the dropping of the atomic bombs on Hiroshima and Nagasaki, that the Japanese surrendered.

Research Questions

1. What events led up to the beginning of World War II?

2. How did Germany become so powerful?

3. Why did the United States initially stay out of the war?

4. Why did President Roosevelt declare December 7, 1941, "A Day of Infamy?"

5. What were some of the major battles in the Pacific?

6. What were some of the major battles in Europe?

7. What was the significance of D-Day?

8. Why was the Yalta Conference such an important event?

# Web Sites

http://tqjunior.advanced.org/4616/

This site serves as an American scrapbook of World War II. Memories that have been passed down to grandchildren and great grandchildren have been documented here. These children recorded their family stories, along with their individual feelings. The site also contains lesson plans for teachers to incorporate the student's stories. (S: 4–6, T: All)

http://www.mrdowling.com/706wars.html

This easy-to-read site contains an overview of important names and places during World War II. Each specific item also has photos and a link for further information that any student can access. Included in the site is a story of the war from a kid's perspective, the diary of a young boy who was 11 when Pearl Harbor was attacked. (S: 4–6, T: All)

http://www.nara.gov/exhall/powers/powers.html

This site, named Powers of Persuasion, deals with poster art from World War II. It examines posters from two different viewpoints. The first section is concerned with patriotism, confidence, and positive outlooks on the war. The second section looks at art that deals with the negative aspects of war, including pictures of dark images like suspicion, fear, and hate. (S: 4–6)

http://www.pbs.org/wgbh/amex/guts/index.html

At this site students can access a fantastic PBS site about the stories and strategies of two monumental events in World War II, D-Day and the Battle of the Bulge. (S: 4–6)

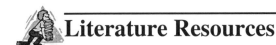# Literature Resources

Cooper, Michael L. (1998). *The Double V Campaign: African Americans and WWII*. New York: Lodestar Books.

This book deals with the two wars that African Americans were fighting in World War II: against the U.S. enemies and against discrimination in America. Maps and photographs accentuate the text of this book.

Devancy, John. (1991). *America Goes to War 1941*. New York: Walker.

This book is written in the form of a diary, allowing readers to witness important moments such as the attack on Pearl Harbor or President Roosevelt reassuring Winston Churchill. Themes such as racism and Japanese economics are introduced.

Dolan, Edward F. (1994). *America in World War II*. Bridgeport, CT: Millbrook Press.

This book focuses on Japan's attack on Pearl Harbor. The United States' response to the attack is also addressed. This book includes excellent photographs of the Pearl Harbor attack.

Sanford, William R., Knapp, Ron & Green, Carl R. (1998). *American Generals of World War II*. Hillside, NJ: Enslow Publishers.

This is a collection of biographies of the generals of World War II. Personal accounts of Eisenhower, Patton, General Ridgway, and others make them more interesting characters to the reader.

Tunnell, Michael O. & Chilcoat, George W. (1996). *The Children of Topaz*. New York: Holiday House.

This unique story consists of 20 diary entries written by a Japanese-American teacher and her third-grade class in Utah. The diary was kept from May until August 1943. This book also contains commentary telling the reader what was happening at the camp and in the war at the time the entries were written.

Activities and Projects

1. Divide the class into several small groups and ask each group to choose an important date in World War II. Prior to the group work, ask students to access information via selected Web sites and literature resources. Each group should then construct a newspaper for that day. They should create a series of articles incorporating real and/or imaginary events. Plan for this activity over a long period of time. If possible, "publish" the newspaper and contribute a copy to the school library.

2. Encourage students to interview someone who either participated in World War II or lived during that time period. With the information gathered small groups of students can combine data and create their own radio broadcast. One student should act as the reporter and another should play the role of someone who lived through the war. The tapes of each pair can then be collected to create one radio show.

3. Have students use the Powers of Persuasion Web site, to explore the use of propaganda during World War II. On a bulletin board, students should create posters and flyers modeled after those used during the war. Ask students to create reproductions of wartime posters or to create a series of original posters inviting the American public to do something (or not do something) related to the war.

4. Ask students to compare and contrast the discrimination against African Americans and Japanese Americans during World War II using a Venn diagram. Students should do this activity after reading selected books or interviewing specific individuals in your local community. Additional information can be obtained via selected Web sites.

5. Have students create an oral time line. Ask a group of selected students to memorize important dates and events in World War II. Instruct the students to line up chronologically. The first student should step forward and recite her or his information, then step back. Continue this process until all students in the line have completed their recitations. This oral time line can be presented to other classes, too.

The Cold War

Introduction

Prior to the end of World War II, plans were being drafted to replace the League of Nations, an international organization formed after World War I, with a new organization. This new organization was the United Nations. Established in 1945, it was a place where nations could work out disagreements and problems. Most unique about this new organization was that it was granted power to raise an army and ensure that its laws were being followed. (The League of Nations had no such power.)

After the war, relations between the United States and the Soviet Union grew tense. This power struggle became known as the Cold War because it was a war of words rather than a war between armed forces. In essence, the Cold War pitted two groups of countries against each other. Democratic countries in the Western world generally supported the United States in its policies. On the other hand, communist countries primarily supported the Soviet Union and its policies. The chief desire of the democratic countries was to halt the spread of communism around the world. It was a time of fevered oration, political maneuvering, and constant power struggles. The Cold War basically ended with the fall of the Eastern bloc and Soviet Union at the end of the 1980s.

Research Questions

1. How did the Cold War get its name?

2. What were other communist countries in the late 1940s?

3. How did Berlin become the center for conflict between the United States and the Soviet Union?

4. Who were some of the U.S. allies in the Cold War?

5. What is the North Atlantic Treaty Organization?

Web Sites

http://turnerlearning.com/cnn/coldwar/cw_thmes.html/
On this Web site, themes of the Cold War are discussed in considerable detail. This would be an excellent tool for beginning classroom discussion on the Cold War. (T: 4–6)

http://www.cnn.com/SPECIALS/cold.war
  This Web site is a CNN® report on people directly involved in the Cold War. An excellent resource for putting names to the people involved at that time, including the Rosenbergs, McCarthy, etc. (S: 4–6, T: 4–6)

 # Literature Resources

Clinton, Susan K. (1993). *The Cuban Missile Crisis*. Chicago: Children's Press.
  This book describes the events and people who were significant in the Cuban Missile Crisis. Lots of information and insights are presented here.

Kort, Michael. (1994). *The Cold War*. Brookfield, CT: Millbrook Press.
  This is a detailed and comprehensive, "battle-by-battle" history of the Cold War. This book is ideal for older readers who want an up-close look at this critical time in U.S. history.

Stein, R. Conrad. (1998). *The Great Red Scare*. Parsippany, NJ: New Discover Books.
  This book is a wonderful reference for those just beginning to learn about communism. There is a whole section on Joseph McCarthy and his attempts to rid the United States of communism.

 # Activities and Projects

  1. After discussing the books on aspects of the Cold War in class, ask students to interview their parents or grandparents about the period of the Cold War. Questions about bomb shelters and air raid drills should be asked and the results shared with classmates. If appropriate, invite selected adults to visit the classroom and share some of their experiences from that time with students. Provide opportunities for students and adults to discuss the events of the day in small groups.

  2. After visiting Web sites and reading books on the Cold War, students can write letters to their local officials about their concerns for future nuclear endeavors by the United States. The letters can include opinions about the history of nuclear proliferation and the consequences—both political and social—of a nuclear proliferation stance by this country or any country.

  3. Form two groups of students and ask them to be the "hawks" and "doves" that President Kennedy had to deal with in making his decision about the Cuban Missile Crisis. Each side should consult various Web sites and library references to find valid arguments for their position (whether to attack or not, the use of nuclear arms, etc.). Engage the class in a healthy debate about this topic.

  4. Ask small groups of students to access Web sites about the fall of the Berlin Wall. Ask students to consider why that was such a momentous event and have them prepare a story about the effects the fall of the wall may have had on people living in East Germany at the time. Post a large sheet of newsprint along one wall of the classroom and ask students to write on the sheet as though it were a large concrete wall (similar to the Berlin Wall). Ask students to post their stories on the wall as well. Provide time for students to discuss their views and interpretations of this momentous event in modern history.

Chapter 10

Our World:
Yesterday and Today

Early Egypt

Introduction

Ancient Egypt is a mysterious place that fascinates scientists and archeologists to this day. The remnants of Egyptian culture that have been discovered reveal an amazingly advanced civilization. The study of hieroglyphics found in pyramids reveal some information about this lost civilization.

The ancient Egyptians were ruled by pharaohs, who had a god-like status while alive and were believed to become gods in the afterlife. The Egyptians worshipped dozens of gods, whose popularity was largely decided by the reigning pharaoh. Ancient Egyptians held a strong belief in the afterlife, so they prepared for it with amazing completeness. Burial rituals were elaborate. The Egyptians mummified their dead, the process taking a full 70 days. The richer a person was, the more elaborate the burial. The pyramids that were constructed for the pharaohs have attracted the most attention in the study of ancient Egypt. Pharaohs were buried with treasures to provide for their comfort in the afterlife. Statues of servants were buried with them so they could do the work there. The walls of the tombs were decorated with hieroglyphics (ancient Egyptian writing). The symbols depicted were spirits and blessings.

The social structure of ancient Egypt was arranged in tiers. The slaves, peasants, and laborers formed the base of the structure. A step up from the base were the craft workers, dancers, professional mourners, and servants. On the third tier existed government officials, scribes, priests, priestesses, soldiers, doctors, and engineers. The second highest tier was composed of the courtiers, generals, high priests, and high-ranking civil servants. The top tier was reserved for the royal families; the periods during which they ruled were called dynasties.

Research Questions

1. Describe the government of ancient Egypt.

2. What are the legends surrounding the tombs of the pharaohs?

3. How did the ancient Egyptians prepare their dead for burial?

4. What are the meanings behind the drawings on the walls of the pyramids and the drawings found on artifacts? What is the name for these drawings?

5. What was life like for a typical Egyptian?

Web Sites

http://www.si.edu/resource/faq/nmnh/pyramid.htm

This Web site offers lots of detailed information that would be excellent in designing appropriate lesson plans about pyramids. It also has numerous links and other resources for further exploration of the topic. (T: 4–6)

http://members.aol.com/egyptmouse/page1.html

Take a virtual tour of Egypt with Mousey. Journal entries take you through his trip step by step, and photographs of Mousey at each location he is describing complement the journal entries. The site is geared toward children and provides wonderful information about some of the more popular places in Egypt. (S: 4–6)

http://members.aol.com/crakkrjack/index.html

This delightful Web site is an excellent resource for teachers and students alike. The Tomb of the Chihuahua Pharaohs is divided into three sections, each led by a different Chihuahua. The sections include general information about ancient Egypt, the mummification process, and Egyptian writing. The information is detailed but presented in a manner that could easily be understood by students. The site also provides ideas for lesson plans and activities for students. (S: 4–6, T: All)

Literature Resources

Aliki. (1979). *Mummies (Made in Egypt)*. New York: Crowell.

This text begins with an explanation of Egyptian beliefs about eternal life and the soul. The book then progresses to an in-depth look at the burial rituals of the ancient Egyptians. This includes a detailed explanation of the mummification process. The illustrations in this book were adapted from actual paintings and sculptures found in the excavated tombs of ancient Egyptian kings.

Hart, George. (1995). *Ancient Egypt*. New York: Time-Life.

This book is a photo essay on ancient Egypt and the people who lived there, documented through the mummies, pottery, weapons, and other objects they left behind. It describes their society, religion, and obsession with the afterlife, and methods of mummification.

Haslam, Andrew. (1997). *Ancient Egypt*. New York: World Book.

Well organized and easy to read, this book introduces readers to all areas of Egyptian life: clothing and dwellings, geography and agriculture, artwork and religion. Numerous color photographs highlight this complete and thorough guide.

Martin, Amanda. (1998). *Ancient Egypt (My World)*. New York: World Book.

This interesting and complete look at life in ancient Egypt is filled with lots of illustrations. Young readers are introduced to the times and culture of this fascinating period of world history.

Millard, Ann. (1996). *Pyramids*. New York: Kingfisher.

A simplified exploration of the ancient Egyptian culture, this book provides explanations of all aspects of that culture. It touches on the social structure, religion, pay system, tasks, traditions, and transportation system, then explains how pyramids were built and decorated and the symbolism behind those decorations. The text is highlighted with beautiful and realistic illustrations.

Watson, Philip J. (1987). *Costumes of Ancient Egypt*. New York: Chelsea House.

This resource book focuses on the costumes and clothing of the ancient Egyptians. By first reviewing some of the history of Egypt, students can gain a better understanding of why these articles were worn. Topics include clothing for people of all statuses: women, kings, gods, laborers, and military officials. Each level of dress is depicted with photographs and diagrams.

 # Activities and Projects

1. After they read selected literature and check Internet sites for explanations of the construction and design of Egyptian pyramids (including meaning of colors and symbols of the hieroglyphics used), have the students design and construct a model of their own burial tomb. They should decide what items to be buried with and what symbolic pictures will decorate their tomb, then write a paragraph or two explaining their choices.

2. Have each student choose a pharaoh of ancient Egypt. The students should gather information on their pharaohs from biographies, articles in magazines, articles from newspapers, the encyclopedia, and other books found in the classroom and local library. Direct them to find out the following: information on the family of the pharaoh, years each pharaoh ruled, year of birth and year of death, burial place, information on the pyramid constructed for the burial (location, types of treasure found in their tombs, etc.), religion of each pharaoh, significant laws or practices she or he adhered to, technological advances made during the reign, and any other information students find of interest. The students should then write and illustrate a biography on their pharaohs. Place these books in an Egyptian display in the library, along with contributions from other classes.

3. After studying the Egyptian hieroglyphics on Web sites and in books found in the school, classroom, or local library, students should create their own stories using hieroglyphics, then translate it into English. Have students write journal entries explaining their choice of symbols. Place the finished hieroglyphics on posterboard with the English translation underneath them and hang it in the hallway outside the classroom.

4. Assign each student one distinct tradition or burial ritual from ancient Egypt (mummification, building of the burial chambers, decoration of the burial chambers, coffins, items chosen to be buried with the person, professional mourners, dances performed, opening of the burial chamber, sealing of the burial chamber, etc.). Students should find information in books and magazines from the library or on the Internet. Then have them write newspaper articles describing their chosen traditions or rituals. Students may also draw comics or other illustrations, write editorials, create recipes for food left in the burial chamber, or write items for other sections of the newspaper (these will be extra credit). Collect all contributions and print them out as a class newspaper. Give each student a copy of the paper to take home and keep a laminated copy in the classroom library.

5. Have students learn about the lives of the ancient Egyptians and how life was so different during this time in history from what it is now by using the Internet and the multiple text sources listed to create journals written as if they were those people during that time. Encourage discussion of who they have chosen to be, what those people do, how they live, and what might happen on a daily basis.

The Rise of Greece

 ## Introduction

The civilization we now know as ancient Greece developed out of years of intense warfare among a variety of competing kings. The ancient Greece we are familiar with came into being around 800 B.C. as a result of trading among a small cluster of city-states such as Athens, Sparta, Thebes, and Corinth. Each of these city-states was like a small nation unto itself. Each was ruled by a small class of people known as aristocrats, usually a group of elderly men. Power was passed down from father to son. Interestingly, an assembly of ordinary citizens took part in the government, too. These citizens had certain rights and responsibilities and, in later years, were given the power to make decisions. It was from these early beginnings that our present-day concept of democratic rule evolved.

 ## Research Questions

1. What is a city-state?

2. What is meant by democratic rule?

3. How was ancient Greek culture similar to ours?

4. What role did merchants play in ancient Greek society?

5. What is meant by Greece's "Golden Age?"

 ## Web Sites

http://www.mrdowling.com/701greece.html
At this short site, students can learn some of the basic information about ancient Greece. This would be a good starting point for further explorations. (S: 4–6)

http://www.princeton.edu/~markwoon/Myth/myth-maps.html
At this site students see a complete map of ancient Greece. The site is ideal for downloading and to begin appropriate map studies of the times. (S: 4–6)

http://www.indiana.edu/~kglowack/athens/
This site is a photographic archive of the city of Athens. Loads of information and descriptive photographs highlight this intriguing site. (S: 4–6)

http://www.richmond.edu/~ed344/webunits/greecerome/
This is a delightful site designed to introduce third-grade students to the culture, civilization, and architecture of ancient Greece and Rome. Complete and thorough. (S: 4–6)

http://www.museum.upenn.edu/Greek_World/Index.html
The Ancient Greek World is filled with tons of interesting information that will energize any lesson plan or unit. A perfect supplement for any classroom teacher. (T: All)

Literature Resources

Connolly, Peter. (1986). *The Legend of Odysseus*. New York: Oxford University Press.
This book tells the story of Odysseus in its entirety. It is extremely informative in addition to being an enjoyable adventure story for children to read. Illustrations support the story of Odysseus and photographs and maps supplement the factual information provided at the end of each individual section of this book.

O'Neill, Cynthia & Casterton, Peter. (1994). *Goddesses, Heroes, and Shamans*. New York: Kingfisher.
This book is the "encyclopedia for children" about mythology from around the world. Any information you need about goddesses, heroes, and shamans can be found in this book. The section on Greece is especially detailed (the myth is a Greek creation). Colorful illustrations and detailed captions are found on each page of this book.

Rees, Rosemary. (1997). *The Ancient Greeks*. Crystal Lake, IL: Reed Educational and Professional Publishing.
This book describes who the ancient Greeks were, how we know about them, what they wore, their family life, their education, their food and how Greece was governed, and provides extensive information on a plethora of other Greek details. Color photographs and illustrations are interspersed throughout the well-written text.

Wilkinson, Philip. (1994). *Mysterious Places: The Mediterranean*. New York: Chelsea House.
This book provides information and extensive knowledge about the Mediterranean and all of its most popular countries. It explains how Greece and Rome have had the most lasting influence on our culture. This book examines and explores some of Greece's most mysterious places and people. Brilliant illustrations fill this book with color and life.

Williams, Susan. (1993). *The Greeks*. New York: Thomson Learning.
This book describes who the Greeks were and provides information on the Greek language, homes, religious beliefs, myths, theater, sports, and the Greeks at war. It explains how the rise of Greece was soon followed by the conquering of Greece by Rome.

Wright, Rachel. (1992). *Greeks*. New York: Franklin Watts.
This book contains numerous facts about ancient Greece: the people, the land, the homes, and the mythology. Also provided throughout this book are creative activities for students to try in addition to crafts from Greece and new vocabulary about Greece, supported by an excellent glossary. Illustrations, maps, and photographs are located throughout the book.

Activities and Projects

1. Ask students to look up the Acropolis in one or more of the Web sites or literature selections listed above. Discuss the purpose of the buildings on the Acropolis. Ask students to think of a modern U.S. city and some buildings that would have the same purposes today. Have students construct a large Venn diagram or oversized poster that compares and contrasts the buildings of the Acropolis and the corresponding buildings of a modern U.S. city.

2. Ask students to consult several of the Web sites above and locate information relative to the Greek system of government. Based on the collected information, students should set up the class as a council of Greek assembly members, who are to debate whether democracy in Athens is a reality or an ideal. Ask students to draw comparisons to democracy in the United States.

3. Have the students decorate the classroom to look like the ancient city of Athens. They should consult Web sites and literature to determine the appropriate structures and/or displays. Ask selected students to act as Athenian guides, leading "tourists" around the classroom. Others students can take on the roles of philosophers, playwrights, and merchants, each of whom can be interviewed (in character) by the visiting "tourists."

4. Ask selected groups of students to design and write fictional newspaper accounts of a day in the life of a single city-state (Athens, Sparta, Corinth, etc.). What events took place, what political decisions were made, how was trade conducted with other city-states? Ask each group to "publish" their city-state's newspaper. Provide sufficient time to discuss and compare the newspapers.

5. Ask selected students to research the gods and goddesses of ancient Greece. Encourage them to take on the role of specific gods and goddesses and allow them to be interviewed by other members of the class.

The Roman Empire

Introduction

Rome was a small village in Italy, founded by an Indo-European people called Latins around 1100 B.C.E. In 509 B.C.E. the Roman senate overthrew a hated king and set up a republic. A republic is a government in which the citizens elect representatives to lead them. Romans believed strongly in their republic as well as in the rights of ordinary citizens.

After 350 B.C.E. the Romans began to extend their rule beyond their city. The Roman government wanted riches, land, and especially power. It began to acquire land, often by moving into a designated area or by waging war on the citizenry. Over many years and through a series of fierce and long-lasting wars Rome eventually ruled much of the Mediterranean area. Money poured into the city, making it quite wealthy and the center of a new empire. By the early 100s C.E. the Roman Empire was vast. It stretched over 2,000 miles from east to west and contained over 100 million people.

Dependent on its armies to maintain its strength and control, Rome's leaders found it increasingly difficult to recruit soldiers. A weakened army meant less control. Eventually the empire was divided into two sections. It was further weakened by the invasion of Germans from the north around the late 400s C.E. After this period the Roman Empire no longer existed.

Research Questions

1. How large was the Roman Empire at its peak?

2. How long did the Roman Empire exist?

3. What countries made up the Roman Empire?

4. What did the Romans contribute to our form of government?

5. What was Roman culture like?

Web Sites

http://www.kent.wednt.edu/curriculum/soc_studies/rome/Rome.html
This site has pictures with good descriptive captions, used to inform students about various Roman sites, cities, and architecture. The pictures are clear and interesting. (S: All)

http://www.roman-empire.net/
This is a complete collection of information, dates, people, and places associated with the Roman Empire. A must-have for any classroom teacher. (T: 4–6)

http://www.mts.net/~aisensee/

This magnificent Web site is set up to resemble a Roman newspaper entitled *The Roman Times*, which tells about the Roman era through sports articles and classified ads. (S: 4–6)

http://http.cs.berkeley.edu/~jhauser/pictures/history/Rome/index.html

This site offers a great assortment of pictures about various aspects of the Roman Empire. (S: 4–6)

 # Literature Resources

Cox, Phil Roxbee. (1993). *Who Were the Romans?* Tulsa, OK: Educational Development Corporation.

This book is full of fun facts and bits of information about the Roman Empire. It also has general to detailed information on the Roman army, dress, homes, education, medicine, religion, and art.

Dineen, Jacqueline. (1991). *The Romans*. New York: New Discovery Books.

This book covers a variety of Roman topics, such as emperors, heroes, and wars. It provides great detail on these topics and includes a complete time line and glossary. The photographs of the actual places and archeological digs are quite impressive.

MacAulay, David. (1983). *City: A Story of Roman Planning and Construction*. Boston: Houghton Mifflin.

In this book the author creates a fictional Roman city called Verbonia. He goes through the Roman strategies and steps used to organize and build a city. The illustrations show how the Romans utilized such things as the structure of the arch and dome, provided water for the city through aqueducts, and organized the city in a grid-like structure.

Rice, Christopher & Rice, Melanie. (1998). *Pompeii: The Day a City Was Buried*. New York: DK Publishing.

The pages of this book are covered with drawings and photographs of Pompeii. Children can learn about this city and its people and the fateful day that the city came to an end.

Simpson, Judith & Bachem, Paul. (1997). *Ancient Rome*. New York: Time-Life.

This book can bring the ancient Roman Empire into the classroom. Children will learn about Roman families, farming, and armies, as well as the empire's rise to and fall from power.

Sis, Peter. (1996). *The Roman Empire*. Chicago: World Book.

This book is filled with activities and information on every aspect of Roman life. The activities include such things as making Roman clothing and dressing up like the different classes of people that lived during this time. The text is easy to understand and the drawings, photographs, and diagrams are informative as well as colorful.

Tanaka, Shelley & Ruhl, Greg. (1997). *The Buried City of Pompeii: What It Was Like When Vesuvius Exploded*. New York: Disney Press.

The authors mix factual information with historical fiction in this book to bring alive the story of a little boy named Pliny, who finds himself in a city struck with disaster. Both drawings and photographs are used to enhance the reader's understanding of what Pompeii was like and what happened one terrible day to end it all.

Activities and Projects

1. After they look at several literature resources and Web sites, ask the children to design several Roman outfits. Divide them into three groups and have each write a play that will use the costumes and Roman dress. Challenge the students to incorporate as many vocations as possible into their plays.

2. Read concepts from *City: A Story of Roman Planning and Construction* to the class. Divide the class into groups and plan a model city. Ask them to build scale models of their cities using clay, wood, paper, cardboard, pebbles, and other necessary materials. Set up tables in a convenient hall area in the school on which the students can display their Roman cities.

3. Ask students to locate appropriate Web sites and literature detailing Roman myths and legends. One example would be the story about Ceres, the Roman Goddess of the Earth, Proserpina, her daughter and Dis, the God of the Underworld. Afterwards, ask students to write their own myths or legends using Roman gods as the characters or to create their own characters. Encourage them to use their stories to explain natural phenomena that the Romans wouldn't have understood fully, such as rain, volcanoes, and earthquakes.

4. Using the Internet site http://www.iei.net/-tryan/deadroma.htm, which is a virtual tour of Rome, have the children write directions from one tourist attraction to another. Students should work in small groups to focus on selected sites in ancient Rome. Have students collect their information in the form of a "tourist brochure" that can be displayed in the classroom or school library.

5. Have children look up the meaning and definition of a mosaic in either *The Romans* or *The Roman Empire*. Also look up *mosaics* in the classroom encyclopedia and show the children other famous mosaics from around the world. Explain how some artists use glass, beads, or painted slabs of pottery for the individual tiles or block pieces, which when put together create an entire image. Have the kids use several different colors of construction paper to create their own Roman mosaics portraying some aspect of Roman life. When they are finished, hang them on the walls to create a mosaic museum.

6. Ask students to investigate the types of food the Romans ate and what they drank, using the Internet and literature listed above. After a thorough investigation has been completed, ask the children to write down their findings on the board and discuss with the class which foods are different from what we eat today and which are similar. After the discussion ask the children to help make Roman grape punch:

Grape Punch

4 tablespoons of honey	crushed bay leaf
2 dates	1 quart of white grape juice
pinch of cinnamon	ground pepper
saffron	lemon.

Chop the dates, then place all of the ingredients in a saucepan and stir the mixture continuously over low heat for half an hour. Allow the punch to cool, then serve with lemons as decoration.

7. Bring several local newspapers into the classroom. Have the children look at the different parts and sections. Then have the children look at the Web site http://www.mts.net/-aisensee/, which is patterned after what a Roman newspaper may have looked like. Ask the class to create their own Roman paper with articles that have to do with the time period and what may have been happening throughout the Roman Empire.

The Middle Ages

Introduction

The Middle Ages is the period in history from about 500 to 1350 C.E. An adjective used to describe this period in history is *medieval*. During medieval times most of the landholders were powerful kings or nobles. Most people were dirt farmers and lived on these lands, scratching out a meager existence. As you might imagine, they had few rights and almost no privileges. There were few cities and most of those only had a few thousand people living in them.

One of the most powerful rulers of the time, Charlemagne, conquered large parts of Western Europe and established monasteries and churches throughout the conquered territories. In 800 he named himself Holy Roman Emperor and declared most of Europe to be the Holy Roman Empire. After his death, raiders from the north and east attacked Western Europe and began their own settlements. Governments broke down and a new system of governance—feudalism—took over. This form of government placed power in the hands of a few nobles, who divided their land among other, less powerful nobles in return for military service and money. Government was a hierarchy, with lords at the top, then lesser nobles (known as *knights*), and at the bottom the peasants, who farmed in and around the villages. The poorest of these peasants were known as *serfs,* who were essentially slaves.

Research Questions

1. What are some of the major events of the Middle Ages?

2. Name the major groups of people during the Middle Ages.

3. Name the four main class positions in a feudal system.

4. What is feudalism?

5. What is the importance of each of the four main class positions in a feudal system?

Web Sites

www.learner.org/exhibits/middleages/
   This very informative site has great links to religion, home life, art, clothing, health, etc., of the Middle Ages. This detailed site is great for teachers to plan lessons and projects for the classroom. (T: 4–6)

http://hyperion.advanced.org/2834/
   This site includes a link to the Middle Ages, Dark Ages, and feudalism. It provides students with knowledge of how feudalism evolved and how it functioned throughout the Middle Ages. (S: 4–6)

http://battle1066.com/

This is a very detailed site about one of the most important battles of the Middle Ages, the Battle of Hastings in 1066. The site suggests that this one event had a profound effect on many other historical events. (S: 4–6)

Literature Resources

Aliki. (1983). *A Medieval Feast*. New York: Crowell.

This book describes medieval feasts and the courts and courtiers of the Middle Ages. Extremely detailed, it book discusses the civilization of the time and the preparation that was involved in the feasts held at English manor houses.

Curry, Jane Louise. (1993). *The Christmas Knight*. New York: Macmillan.

This well-illustrated book tells of an impoverished knight who finds a miracle when his cherry tree blooms on Christmas Day. Not only does this book provide insight into the Middle Ages, it also accurately presents the life and times of the poor.

Hindley, Judy. (1993). *The Time Traveler Book of Knights and Castles*. London: Usborne Publishing.

Readers of this book get to journey to a castle, go hunting, train to be a knight, and much more. Well thought out and organized, this book covers many aspects of this time period.

Howarth, Sarah. (1993). *The Middle Ages*. New York: Penguin.

Beginning with the fall of the Roman Empire, this book takes the reader through the Middle Ages and covers every aspect in great detail. It allows the reader to live as a lord and peasant and offers a taste of art and education.

Quindlen, Anna. (1997). *Happily Ever After*. New York: Penguin.

Kate loves to dream she is a princess. One day her dream turns into reality, and she is transported back in time to the Middle Ages. There she is a princess, but finds it less desirable than she had imagined.

Slavin, Bill. (1996). *The Stone Lion*. Alberta, Canada: Red Deer College Press.

Set in medieval Europe, this book tells the story of a country boy apprenticed to a silversmith in a cathedral town. Magic comes to life when the young boy sits on top of the stone lion and discovers a connection between the lion and the boy's grandmother.

Steel, Philip. (1995). *Castles*. New York: Kingfisher.

In this book the reader is able to view the inside and outside of castles, along with detailed pictures of the rooms of the castles. While exploring this book, the reader will feel a part of this magnificent building.

Wise, William. (1971). *Monsters of the Middle Ages*. New York: Putnam.

This book discloses the fantastic tales that people in the Middle Ages made up to explain things that frightened them. Humorously, the author has brought the medieval monsters to life to help depict what life was like for people at the time.

Activities and Projects

1. After they explore books such as *The Middle Ages,* Web sites like http://hyperion. advanced.org/2834/, and class discussions, students should have an understanding of the class structure of the feudal system. Ask students to write a play or skit about the different positions in the class system. The lords, ladies, knights, and serfs were the main classes, so each position will have to be filled. Have students select the audience for the play, such as other classes in the school, family members, or members of the community.

2. Have students choose positions from the class system of the Middle Ages. Ask them to write stories about their lives as lords, ladies, knights, or serfs. They should include information about their normal daily activities, relying on literature sources such as *A Medieval Feast, The Christmas Knight,* and *The Stone Lion,* and Web sites like www.learn.org/exhibits/middleages/ and http://guest.btinternet.com/-mark.furnival/ darkage.htm.

3. After discussing *The Middle Ages* and *The Time Traveler Book of Knights and Castles,* ask students to design a time line of the Middle Ages on a bulletin board. Allow them to select events they feel are important to add to the bulletin board.

4. Some students may be interested in looking through books such as *The Time Traveler Book of Knights and Castle* and Web sites such as http://guest.btinternet. com/-mark.furnival/darkage.htm for more information about people during the first 500 years of the Middle Ages (e.g., Angles or Saxons). Encourage students to present their findings to the class.

5. Ask students to contribute to a "Medieval Mural" by drawing pictures of life in the Middle Ages (a manor with fields, a castle, huts, knights jousting, etc.) Students should label and describe each of their illustrations.

The Renaissance

Introduction

The word *renaissance* means "rebirth." A renaissance is a period of new interest in something. During the 1300s many changes were taking place throughout Europe. Towns and cities were growing, trade flowed into the cities, and many of the cities (particularly those in Italy) were becoming exciting places to live and work.

During this time wealthy Italians began to take interest in art and learning. They could afford to support the arts and did so by donating large sums of money to museums and galleries. With this financial support, many artists and writers were freed to do their work instead of taking menial jobs just to get by. It was not long before Italy became a center for art and literature—new styles were developed, work was getting out to the "masses," and people were paying more attention to the cultural side of their lives.

The Renaissance extended throughout Europe and spanned the next two centuries. It spawned inventors such as Leonardo da Vinci, painters such as Rembrandt, sculptors such as Michelangelo, and writers such as William Shakespeare. It was indeed a time of innovation and rebirth.

Research Questions

1. Who are some of the major artists of the Renaissance?

2. Who are some of the major writers of the Renaissance?

3. What effect did the Renaissance have on everyday people?

4. What influence does the Renaissance have for people today?

5. What were some of the "causes" of the Renaissance?

Web Sites

http://www.nmhu.edul/departments/english/homepages/shana/re.htm
This Web site provides resources on literature, the art of Renaissance science, and the Florentine Renaissance. It also covers Renaissance authors such as William Shakespeare, John Milton, and Thomas Middleton. (S: 4–6, T: All)

http://www.luminarium.org/renlit
This is a comprehensive guide to the British literature of the Renaissance. This Web site also includes several hundred links to additional resources. (S: 4–6, T: 4–6)

http://www.learner.org/exhibits/renaissance/

This is a great site with loads of valuable information about the Renaissance. Ideal for any unit. (T: 4–6)

http://library.thinkquest.org/3588/Renaissance/

Students can take a virtual journey to the time of the Renaissance at this Web site. Lots to see and do here. (S: 4–6)

http://www.yesnet.yk.ca/schools/projects/renaissance/

At this Web site students can learn about some of the famous "personalities" of the Renaissance. (S: 4–6)

Literature Resources

Clare, John. (1995). *Italian Renaissance*. San Diego: Gulliver.

A compelling and thorough introduction to the Italian Renaissance, this book packs a lot into its 64 pages.

Halliwell, Sarah. (1997). *The Renaissance: Artists and Writers*. Austin, TX: Steck-Vaughn.

This book provides older readers with lots of data and a plethora of information about the major figures of the Renaissance.

Howarth, Sarah. (1992). *The Renaissance People*. Brookfield, CT: Millbrook Press.

This book discusses thirteen walks of life in the Renaissance, including banker, artist, and explorer. It also includes quotations from contemporary sources.

Langley, Andrew. (1999). *Renaissance*. New York: Knopf.

Another entry in the Eyewitness series, this book is filled with photos and eye-catching drawings, all accompanied by snippets of information and pertinent facts.

Merlo, Claudio. (1999). *Three Masters: Leonardo, Michelangelo, Raphael*. Hauppage, NY: Barrons.

This is a profusely illustrated text, with detailed drawings and photographs that complement an extensive review of three Renaissance masters.

Walker, Robert (1995). *The Italian Renaissance*. New York: Facts on File.

This book covers the major artists and sculptors of the Italian Renaissance. Thorough and complete, it overflows with information.

Activities and Projects

1. Ask small groups of students to select one of the following four people: John Calvin, Leonardo da Vinci, Michelangelo, or Shakespeare. (You may want to select other individuals depending on the resources available.) Ask each group to access the Web sites and literature above, supplementing their information with appropriate library resources. Then have each group take on the persona of their selected individual. After the appropriate research time, ask other students to interview the "individual." They may want to pose the following questions: Who are you? When did you live? Where

do you live? What kind of work do you do? What should people remember about you? What is your most famous work? Allow sufficient time for students to discuss the responses of each "individual" person relative to the time in which he lived.

2. Ask students to tie a piece of string from one end of the room to the other. The string should be at eye level (along one wall of the classroom) or may be placed near the ceiling. Have small groups of students select important events of the Renaissance and describe or illustrate them on a series of 3-by-5-inch index cards. Provide the groups with several clothespins and ask group members to post their cards along the string in the proper chronological order. Take time to discuss the order of events and their impact on society at that time in history.

3. Work with the art teacher to bring in several examples of Renaissance paintings over an extended period of time. You could contact the local art association to see if they know of any experts on Renaissance painters who would be willing to visit your class and share some paintings and historical information with your students.

4. One of the best software programs on the Renaissance is a CD-ROM produced by the National Geographic Society (P.O. Box 10597, Des Moines, IA 50340; 1-800-368-2728, cost $59.95). This program (catalog No. U82774; Mac/Windows) lets students travel back to the time of the Renaissance. They'll meet famous people who shaped the era, including the Medici family, Michelangelo, and Leonardo da Vinci. Students will gain an appreciation for the stunning paintings, sculptures, and architecture that are hallmarks of the Renaissance.

The Countries of Western Europe

Introduction

There are many countries in Western Europe. From Finland and Norway in the north to Spain and Portugal in the west to Italy and Austria in the east, this part of the world is distinguished by an array of languages, a panorama of geographical and geological features, and a host of traditions and customs to be found nowhere else in the world. That these countries exist peacefully together today is a testament to their determination and direction. For centuries this part of the world was been embroiled in battles and wars, with territories changing hands and being ravaged by years of conflict.

Interestingly, the peoples of Western Europe and the people of the United States have a great deal in common. Most of the countries in this part of the world have modern industries, just like in the United States. Their governments are also quite similar to ours. Just as important is the fact that many Americans have their ancestral roots in the countries of Western Europe. We may be separated by a great ocean, but we are connected by both ancestors and actions.

Research Questions

1. What are the Scandinavian countries?

2. What are the island nations of Western Europe?

3. What are the Mediterranean countries?

4. Which countries are located on the Iberian Peninsula?

5. Which country has the largest city?

6. Which country has the greatest number of people?

7. Which country has had a democratic form of government for the longest period of time?

Web Sites

http://lcweb2.loc.gov/frd/cs/detoc.html
This site has all the information a student could need on Germany. It includes topics such as economy, society, and transportation. (S: 4–6, T: 4–6)

http://www.Zipzapfrance.com/anglais/top_ten/index.html
This site presents an abundance of information about France. Customs, traditions, important sites, and an inside look at the people are all included. (S: 4–6)

http://www.odci.gov/cia/publications/factbook/it.html
    This site offers lots of information about Italy. Many aspects such as geography, economy, and the military are discussed. (S: 4–6)

http://lcweb2.loc.gov/frd/cs/estoc.html
    Lots of information and a complete examination of the country of Spain are on this site. (T: 4–6)

http://www.castles-of-britain.com/
    Students can learn all about the castles of England at this engaging and informative site. (S: 4–6)

http://www.odci.gov/cia/publications/factbook/sw.html
    Filled with lots of information about the people, geography, history, and economics of Sweden, this is a very detailed site. (T: 4–6)

http://www.odci.gov/cia/publications/factbook/nl.html
    Teachers can get loads of details and information about the Netherlands at this all-purpose Web site. (T: 4–6)

http://www.swissemb.org/kids/
    Switzerland for Kids offers many insights and loads of information about this European country. (S: All)

http://library.advanced.org/18802/
    The Global Gazette has been created by three girls in Norway, the United States, and Hong Kong. It's a great resource for "compare/contrast" studies. (S: 4–6)

 # Literature Resources

Note: The number of children's books on the countries of Western Europe is extensive. Several publishers produce series of books about European countries. These books are available at most public libraries or through your school library. Following are some representative series titles:

Cooking the _____ Way (Minneapolis, MN: Lerner)

Country Fact Files (Austin, TX: Raintree/Steck-Vaughn)

Major World Nation Series (New York: Chelsea House)

Modern Industrial World (New York: Thomson Learning)

Picture a Country (New York: Franklin Watts)

Amos, Janine. (1993). *Getting to Know Germany and Germans*. Hauppauge, NY: Barrons.
    This book is a basic introduction to Germany. It describes the people, landscape, and language. There is also a section with German words and phrases.

Ayer, Eleanor H. (1990). *Germany*. Vero Beach, FL: Rourke.
    This book describes the history of the old East and West Germany after WWII, the fall of the Berlin Wall, and the prospects for reunification of Germany.

Clark, Colin. (1994). *Journey Through Italy*. Mahwah, NJ: Troll Associates.
This book describes some distinct features of life in Italy. Lots of information on the major cities is also included.

Denny, Roz. (1994). *A Taste of France*. New York: Thomson Learning
This cookbook describes French foods. Also included are recipes for readers to make.

Haskins, Jim. (1990). *Count Your Way Through Germany*. Minneapolis, MN: Carolrhoda Books.
This story-by-numbers book, part of a series, presents the country of Germany in a most interesting way. Readers will learn about customs, traditions, and the people.

Sansone, Emma. (1992). *Getting to Know Italy and Italian*. Hauppage, NY: Barrons.
This guide to Italian life describes the people, their landscapes, and their language. There is a special section on the Italian language.

Sookram, Brian. (1999). *France*. Philadelphia, PA: Chelsea House.
This is a quick reference guide about the country of France. This volume is filled with lots of details and facts.

Activities and Projects

1. Ask students to become travel agents. They should select a country of Western Europe, then access several of the Web sites and literature choices above to determine airplane prices and the times of flights, hotel information, the sites to visit, transportation while on the trip, and much more. After locating the appropriate information, students should assemble it in the form of newsletters or travel brochures. If possible, obtain selected travel brochures from a local travel agency and present these to the class as examples. Ask students to design their brochures so that they are "kid friendly."

2. Students may enjoy logging onto http://www.epals.com to obtain an e-mail pen pal from a European country. If this is possible, provide sufficient opportunities for students to review materials, Web sites, or literature resources about selected countries. Additional information can be gathered from the e-mail pen pals and added to a classroom display or mural. This can be a wonderful long-term project throughout the school year.

3. Ask students to consult with the school's music teacher to obtain recordings of music from several selected European countries. Encourage students to consult relevant Web sites or children's literature to learn about the traditional music of selected countries. How is that music similar to or different from the music listened to by people in the United States? Provide sufficient opportunities for students to share specific musical selections with the entire class.

4. Ask students to read several books from the Cooking the _____ Way series (see above). If possible, have students prepare a complete meal focusing on the foods or recipes from one or more selected countries (you may need some additional adult help). To get you started, following is an easy-to-make recipe for homemade pasta, an all-time favorite in many European countries:

Pasta

Beat three eggs in a medium-sized bowl with a table fork. Mix in 2 pinches of salt and add 1 3/4 cups of pasta flour (available in many larger grocery stores, gourmet stores, or health food stores), one handful at a time (mixing well each time). Knead the dough for about five minutes and wrap it in waxed paper. Let it rest for about 10 minutes. Roll out the dough (on a floured surface) as thin as possible with a rolling pin. Use a sharp knife to cut the dough into long, thin strips about 1/4 inch wide. Bring a large pot of water to a boil. Add the homemade pasta to the boiling water and cook for approximately 2 minutes. Strain and serve with butter or pasta sauce.

The Countries of Eastern Europe

 ## Introduction

The Eastern European countries are a political hot spot in the world, perhaps rivaled only by the Middle East. Defining Eastern Europe is a constant challenge simply because political boundaries are shifting, war is being waged constantly, and territories are being annexed and lost. What is true as this is being written may not be in effect a year from now. However, at this writing the countries of Eastern Europe are Poland, the Czech Republic, Slovakia, Hungary, Romania, Slovenia, Croatia, Bosnia and Herzegovina, Serbia, Bulgaria, and Albania. It is important to consult current periodicals and newspapers to ensure that the names in effect now are also in effect during your study of this region.

This area of the world is steeped in history, and its landscape ranges from fields used by farmers and cattle breeders to majestic waterfalls and crystal lakes. Its culture is as diverse as the land. It could be said that Eastern Europe has served as a melting pot. The people of this area have had to start over because of wars caused by discrimination, religion, and political power struggles. Simply stated, it is a region of conflicts and contrasts, one that has evolved and one that will continue to evolve.

 ## Research Questions

1. What countries are included in Eastern Europe?

2. What do the countries have in common?

3. How are they similar to the United States?

4. How do they differ from the countries of Western Europe?

 ## Web Sites

http://www.odic.gov/cia/publications/factbooks/pl.html
This very thorough site provides detailed information on the geography, people, economy, communications, transportation, military, and current issues of Poland. It is an excellent site and can be used as a valuable teacher resource. (T: All)

http://www.odci.gov/cia/publications/factbook/hu.html
This is a complete and valuable site about Hungary. Loads of information and lots of factual details make this a perfect resource for any classroom teacher. (T: 4–6)

http://www.croatia.hr

The stunning photos will amaze students who visit this Web page. This tourist page provides wonderful and in-depth information about Croatia, including history, geography, attractions, and places of interest. (S: 4–6, T: All)

http://www.odci.gov/cia/publications/factbook/ro.html

At this site teachers can obtain the most up-to-date information about Romania. This site is thorough and complete. (T: 4–6)

http://www.odci.gov/cia/publications/factbook/bu.html

A site from the files of the CIA, this one includes basic information and details about Bulgaria. (T: 4–6)

http://www.odci.gov/cia/publications/factbook/ez.html

A complete and thorough description of the Czech Republic from the files of the CIA can be found on this site. (T: 4–6)

http://www.odci.gov/cia/publications/factbook/lo.html

Up-to-the-minute information and important facts about Slovakia can be found on this site. (T: 4–6)

http://www.odci.gov/cia/publications/factbook/al.html

Facts, figures, and loads of information about Albania are located on this all-inclusive site. (T: 4–6)

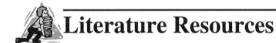

Literature Resources

Burke, Patrick. (1997). *Eastern Europe*. Austin, TX: Steck-Vaughn.

This thorough and complete book looks into various countries in this region, covering geographical, political, and economic facets.

Hintz, Martin. (1998). *Poland (Enchantment of the World Series)*. New York: Children's Press.

This book addresses not only the history, geography, and economy of Poland, but also the plants and animals, language, religion, sports, and arts of its people.

Isaac, John. (1997). *Bosnia: Civil War in Europe (Children in Crisis)*. Woodbridge, CT: Blackbirch Marketing.

This book shows the struggles of children and their families in a controversial region. Vivid photos are enhanced by the personal stories of these people. This is an eyewitness account of Bosnia and the events that surrounded the lives of its inhabitants.

Lear, Aaron. (1999). *Albania*. New York: Chelsea House.

Part of a series of books (Major World Nations), this compelling volume takes a peek inside a little-known country of Eastern Europe.

Waterlow, Julia. (1998). *A Family from Bosnia*. Austin, TX: Steck-Vaughn.

Part of a series of books (Families Around the World), this book offers a glimpse into the life and times of a single family in Bosnia.

Activities and Projects

1. Provide students with a randomly ordered list of events dealing with the creation of selected countries in Eastern Europe (consult the Web sites offering information from the files of the CIA for pertinent data). Ask students to list these events chronologically on individual index cards posted along one wall of the classroom.

2. Ask students to create a chart of Slavic languages. They should work in small groups to access necessary data from the Web sites and literature resources listed above. Have each group use a variety of graphic aids to present their findings. For example, student groups may wish to make a diagram or they may want to write the different languages on an outline map of Eastern Europe.

3. Ask students to consult several of the Web sites above. Have one group of students create an outline map of the Eastern European countries as they were 100 years ago, a second group a map of the countries as they were 50 years ago, and a third group an outline map of the countries as they are today. Allow sufficient opportunities for students to discuss the changes they see among the three maps.

4. Work with the school music teacher to introduce your students to some of the music of this region of the world. You could play the music of selected Hungarian composers such as Franz Liszt or Bela Bartok. Another possibility would be the waltzes of Franz Lehar or the operettas of Sigmund Romberg. Ask students to discuss the feelings or emotions evoked by these composers and their work.

5. Ask students to collect an assortment of old magazines. Have small groups of students create individual collages of the scenes and sights from a selected Eastern European country. When completed, ask students to discuss any similarities and/or differences in the collages they created.

Commonwealth of Independent States

 Introduction

Simply put, the former Soviet Union is a land of contrasts and conflicts. Dozens of ethnic groups, a wide and varied terrain, constant battles and wars, breakaway republics, an economy that barely exists, a country that spans 11 separate time zones, and a bitterly cold climate mark this extensive region as one of both non-stop change and a static government. Perhaps this is a conflict in terms, but in many respects the former Soviet Union has always been a paradox, both internally and externally. Held together by patches of communism, yet reaching out for the democratic ideals of its smaller, neighbors in Europe, the former Soviet Union is engaged in a fight for growth and survival that is seemingly endless.

 Research Questions

1. What caused the breakup of the Soviet Union?

2. What are some of the most prominent physical features of the former Soviet Union?

3. What is the largest city?

4. What is Moscow known for?

5. Who was Joseph Stalin?

6. How does the Russian economy compare with the United States?

7. What is Russia's major export?

 Web Sites

http://www.mrdowling.com/707russia.html
This site provides a fact list about Russia. There are links to all of the major events that have happened in Russia. The site goes in-depth into the lives of the most notable people that lived in Russia. (T: 4–6)

http://www.alexanderpalace.org/palace/
This Web site shares the many lost treasures of the Romanovs, the last royal family to rule in Russia. There are a variety of rooms that the student may enter to learn about each of the Romanovs and their history. (S: 4–6)

http://www.learner.org/exhibits/russia/
This site describes the changes that Russia went through after the breakup of the Soviet Union. The Web site goes into detail about how the various countries were run after the breakup and what the impact of the breakup was on those countries. (T: 4–6)

http://www.odci.gov/cia/publications/factbook/rs.html

This site has loads of information and fascinating facts about Russia, perfect for any lesson or unit. (T: 4–6)

http://lcweb2.loc.gov/frd/cs/rutoc.html

Russia: A Country Study will provide classroom teachers with a plethora of data and pertinent facts about Russia. (T: 4–6)

http://www.learner.org/exhibits/russia/

Lots and lots of information about Russia can be found on this site that covers history, geography, people, culture, and economics. (S: 4–6, T: 4–6)

http://www.nationalgeographic.com/resources/ngo/maps/view/images/russiam.jpg

This site offers a physical map of Russia from the National Geographic Society. Cities and principal landmarks are identified and labeled. (S: 4–6, T: 4–6)

 # Literature Resources

Jacobson, Peter Otto. (1986). *A Family in the USSR*. New York: Bookwright Press.

This book tells the story of a family that lives in Leningrad. The book shows the reader the home, work, school, recreation, and day-to-day activities of the family.

Murrell, Kathleen. (1998). *Russia*. New York: Knopf.

Part of the Eyewitness series, this completely illustrated and detailed book provides readers with loads of valuable information about Russia and its people.

Pluckrose, Henry. (1999). *Russia (Picture a Country)*. New York: Franklin Watts.

This slice-of-life photo essay follows a child as he attends school and participates in other activities. A nice "compare and contrast" book for younger readers.

Popescu, Julian. (1998). *Russia (Major World Nations)*. New York: Chelsea House.

This descriptive and most informative look at modern Russia today provides young readers with lots of first-hand data.

Price, Susan. (1992). *Ghost Song*. New York: Farrar, Straus & Giroux.

This is a Russian tale of the mysterious creatures of the night. This piece of literature will give the reader insight on what it is like to live in Russia, with all of the folklore that surrounds the people.

Sallnow, John. (1997). *Russia*. Austin, TX: Steck-Vaughn.

A broad variety of arranged and categorized facts provide readers of this book with overviews of Russia: its economy, geography, culture, and people.

Whyte, Harlinah. (1997). *Russia (Festivals of the World)*. Milwaukee, WI: Gareth Stevens.

In this book students will learn about some of the celebrations and festivals that are so much a part of the Russian culture.

Activities and Projects

1. Ask students to access several of the Web sites and literature resources above. Encourage them to construct and prepare a series of "Compare and Contrast" charts (on large sheets of newsprint) that illustrate the differences and similarities between children living in Russia and children living in the United States. Ask students to discuss whether there are more similarities or more differences between the two groups of children.

2. If possible, obtain a large, oversized wall map of the former Soviet Union. Post the map along one wall of the classroom. Ask students to check out the information available on some of the Web sites listed above, with special reference to the cities of the former Soviet Union. Have students write down pertinent facts about selected cities on individual index cards and post those cards around the perimeter of the map. Use lengths of different colored yarn to "link" each card with the specific location of the city it describes.

3. Ask students to check out the Web site http://www.mrdowling.com/707/russia.html/. Based on the information they obtain, they should invent, construct, or design a comparable Web site for the United States. What specific types of information should be on the new site? What data would be most useful for a student in Russia who was doing some research for a class assignment on the United States?

4. Ask students to plan an imaginary tour through the former Soviet Union. Divide the class into several small groups and encourage each group to plan an itinerary for a two-week journey. Ask each group to identify selected sites and attractions they would like to see on a railroad trip. Students may wish to "take" their trips and send "home" some imaginary postcards describing the natural environment and the weather conditions of each place they visit.

The Countries of Northern Africa

 ## Introduction

Northern Africa stretches from the Atlantic Ocean on the west to the Egyptian desert on the east. This area includes the countries of Libya, Tunisia, Algeria, Egypt, and Morocco. These five countries occupy an area of 1,835,000 square miles. The population in all the countries of Northern Africa is predominantly Arabic and Muslim. Northern Africa's inhabitants are confined chiefly to the narrow Mediterranean coastal belt and scattered Saharan oases with their characteristic date palms. Most of Northern Africa has a marked dry season, and cultivation depends on frequent, intensive irrigation. Wheat, barley, potatoes, olives, tomatoes, oranges, dates, and grapes are grown in this region. Sheep and goats are the principal livestock. There are important mineral deposits, such as iron ore, phosphates, petroleum, and natural gas.

 ## Research Questions

1. Who were the earliest known inhabitants of Algeria?

2. What is the most famous river in Egypt?

3. What is the name of the African people who are world famous for their beadwork?

4. What are some foods that can be found in North Africa?

5. What are the names of some of the ethnic groups found in Sudan?

 ## Web Sites

http://lcweb2.loc.gov/frd/cs/lytoc.html
This site is dedicated to the study of Libya. It's very detailed and descriptive and contains very useful information. It explains specific subjects, such as evolutionary changes in traditional society, education, and foreign trade. (T: 4–6)

http://www.odci.gov/cia/publications/factbook/eg.html#gov
One of the four great ancient civilizations, Egypt, made numerous advances in technology, science, and the arts, which this site explores in detail. It also contains information about the country's geography, people, government, economy, communications, transportation, military, and transnational issues. (S: 4–6, T: 4–6)

http://www.arab.net/algeria/algeria_contents.html
This site explores the country of Algeria. It contains information on its history, geography, business, culture, government, and transportation and offers links to obtain further information at additional sites. (T: 4–6)

http://www.mrdowling.com/607/mana.html

This site provides an interesting overview of Northern African countries. It contains a vast array of color photographs of the land, it has a variety of maps, and it also contains information about the people. In addition, this site gives information on Northern African countries' primary resources, oil, and major accomplishments, such as the Suez Canal. (S: 4–6)

 # Literature Resources

Brown, Marcia. (1982). *Shadow*. New York: Scribner.

This book is an actual tale captured in text from the storytellers and shamans; it was once only heard around a fire, but now can be read by everyone.

Hermes, Jules. (1995). *The Children of Morocco*. Minneapolis, MN: Carolrhoda Books.

This is an introduction to many different Moroccan children, including nomadic Berbers, village dwellers, and various city children.

Loveridge, Emma. (1997). *Egypt*. Austin, TX: Steck-Vaughn.

This book is a broad examination of Egypt that focuses on the geography, climate, natural resources, cultures, and economy of this ancient country.

Musgrove, Margaret. (1976). *Ashanti to Zulu: African Traditions*. New York: Dial Press.

This book uses the alphabet to guide the reader through 26 African traditions. This is an excellent book for the young reader. It not only teaches the student about African traditions, but it also incorporates the alphabet.

Onyefulu, Ifeoma. (1997). *Chidi Only Likes Blue*. New York: Cobblehill Books.

This book can be an excellent tool for incorporating learning about Africa into the recognition of colors. As the book goes through each color an African tradition is explained, ways of cooking are shown, or types of foods are pictured.

Rodgers, Mary. (1988). *Sudan in Pictures*. Minneapolis, MN: Lerner.

This book describes the country of Sudan. It contains information about the land, flooding, rainfall, and climate. It also contains a section on the history and government, which includes the ruling kingdoms, major influences from other countries, and the development of its current government.

Sayre, April. (1999). *Africa: The Seven Continents*. New York: 21st Century Books.

This thorough introduction to the continent of Africa is filled with photos and descriptive information. It is a good first book for young explorers.

Stalcup, Ann. (1999). *Ndebele Beadwork: African Artistry*. New York: PowerKids Press.

The Ndebele women of Africa are famous for their artistic beadwork. This book shows how the Ndebele women use beadwork to decorate clothing. The beading technique is also used in the making of jewelry, fine costumes for special ceremonies such as weddings, the decoration of headdresses, and in the making of dolls.

Targ-Brill, Marlene. (1993). *Algeria (Enchantment of the World)*. New York: Children's Press.

This book discusses the geography, history, people, and culture of this large country in Northern Africa.

Activities and Projects

1. Ask each of several small groups of students to select a country in North Africa. Encourage them to collect as much information as they can using several Web sites and literature resources. Afterwards, ask each group to construct a Venn diagram that compares life in their selected country with life in the United States. What similarities and/or differences do they note?

2. Ask students to create a time line of some of the major events in Egyptian history. Some students could post an extra-long strip of newsprint along one wall of the classroom to record the significant historical events. Other students could illustrate selected events with original drawings or pictures cut out of old magazines (copies of *National Geographic* would be ideal).

3. Divide the class into groups of two. Ask each pair to choose a country located in Northern Africa. Ask the pairs to list the pros and cons of living in their specific country. They can find the information in books or on the Internet. After they have constructed a list for each, bring the class back together. Ask each group to share with the rest of the class the advantages and disadvantages of living in their chosen country.

4. Have students create a tabletop model of a Berber encampment. They can combine cardboard cutouts of animals with pipe-cleaner people and toothpick structures to create the scene. Ask students to label various parts of their model for exhibition in a school display case.

5. Although your students may never be able to visit a northern African country, they can enjoy a typical food from Africa. Following is a recipe for *kanya*, a popular sweet in many African countries:

> **Kanya**
>
> Thoroughly mix 1/2 cup smooth peanut butter and 1/2 cup of superfine sugar in a large bowl. Press any remaining granules of sugar against the side of the bowl with a wooden spoon until they are completely crushed and mixed with the peanut butter. Slowly add 2/3 cup of uncooked Cream of Rice and continue stirring until the mixture is completely and thoroughly blended. Spread the mixture in a loaf pan and press down with your hands until it is evenly spread. Cover the pan with plastic wrap and refrigerate for two to three hours until firm. Cut into small bars with a knife and enjoy!

The Countries of Sub-Saharan Africa

Introduction

Sub-Saharan Africa is the land to the south of the Sahara Desert. It is an enormous area, stretching more than 3,500 miles from the grasslands and forests of central Africa to the narrow coastal plain of Southern Africa. This area is typically divided into three separate and distinct regions. These include the western and central forest countries, the countries of Eastern Africa, and the countries of Southern Africa.

There are 17 countries in the western and central region of Africa. These include the Central African Republic, Senegal, Angola, Niger, Ivory Coast, Liberia, and Gambia. For the most part people living in these countries make their living through subsistence farming. As a result, the economies in these countries are weak and subject to enormous fluctuations.

The Great Rift Valley separates eastern Africa from the rest of Africa. Eight countries, including Kenya, Tanzania, Mozambique, and Madagascar, make up Eastern Africa. Much of Eastern Africa is a high plateau. This part of Africa has the highest mountains and largest lakes. Most of the area has a hot climate, with one dry season. Grasslands are the predominant form of vegetation.

Southern Africa has many different climates and an equal diversity of countries. Countries in this region include Zambia, Zimbabwe, Swaziland, Botswana, and South Africa. Interestingly, this part of Africa has both the richest and poorest countries on the entire continent. Vegetation ranges from vast expanses of grasslands to desert environments to rich coastal plains.

Research Questions

1. What are the countries that make up Sub-Saharan Africa?

2. What are some of the different customs and traditions of this region?

3. What is the predominant climate?

4. Describe different forms of agriculture in Southern Africa.

5. What types of religious differences exist in the western and central forest countries?

6. What are the major landforms of Eastern Africa?

7. Describe the economy of South Africa.

 # Web Sites

http://www.geographia.com/south-africa

This site includes extensive information that is easily accessible to both students and teachers. The site covers travel and South Africa. It also has detailed pictures and photographs. (S: All, T: All)

http://www.hmnet.com/africa/1africa.html

The African Information Center is an all-inclusive Web site that offers detailed and complete information on every African country. This is simply an incredible site that has everything students or teachers would want to know about this amazing continent. (S: All, T: All)

http://www.africaonline.com/AfricaOnline/coverkids.html

From Africa Online, students can acquire loads of information and discover tons of amazing facts about the countries of Africa. Complete and thorough! (S: 4–6)

http://library.advanced.org/16645/

This phenomenal site has a wealth of information and lots of interactive data on the countries of Africa. This is a super resource. (S: 4–6, T: All)

http://www.nationalgeographic.com/resources/ngo/maps/view/images/africam.jpg

At this site, from National Geographic, students can view satellite images of all the African countries. Great for map studies! (S: All, T: All)

 # Literature Resources

Cowen-Fletcher, Jane. (1994). *It Takes a Village*. New York: Scholastic.

This book is about an African family living in a village. It tells of their customs and way of life and can show students how people in other countries live differently than we do.

Fredericks, Anthony D. (1999). *Elephants for Kids*. Minnetonka, MN: NorthWord Press.

This book provides readers with facts and information about the world's largest land animal. In this book filled with an array of awe-inspiring details, the narrator (a native of Kenya) offers readers lots of insight about this delightful creature.

Leigh, Nila K. (1993). *Learning to Swim in Swaziland*. New York: Scholastic.

This book is about a young girl from the United States whose parents moved to Swaziland, Africa, when she was in second grade. She tells about the differences between here and there. She discusses and illustrates school, language, clothing, and food, and shows pictures of her new culture.

Nicholson, Robert. (1994). *The Zulus*. Philadelphia, PA: Chelsea House.

This book is about an African tribe called the Zulus. It tells of their customs, spirits and sacrifices, crafts, meals, and child rearing. It also tells stories about the chiefs and warriors of this tribe.

Sammis, Fran. (1998). *Colors of Kenya*. Minneapolis, MN: Carolrhoda Books.

This beautifully illustrated book is filled with loads of fascinating descriptions and colorful details about Kenya. A fabulous resource.

Schneider, Elizabeth Ann, Ph.D. (1997). *Nebele*. New York: Rosen Publishing Group.

This book is about African customs and youth activities and contains a glossary, pictures, and an early history of South Africa.

Activities and Projects

1. Ask students to log on to several of the Web sites listed above. Have them work in small groups to obtain important information about a selected country or group of countries in Sub-Saharan Africa. After the data have been collected, ask each group to set themselves up as a travel agency. Each group can develop a series of brochures, newsletters, posters, and informational guides to their selected country. If you wish, ask students to write the information as though students their own age would be using it. You may want to ask another class to visit your "travel agency" to talk with the "agents" and plan appropriate journeys to designated countries.

2. Divide the class into two large groups. Have each group use the Internet, encyclopedias, and trade books to find facts about Sub-Saharan Africa. Each group or team should then construct a series of trivia cards. With the teacher as the game show host, have each team pick a trivia card from the other and accumulate points for correct answers.

3. Ask selected students to each assume the role of the president of a selected African country. After appropriate research via Web sites and literature, ask each "president" to present facts to the class, such as location of the country, neighbors, exports and imports, geographical features, ethnic groups, and/or political structure.

4. Divide the class into several groups. Ask each group to select one or more countries and locate important information about their designated country(ies). Ask each group to develop a "filmstrip" about their country by drawing pictures on a roll of adding machine paper. As they unwind their "film," one member of the group can be the narrator and describe the scenes pictured.

5. Ask small groups of students to create charts or graphs that list the exports of selected countries. Using appropriate Web sites and the literature above, students can identify important crops, minerals, or other items that represent the economy of designated countries. Ask youngsters to post their data on oversized posters or sheets of newsprint.

6. Have selected youngsters use Web sites to construct a series of weather maps for specific countries. How is the weather different in the western countries when compared with the countries in Southern Africa?

7. The National Geographic Society (http://www.nationalgeographic.com) sells a variety of videos that offer an intriguing look into the richness and vastness of the African continent. Try to obtain one or more of the following: *Africa's Animal Oasis* (No. 51529), *Africa* (No. 51440), *Journey to the Forgotten River* (No. 51461), *Serengeti Diary* (No. 51388), *African Odyssey* (No. 51336), *Bushmen of the Kalahari* (No. 51027), *African Wildlife* (No. 50509), *Africa's Stolen River* (No. 51373), and *Lions of the African Night* (No. 51331).

The Countries of South Asia

Introduction

The countries of South Asia include India, Pakistan, Bangladesh, Sri Lanka, Nepal, and Bhutan. South Asia extends from the slopes of the Himalayan Mountains in the north to the island of Sri Lanka in the south. The northern part of the Indian subcontinent contains plains, and plains also run along the eastern coast.

The climate of most of South Asia is affected by monsoons, seasonal winds that occur in the Indian Ocean and South Asia. From April through October, the wind blows from the southwest, off the warm Indian Ocean. This wind carries moisture inland and dumps large amounts of rain across the landscape. The monsoon wind produces a large area with a hot or warm climate and one dry season.

The northwestern part of South Asia does not benefit from the monsoon. This part of South Asia is dry or semi-dry for the entire year.

Research Questions

1. What countries make up South Asia?

2. What effect do monsoons have on the agriculture of the region?

3. Why are many of these countries so poor?

4. Which of the countries has the largest population?

5. How are the countries of Pakistan and Bangladesh similar?

Web Sites

http://geocities.com/ResearchTriangle/Lab/1604/country.html
This is a wonderful Web site containing a host of information on Bangladesh. It includes a brief history, physical description, climate summary, and a multitude of other information. (S: 4–6)

http://www.green-lotus-trekking.com/engels/info-nepal.html
This is a Web site on Nepal. Scrolling down this Web site provides students with an abundance of information on the geography, history, people, and various other aspects of Nepal and its culture. (S: 4–6)

http://www.interknowledge.com/india/
This site offers a great introduction to the country of India. There's lots of material here for plenty of lesson plans. (T: 4–6)

http://www.lex5.k12.sc.us/ces/Indiamn.htm

This is a great site on the history, geography, people, and cultures of India as written by a class of fifth grade students. (S: 4–6)

http://www.interknowledge.com/nepal/

This site offers classroom teachers lots of good information on the country of Nepal. (T: 4–6)

http://www.vic.com/nepal/

Journal entries and photographs highlight one man's visit to Nepal. (S: 4–6)

http://www.oxfam.org.uk/coolplanet/kidsweb/world/bangla/banghome.htm

This all-inclusive site on the country of Bangladesh will provide students and teachers with lots of valuable data. (S: 4–6, T: 4–6)

 # Literature Resources

Bash, Barbara. (1996). *The World of the Banyan Tree*. Boston: Little, Brown.
This wonderful tale combines fiction and nonfiction into a captivating read-aloud book ideal for every classroom.

Bickman, Connie. (1996). *Nepal (Through the Eyes of Children)*. New York: Abdo Publishing.
As the series title suggests, this book provides readers with an examination of the country of Nepal as viewed by some of its youngest residents.

Brace, Steve. (1995). *Bangladesh*. New York: Thomson Learning.
Profusely illustrated with color photographs, this book examines the landscape, climate, and urban and rural life of Bangladesh.

Chin-Lee, Cynthia. (1997). *A Is for Asia*. New York: Orchard Books.
Using the alphabet, this book explains a characteristic belonging to some country or culture of Asia. The illustrations creatively highlight the characteristics described.

Kagda, Falaq. (1997). *India (Festivals of the World)*. Milwaukee, WI: Gareth Stevens.
This is a delightful overview of India's heritage, customs, and lifestyles.

Littlefield, Holly. (1999). *Colors of India*. Minneapolis, MN: Carolrhoda Books.
This delightful book examines the culture and geography of India and its people. Part of a series.

Pluckrose, Henry. (1998). *Picture a Country: India*. New York: Franklin Watts.
As the name implies, this book is full of photographs of India. The text is simple and the book presents many facts about the people, culture, and geography of India.

Siddiqui Ashraf. (1998). *Pakistan: Toontoony Pie and Other Stories*. New York: Hippocrene Books.
Filled with stories and folktales of Pakistan, this book will delight and engage young learners for many hours.

Zwier, Lawrence. (1998). *Sri Lanka: War-Torn Island*. Minneapolis, MN: Lerner.
As part of a series (World in Conflict), this book offers young readers an insight into a little known country's history and conflicts.

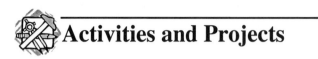# Activities and Projects

1. Ask small groups of students to draw the borders of India, Pakistan, and Bangladesh on an outline map of South Asia. Afterwards, ask them to access the Web sites and literature above to mark each country's capital, major crops, and natural resources. Students should post illustrations of the items directly on the map or cut out photos from old magazines and post them around the perimeter of the map.

2. Ask several students to post a large map of South Asia along one wall of the classroom. Have them access information on monsoons at various Web sites (for example, http://www.kjc.gov.my/ns-home/docs/monsoon.htm or http://iri.ldeo.columbia.edu/~krishna/talk/krishna.html). Afterwards, have them draw the path of the monsoon on the map.

3. Ask students to access several of the Web sites listed above. Divide the class into several small groups and ask each group to focus on a different religious group of the area (i.e., Hindu, Muslim, Buddhist). Ask each group to develop an informative brochure or poster about their identified religion and/or some of the special celebrations or holidays related to that religion.

4. Ask students to consult several of the Web sites listed above to obtain information on the various crops grown in South Asia. Have them present their findings in the form of a brochure or leaflet. Students could also construct a three-dimensional museum display showcasing the different crops (tea, cotton, wheat, rice).

The Countries of Middle East

Introduction

The Middle East includes the countries of southwest Asia. It got its name from Europeans primarily because of its location between the Far East (as East Asia is sometimes called) and Europe. The countries of this region include Saudi Arabia, Syria, Jordon, Lebanon, Iran, Iraq, Turkey, Afghanistan, and Israel. With the exception of Israel, all of these countries are Muslim.

The climate of the Middle East is predominantly dry, with little rainfall. The Arabian Desert is the dominant geographical feature in this part of the world. Because so little rain falls agriculture is quite limited. Irrigation has helped in some areas, but farming for the most part is a constant struggle against the elements. Countries that lie close to the Mediterranean Sea—Israel, Lebanon, Syria, and Turkey—have climates that are quite similar to other Mediterranean countries: warm with one dry season.

Research Questions

1. Which Middle Eastern country is the most desolate?

2. What goods does Israel export?

3. Where in Saudi Arabia is oil found?

4. What religion is practiced in Iraq?

5. What is an open-air market?

6. Which Middle Eastern country has the largest population?

Web Sites

www.odci.gov/cia/publications/factbook/is.html
This is a comprehensive site on Israel. It describes the geography, people, history, government, economy, communications, transportation, and military. (T: 4–6)

http://lcweb2.loc.gov/frd/cs/trtoc.html
This site has all the information any teacher would need on the country of Turkey. (T: 4–6)

http://www.odci.gov/cia/publications/factbook/ir.html
Complete information and factual data about Iran can be located on this site. (T: 4–6)

http://www.odci.gov/cia/publications/factbook/af.html
Loads of information about Afghanistan can be found at this Web site. (T: 4–6)

http://lcweb2.loc.gov/frd/cs/sytoc.html
    Complete information about the history, geography, and economy of Syria is provided on this site. (T: 4–6)

Literature Resources

Baralt, Luis. (1997). *Turkey*. New York: Children's Press.
    With a balanced viewpoint and plenty of photos, this book is an informative introduction to an ancient country.

Bickman, Connie. (1994). *Through the Eyes of Children*. Edina, MN: Abdo and Daughter.
    This book explains Israel in very basic terms. It presents the children, foods, clothes, school, work, city life, and traditions.

Foster, Leila. (1997). *Afghanistan*. New York: Children's Press.
    A complete and thorough overview of this Middle Eastern country is presented in the pages of this book.

Haskin, Jim. (1990). *Count Your Way Through Israel*. Minneapolis, MN: Carolrhoda Books.
    This book details the nine products that Israel exports.

Honeyman, Susannah. (1995). *Saudi Arabia*. Austin, TX: Steck-Vaughn.
    Daily life, climate, landscape, population, laws, industry, environment, and the country's future are all discussed in this book .

South, Coleman. (1995). *Syria*. New York: Benchmark Books.
    The geography and long, complex history of this country are accurately detailed in the pages of this book.

Teta, John. (1990). *Iraq in Pictures*. Minneapolis, MN: Lerner.
    This book presents Iraq through pictures. Its history, economy, climate, religion, resources, and people are all described.

Whitehead, Susan. (1998). *Jordan*. New York: Chelsea House.
    Lots of interesting information about the history, geography, and people of Jordan can be found in this book.

Activities and Projects

1. Ask students to make an oversized chart of all the Middle Eastern countries. The countries should be listed down the left-hand side of the chart and categories such as the following should be listed across the top: "Religion," "Geography," "Climate," and "Principal Cities." Ask students to access information via the Web sites and literature listed above and record their data on the chart. What similarities do they note? Are there any trends?

2. One of the staples in many Middle Eastern meals is pita bread. The following recipe gives students an opportunity to create their own version of pita bread from scratch:

> ## Pita Bread
>
> Dissolve 1 tablespoon of yeast in 2 cups of warm water. Stir in 1 tablespoon of honey and add 2 teaspoons of salt and 6 cups of all-purpose flour (one cup at a time). Stir until the mixture can't be stirred any longer. Turn the dough onto a lightly floured tabletop. Knead for about 10 minutes. Place the dough in a bowl that has been buttered on all sides and coat the dough thoroughly. Cover the bowl with a damp cloth and allow it to rise until it has doubled in size (about 2 hours). Push it down and shape it into individual balls (about 10-15). Allow the balls to rest for 15 minutes, then shape them into small flat spheres. Preheat the oven to 450 degrees and bake the loaves on a cookie sheet placed on the lowest rack in the oven for about 10 to 12 minutes. Allow to cool and serve.

3. Ask students to take on the role of a child in a specified Middle Eastern country. After obtaining necessary information from one or more Web sites listed above, each student should provide a "guided tour" of her or his country, "pointing out" the historical features, tourist sites, architecture, and customs and traditions of that country. Ask other students to question each "tour guide" about selected aspects of the country.

4. Ask students to locate as much information as they can about the Arabian Desert. Have small groups of students create a series of posters showing some of the most common characteristics of this region. Students can focus on plant life, animal life, people, historical sites, or important cities. Allow sufficient time for students to share and discuss their respective posters.

The Countries of East Asia

Introduction

Perhaps no other region of the world has changed as much in the last 100 years—or as often—as the countries of East Asia. It is an area beset by wars and influenced by an industrial revolution that has been a part of Western culture for many decades, a revolution that has opened up new avenues of economic prosperity unseen in this part of the world. Yet it is still a region of enormous poverty and a burgeoning population that strains the governments of almost every country in the region. It is an area of problems and challenges, faced with the realities of the twenty-first century, yet holding fast to the customs and traditions of a bygone era.

The countries of China, Taiwan, Mongolia, Japan, and the two Koreas make up East Asia. Although they are grouped together for geographic purposes, they are probably more dissimilar than they are alike. A host of religions, a demanding landscape, and a population that outpaces any other region of the world is causing stresses and strains both nationally as well as internationally. This is both a land of history and of potential, of promise as well as diversity.

Research Questions

1. Which East Asian country has the largest population?

2. Which East Asian country is the most isolated?

3. Which East Asian country is the most technologically advanced?

4. What are some of the major religions of this region?

5. What are the major languages of this region?

6. What is the most prosperous city in this region?

Web Sites

http://zhongwen.com

This site offers a Chinese dictionary, some readings from China (such as Ballad of Mulan), and facts about the Chinese culture. There is a very thorough explanation of the Chinese language. (S: 4–6, T: All)

http://asterius.com

This site focuses on the history of China—a condensed version from 2200 B.C.E. to the present. This site could serve as a valuable resource for teachers who need to brush up on their history of China. (S: 4–6, T: All)

http://library.advanced.org/26469/index.2.html

This is a fantastic site, with very detailed information about and pictures of China. Entitled Discovering China, it presents topics such as cities, history, culture, and important people. (S: 4–6, T: 4–6)

http://tqjunior.advanced.org/5110/

This site presents comparisons between China and Korea. There are links to information about language, history, art, food, etc. (S: 4–6)

http://lcweb2.loc.gov/frd/cs/mntoc.html

Just about everything a teacher would need on the history, culture, and geography of Mongolia can be found on this site. (T: All)

 # Literature Resources

Bornoff, Nick. (1997). *Japan (Country Insights)*. Austin, TX: Steck-Vaughn.
  This balanced overview of life in Japan explains how technology and tradition coexist in two diverse settings: an urban environment and a rural village.

Brenner, Barbara. (1999). *Chibi: A True Story from Japan*. New York: Clarion Books.
  This is an engaging read-aloud book that is well suited for any study of Japan and its people.

Chang, Cindy. (1994). *The Seventh Sister*. Mahwah, NJ: Troll Associates.
  This is an interesting Chinese legend, originating from the eastern side of the country, that explains how the night sky formed. The bits of Chinese culture described provide a taste of what life is like on "the other side of the world."

Cromie, Alice. (1994). *Taiwan (Enchantment of the World)*. New York: Children's Press.
  The culture, geography, history, and economics of this island nation are detailed in this book.

Ingpen, Robert et. al. (1994). *Folktales & Fables of Asia & Australia*. New York: Chelsea House.
  This colorful gathering of folktales offers a variety of stories from across the continents of Asia and Australia. The folktales from Asia paint vivid mental pictures of brave warriors, wise servants, and fantastic animals.

McMahon, Patricia. (1993). *Chi-Hoon, A Korean Girl*. Honesdale, PA: Caroline House.
  This story follows an eight-year-old Korean girl named Chi-Hoon in Seoul, South Korea. It describes her daily schedule, which includes school, family time, and playtime.

Scoones, Simon. (1998). *A Family from Japan*. Austin, TX: Steck-Vaughn.
  A descriptive and informative review of family life in Japan fills this engaging book.

Targ-Brill, Marlene. (1992). *Mongolia (Enchantment of the World)*. New York: Children's Press.
  This book presents the geography, history, culture, industry, and people of Mongolia.

Zhang, Song. (1997). *Cowboy on the Steppes*. Seattle, WA: Tundra Books.
  This story of a young boy forced to herd sheep on the steppes of Mongolia is both authentic and captivating.

Activities and Projects

1. If possible, prepare a traditional Japanese meal, or *gohan*. Use books, the Internet, and other sources to gather Japanese recipes to prepare. With the cooperation of parents, have students bring in supplies (cups, plates, utensils, chopsticks) and food (white rice, meat, and vegetables). When the meal is ready, have the students sit on the floor and recite the traditional sayings ("I receive this food" and "It was quite a feast"). Following are three recipes to get you started:

Black and White Salad

4–6 leftover boiled potatoes   pinch of dill
2 tablespoons of white vinegar   mace
juice from 1/2 lemon   salt and pepper
1 can of cooked mussels   walnut halves
1 can button mushrooms   parsley (large handful)

Slice the potatoes. Mix the next four ingredients and marinate the potatoes in the mixture. Add a pinch of dill and a little powdered mace. Drain the mussels and the mushrooms. Mix gently with the potatoes. Garnish with a few walnut halves.

Eggdrop Soup

1 egg
2 tablespoons scallions, finely chopped
3 cups basic clear soup (see below)

Beat the egg and the scallions together in a small bowl. In a saucepan, bring the basic clear soup to a boil. Swirl the egg mixture around the inside of the pan in a small stream, making a circle. Remove the soup from the heat, pour into small bowls, and serve.

Basic Clear Soup

Bring three cups of water to a boil in a medium sauce-pan. Stir in 1 heaping teaspoon of dashinomoto, 1/2 teaspoon of salt, and 1/2 teaspoon of soy sauce. Remove the pan immediately from the heat and pour into several small bowls.

2. Work with students to make a map of Japan using burlap. Cut a large piece of blue burlap to serve as the backing and to represent the ocean. Cut another piece of burlap in a different color in the shape of the islands of Japan. Ask students to make a key and sew symbols on the map with yarn and simple stitches. Include bodies of water, large cities, and lines of latitude and longitude. Sew the islands to the burlap, leaving an opening of 4 inches along one edge. Stuff a thin layer of polyester fiberfill into the spaces between the islands and the backing (this will give the map a three-dimensional effect). Sew the openings shut and display.

3. Create a travel guide for East Asia. Divide the class into groups of three students each and assign a different country to each group. The groups are responsible for collecting information (by using encyclopedias, the Internet, etc.). Information should include points of interest, culture, travel tips, and other important facts. They can compose their guides and include maps and pictures from the assigned country. Once complete, each group should present their guide to the class.

4. To obtain the most current information about China, students can access the following Web sites:

   http://www.chinatoday.com

   http://www.nationalgeographic.com/resources/ngo/=maps/view/images/chinam.jpg

   http://www.kiku.com/electric_samuri/virtual_china/index.html

   http://www.globalfriends.com/html/world_tour/china/china.htm

   http://lcweb2.loc.gov/frd/cs/cntoc.html

5. Based on library investigations and the information obtained from the Web sites listed above, have students put together a diary on a "Day in the Life of a Chinese Student." What does a Chinese boy or girl (at the same age as your students) do during the course of a typical day? How is her or his school day different from or similar to a U.S. student's day? Construct oversized Venn diagrams of the information using large sheets of newsprint.

The Countries of Southeast Asia

Introduction

Southeast Asia includes the mainland countries of Burma, Thailand, Laos, Cambodia, and Vietnam. It also includes the island nations of Singapore, Indonesia, the Philippines, and Brunei. Also included is the country of Malaysia. Southeast Asia is an extensive group of countries that is home to more than 452 million people. It is extremely diverse, with nine major languages, numerous dialects, and six major religions. This region of the world depends largely on farming and agriculture to support its staggering population; some of its major exports are rice, rubber, timber, fish, textiles, and minerals. Oil, gas, and copper are particularly important. All of this area has a hot, humid climate with lots of vegetation and an enormous diversity of animal life.

Research Questions

1. How many countries are there in Southeast Asia?

2. What animals are native to Southeast Asia?

3. What are the major religions?

4. In square kilometers, what is the area of Southeast Asia?

5. What is the largest city in this region?

6. Which Southeast Asian country has the highest population?

Web Sites

http://www.accessasia.com/xroad/xrasnet.html
Students can use e-mail to find resources and related sites that will help them learn about Southeast Asia. Valuable travel information, maps, and virtual tourist guides are also available at this site. (S: 4–6)

http://www.darkwing.uoregon.edu/-bkrish/
This site provides general information about Southeast Asian education, climate, geography, and population. (T: All)

http://sunsite.nus.edu.sg/
This informative Web site has a map that displays all the countries of Southeast Asia. Each country is clearly labeled and its respective flag is also shown. (T: All)

http://www.odci.gov/cia/publications/factbook/vm.html

Clearly presented, this Web site provides a detailed list of various aspects of Southeast Asia. It includes facts about geography, people, government, economy, transportation, military, and transnational issues. (S: 4–6)

http://lcweb2.loc.gov/frd/cs/phtoc.html

Loads of information about the Philippines can be found on this extensive Web site. (T: 4–6)

http://www.interknowledge.com/vietnam/

At this site students and teachers can obtain lots of valuable information about the people, culture, and geography of Vietnam. (S: 4–6)

http://www.sg/

This captivating Web site presents the history of Singapore, its ethnic groups, its major religion, and a variety of popular activities. (S: 4–6)

Literature Resources

Brown, Marion. (1989). *Singapore*. New York: Children's Press.

This book has a wide variety of fascinating information and factual details about one of the smallest countries in the world.

Hansen, Ole. (1997). *Vietnam*. Austin, TX: Steck-Vaughn.

This is a thoughtful and fact-filled look into a country that has long symbolized the people and customs of Southeast Asia.

Lorbiecki, Marybeth. (1997). *Children of Vietnam*. Minneapolis, MN: Carolrhoda Books.

This is an insightful look at the children of this war-torn country, including their daily lives and daily challenges.

Major, John S. (1991). *The Land and People of Malaysia and Brunei*. New York: HarperCollins.

This book discusses the major problems faced by many Southeast Asian nations. Readers also learn about sea gypsies, headhunters, weavers, Chinese merchants, Malay sultans, Indian lawyers, and rubber tappers.

Rigg, Jonathan. (1995). *Southeast Asia*. Austin, TX: Steck-Vaughn.

This book is loaded with facts about Southeast Asia and has wonderful color pictures of its people. Fascinating facts and colorful photos highlight this book.

Rowell, Jonathan. (1997). *Malaysia*. Austin, TX: Raintree/Steck-Vaughn.

History, geography, and culture are succinctly examined in this thoroughly researched book.

Shalant, Phyllis. (1988). *What We've Brought You from Vietnam*. New York: Julian Messner.

This wonderful "hands-on, minds-on" book presents information about Vietnam's culture through the use of crafts, folklore, puppetry, games, and recipes.

Wee, Jessie. (1998). *Philippines*. New York: Chelsea House.

The author presents readers with loads of information about this island nation and the people who inhabit it.

Activities and Projects

1. Ask students to create one or more dictionaries, each focusing on the language of a specific Southeast Asian country. Using the Web sites and literature above, as well as other library resources, students should assemble a brief dictionary of terms and words that an "average" tourist would need to know when visiting a selected country. Students may wish to assemble their dictionaries with other students in mind. If appropriate, these dictionaries can be donated to the school library.

2. Ask students to imagine that a local governmental agency has asked them to put together a travel guide for youngsters who are visiting one or more of the countries in Southeast Asia. Arrange the class into several small groups and ask each group to consult Web sites and literature to obtain necessary information for a "child's-eye" view of a specific country. What features should be emphasized? Which sites would be most interesting for other children to see?

3. Following a recipe for fried rice that your students will enjoy:

Fried Rice

1 small onion, chopped
2 tablespoons of chopped green pepper
2 tablespoons of vegetable oil
2 cups of cooked rice
1 can of water chestnuts, thinly sliced
1 can of mushroom stems and pieces
2 tablespoons of soy sauce
3 eggs, beaten

Cook and stir green pepper and onion in oil in a skillet for about 3 minutes. Stir in rice, water chestnuts, mushrooms, and soy sauce. Cook over low heat, stirring frequently, for about 5 to 7 minutes. Stir in eggs. Cook and stir 4 to 5 minutes longer. Makes 4 to 5 servings.

---

4. Ask students to create a transportation bulletin board. Have them cut drawings and photographs from old magazines (*National Geographic* is ideal), each representing a form of transportation in a Southeast Asian country. Students should arrange the pictures in a collage or separate them into selected categories (e.g., "Transportation 1,000 Years Ago," "Transportation 100 Years Ago," "Transportation Today"). Ask students to discuss any differences among the three categories and to compare transportation in Southeast Asian countries with that in some of the industrialized countries of the world.

The Countries of Oceania

Introduction

Oceania refers to the islands located in the Southern Hemisphere below Asia. They include Australia, New Zealand, and the independent countries of Papua New Guinea, Fiji, Tonga, Kiribati, Tuvalu, Nauru, the Solomon Islands, and Western Samoa. Spread out across the vastness of the south Pacific Ocean, they are as culturally and economically diverse as any group of countries in the world.

Australia, often referred to as the island continent, is mostly flat, dry, and hot. Early settlers established their cities along the eastern part of the country. These include the principal cities of Sydney, Melbourne, and Brisbane. Australia's dry climate proved to be ideal for sheep herding and cattle grazing, so large ranches were established across the outback (Australia's interior). Rich mineral resources have also contributed to Australia's economy.

To the southeast of Australia lies New Zealand. Consisting of two main islands and dozens of smaller ones, New Zealand's economy is primarily agricultural. Exports include dairy products, meat, and wool. About 80 percent of the three million people who live in New Zealand live in cities such as Wellington, Auckland, and Christchurch.

Research Questions

1. What are some of the island nations of Oceania?

2. Why is Australia called the island continent?

3. What is the primary export of New Zealand?

4. Who are the aborigines?

5. How were most of the Polynesian islands formed?

6. What is the population of Australia?

Web Sites

http://www.odci.gov/cia/publications/factbook/cw.html
This Web page provides several facts and statistics about the Cook Islands. This site also provides a map of these very spread-out and differentiated, tiny islands. (T: All)

http://www.kdu.com.ausform.html
This Web page has several links to other sites and exciting pictures of Australia and the "land down under." There are a teacher's page, sites on mammals and sheep, and pages on the Australian people and Australia's history. (T: 4–6)

http://australia-online.com/

At this site teachers and students can locate just about everything they wanted to know about Australia. Complete and thorough. (S: All, T: All)

http://library.advanced.org/28994/

Wow! This is a super site overflowing with information and data. This site is complete and thorough. (S: All, T: All)

http://www.exploring.nu/

The Exploring Travelogue has just about everything the armchair traveler would want to know about the countries of Oceania and Micronesia. (S: 4–6, T: 4–6)

http://hike.org/nzataglance/index.html

New Zealand at a Glance is a complete map of this country. Perfect for downloading and printing. (S: 4–6)

Literature Resources

Ball, John. (1984). *We Live in New Zealand*. New York: Bookwright Press.

This book introduces people who live and work in New Zealand. Each person describes her or his job and the way she or he lives. Some of the people introduced are a schoolgirl, a dairy farmer, an artist, and a fisherman. There are also facts about New Zealand and a glossary.

Bickman, Connie. (1994). *Children of Australia*. Minneapolis, MN: Library of Congress.

This book visits the different areas of Australia and the children who live there. In the book the children describe what is good to eat, what to wear, traditions, school, animals, and fun things to do. The book also contains a glossary and an index.

Browne, Rollo. (1987). *A Family in Australia*. Minneapolis, MN: Lerner.

This book introduces a family that lives in Nhulunbuy in the Northern Territory of Australia. The book takes us through a family's everyday activities. The book shows us where they work, go to school, play, and live.

Cavendish, Marshall. (1991). *Cultures of the World: Australia*. New York: Times Book International.

This book provides a complete look at Australia. It covers topics such as geography, history, government, economy, lifestyles, religion, language, food, and leisure activities. There is also a map at the back of the book so the reader can get a better idea of where Australia is located.

Dolce, Laura. (1997). *Australia (Major World Nation)*. New York: Chelsea House.

This book is illustrated with beautiful black-and-white photographs of vistas, wildlife, and scenery. The achievements of modern Australians are described. Covered as well are the problems of drug and alcohol addiction and treatment of the aborigines.

Knowlton, M. & Sachner, M. J. (1987). *New Zealand*. Milwaukee, WI: Gareth Stevens.

This book provides a complete look at New Zealand. It covers topics ranging from history, language, population, natural resources, art and music, to the people. It also includes various photographs of the people, places, and animals of New Zealand.

Lowe, D. & Smith, K. D. (1995). *The Australian Outback and Its People*. New York: Thomson Learning.

The large, dry regions of Australia, known as the outback, are introduced through brief discussions of the history, environment, inhabitants, and future. The aboriginal culture and the European impact on it are explored at a greater length.

North, Peter & McKay, Susan. (1999). *Welcome to Australia*. Milwaukee, WI: Gareth Stevens.

This book includes everything that you would want to know about Australia and its people. In the back of the book are quick facts, a glossary, lists of reference material such as videos and Web sites, and an index. The photographs are large, detailed, and bright and bring the people of Australia to life.

Paul, Teresa. (1998). *Down Under*. New York: Crabtree.

This book describes the lives of various animals in Australia, including the platypus, dingo, kiwi, kangaroo, emu, koala, and Tasmanian devil. The book includes interesting facts about where and how they live and what they eat.

 # Activities and Projects

1. Using one or more of the Web sites listed above, small groups of students can assemble dioramas of Australia and New Zealand. Students will need to collect relevant facts about each of the two countries and decide on the features to include in each of the dioramas. For example, one group may elect to construct a diorama of an Australian sheep ranch, a view of Sydney, or the Great Coral Reef. Another group may wish to assemble a diorama of Christchurch, a Maori dance, or a farm in New Zealand.

2. Ask each of two groups to imagine that they are settlers in Australia or New Zealand. Ask each group to describe the reasons they decided to settle in the country they did, what factors influenced their decision, and how they plan to survive the first crucial months. Students may need to access information via the Web sites above or selected literature.

3. Ask students to create individual salt maps of the countries of Oceania or a composite map of all the countries, using the following recipe:

> **Salt Map**
>
> 4 cups of flour   1 cup of salt
> 1 egg yolk   1 1/2 cups of warm water
> 1 tablespoon of water
>
> Combine the first three ingredients and knead for about 10 minutes. The mixture should be stiff but pliable. Spread the mixture out on a cookie sheet or piece of aluminum foil, forming it into various landform and ocean areas. Brush with egg yolk mixed with 1 tablespoon of water and bake at 325 degrees until very dry, about an hour, depending on size. Paint various areas with tempera paint and label them, then seal with two or three coats of polyurethane.

4. Ask students to pretend that they are visiting one of the countries in Oceania. Have them create postcards that they would send back to their families at home. Ask students to post these cards on the bulletin board.

5. Ask students to write to the consulate or foreign embassy of some of the countries of Oceania. Students can ask for travel details and other pertinent information that would be useful in planning a trip to those countries. Students can also prepare a travel plan for selected countries (length of stay, required documents/inoculations, necessary clothing, etc.).

6. Ask students to create costumes worn by natives in any of the countries of Oceania. What differences do they notice between the costumes of one culture and those of another culture? How are the costumes symbolic of the traditions or customs of a particular ethnic group?

The Countries of Canada and Mexico

 ## Introduction

The two closest neighbors to the United States are Canada and Mexico. To the north, part of our boundary with Canada is formed by the Great Lakes. To the south, our border with Mexico is defined partially by the Rio Grande. Although the policies and politics of these three neighbors are often at odds, they have remained friends and allies.

Canada is one of the largest countries in the world (it is the second largest). Most of Canada is vast stretches of uninhabited land. Located in high latitudes, Canada is a country with a very cold climate, yet an abundance of flora and fauna. Canada's population is relatively small for its land area, with a population density of only six to seven persons per square mile.

Mexico is a low latitude country, and as such it experiences a more temperate climate year-round. Although it is only one-fifth the size of Canada, it has three times as many people (its population density is about 94 persons per square mile). Most of the population of Mexico lives in the southern end of the Mexican Plateau. It is here that the world's largest city, Mexico City, is located.

 ## Research Questions

1. What is the capital of Canada?

2. What is the capital of Mexico?

3. What is the largest city in Canada?

4. Why do so few people (in comparison to Mexico) live in Canada?

5. What is the chief economic export of Mexico?

6. How is Canada's form of government similar to ours?

 ## Web Sites

http://infocan.gc.ca
This Web site offers children a look at Canada's history from its early days to modern times. Topics discussed include society and culture, government and the law, the land, and industry and resources. (T: All)

http://explora.presidencia.gob.mx/index_kids.html
    Mexico for Kids is an all-inclusive Web site that provides students with loads of fascinating facts and detailed information about this country. (S: All)

http://lcweb2.loc.gov/frd/cs/mxtoc.html
    Loads of information about Mexico can be accessed from this site. (T: 4–6)

http://canada.gc.ca/canadiana/cdaind_e.html
    Facts and figures, national symbols, and important historical events about Canada can be located at this extensive site. (T: All)

Literature Resources

Barias, Robert. (1997). *Canada (Festivals of the World)*. Milwaukee, WI: Gareth Stevens.
    This volume provides detailed information on the geography, wildlife, history, government, and economy of Canada.

Coronado, Rosa. (1989). *Cooking the Mexican Way*. Minneapolis, MN: Lerner.
    Recipes galore highlight this delicious (and nutritious) book about Mexican culture.

Hamilton, Janice. (1999). *Canada (A Ticket To)*. Minneapolis, MN: Carolrhoda Books.
    This introduction to Canada touches briefly on the country's geography, people, language, customs, and lifestyles.

Law, Kevin. (1997). *Canada (Major World Nations)*. Philadelphia, PA: Chelsea House.
    This is an introduction to the geography, history, government, economy, and people of the second largest country in the world.

Madrigal, Antonio. (1997). *The Eagle and the Rainbow*. Golden, CO: Fulcrum Publishing.
    This is a treasury of hard-to-find Mexican folktales that provide a wonderful accompaniment to any study of Mexico.

Olawsky, Lynn. (1997). *Colors of Mexico*. Minneapolis, MN: Carolrhoda Books.
    This is a very brief, yet colorful, introduction to the culture and people of Mexico.

Stein, Conrad. (1998). *Mexico (Enchantment of the World)*. New York: Children's Press.
    This is introduction to the geography, history, economy, culture, and government of Mexico.

Sylvester, John. (1996). *Canada (Country Fact Files)*. Austin, TX: Steck-Vaughn.
    This is a brief but thorough introduction to our neighbor to the north.

Wright, David. (1992). *Canada Is My Home*. Milwaukee, WI: Gareth Stevens.
    This true story is about a girl living in Canada who tells about the sites of the country and the beauty that surrounds her.

Activities and Projects

1. If possible, obtain examples of travel visas from parents or colleagues. Ask students to note the various features on the visas. Ask them to create their own original visas for travel into Mexico. What information should be recorded on the visas? How long are the visas valid for?

2. Ask students to access one or more of the Web sites listed above. Provide small groups of students with either a map of Canada or a map of Mexico. Encourage each of the groups to list five major cities of the country they are studying. Ask each group to plot the distances between those major cities and graph their results on a large wall chart. Encourage some class discussion on the distances within the country of Canada in comparison to the distances within the country of Mexico.

3. Ask students to log onto the following Web site: http://www.go2mexico.com. After they have gathered sufficient information about various tourist spots throughout Mexico, encourage pairs of students to design a Mexican vacation. Where would they want to go during a two-week vacation? What would they like to see? What would they like to do? After each pair has prepared its itinerary, provide opportunities for students to share their "vacations" with each other.

4. Ask students to log on to http://www.parkscanada.pch.gc.ca/. After gathering the appropriate information, students should make a chart of Canada's endangered species, indicating their habitats, features, behaviors, and the reasons they have become endangered. Create opportunities for students to discuss how humans have affected the environment and caused problems for both flora and fauna.

5. Ask students to log on to http://www.embassy.org. This site lists all the embassies of major countries around the world. Have students obtain additional information about Canada and Mexico from this site that could be used for an appropriate library display. What type of information would be most useful for students? For teachers? For parents? For travelers? Provide opportunities for students to discuss their findings.

The Countries of South America

 ## Introduction

South America is the fourth largest of the seven continents, yet it contains just 6 percent of the world's population. This continent contains 13 individual nations, each with its own story. There is a variety of natural resources that are exported throughout the world. The dominant language is Spanish, with the exception of Brazil, whose language is Portuguese.

The countries of South America are as diverse as its landscape and as unique as its people. They range from the arid deserts of Chile, to the soaring mountain peaks of Peru, to the damp and steamy rainforests of Brazil, to the sweeping panoramic plateaus of Argentina. South America can truly be called a continent of contrasts and of enormous diversity. It is both spectacular and grand and offers young adventurers a pleasing journey through time and treasures.

 ## Research Questions

1. What are the countries in South America?

2. Name some of the important land features that are found in South America.

3. What are some of the traditions practiced by people living in South America?

4. Describe the climates in the countries of South America.

5. What is the longest river in South America?

 ## Web Sites

http://lcweb2.loc.gov/frd/cs/cotoc.html
This site offers general facts and information about Colombia. It presents the government, population, climate, traditions, and physical geography of this country. This teacher-friendly site can also be used by students if they need to research specific information. (T: All)

http://lcweb2.loc.gov/frd/cs/vetoc.html
This site offers general facts about Venezuela. It is a good place to gain some general knowledge about the country. This is a site mainly for teachers, but students could also use it for research purposes. (T: All)

http://www.lonelyplanet.com/road/witness/sld-per.htm
This site has general information about Peru. There are pictures that can be shown in a slide show format so that students can gain a visual perspective on the country. It is a good research site for older students. (S: 4–6)

http://www.care.org/virtual_trip/bolivia/index.html

This is an excellent site for children. It is a virtual field trip that covers all of Bolivia. The pictures are very clear and provide a sense of what the landscape and people of Bolivia are like. It also has captions explaining all the pictures so that children understand what they are looking at. (S: 4–6)

http://www.lib.utexas.edu/Libs/PCL/Map_collection/americas/Venezuela.GIF

The University of Texas provides information on Venezuela at this site. Its most special feature is a grid map of Venezuela that includes large cities and rivers. This student-friendly site makes it easy for students to locate metropolitan areas and geographical features of Venezuela. (S: 4–6)

http://www.atlapedia.com/

This site contains full-color physical and political maps as well as key facts and statistics on countries of the world. All South American countries can be accessed from this site. (S: 4–6)

http://odci.gov/cia/publications/factbook/br.html#top

This site provides general information on Brazil. It is divided into categories, which students can click on to access basic knowledge for research purposes. (S: 4–6)

Literature Resources

Alexander, Ellen. (1994). *Chaska and the Golden Doll*. New York: Arcade Publishers.

This book is about a young girl, Chaska, and her dog Kusi, who uncover a precious golden Inca icon that helps her and her village achieve their greatest dreams and goals.

Ancona, George. (1999). *Carnaval*. San Diego: Harcourt Brace.

Carnaval is about the people in the Brazilian town of Olinda. The villagers have been preparing for weeks for the carnaval, a five-day festival of parades, dancing, and singing. The town still celebrates the traditions and folklore of the people and the shared cultures that make up Brazil.

Ancona, George. (1994). *The Golden Lion Tamarin Comes Home*. New York: Simon & Schuster.

A family of four golden lion tamarins is reintroduced into the wild. From the National Zoo in Washington, D.C., to their independent life in the Brazilian rainforest, this story captures the tamarins' journey back to their natural habitat.

Despain, Pleasant. (1998). *The Dancing Turtle: A Folktale from Brazil*. New York: August House Little Folk.

This Brazilian folktale is about a turtle who is captured by a hunter. The hunter would like to make turtle soup, using the turtle as the main ingredient. The turtle's only hope for survival is the hunter's children and her own common sense.

Fredericks, Anthony D. (1996). *Exploring the Rainforest: Science Activities for Kids*. Golden, CO: Fulcrum Publishing.

With this detailed activity guide students will learn an abundance of information about the amazing and intriguing ecosystem known as the rainforest. A "must have" book for any study of rainforest life!

George, Jean Craighead. (1990). *One Day in the Tropical Rain Forest*. New York: Crowell.
   For a young Venezuelan Indian boy, the rainforest, and all of its wildlife, their last day together has come very quickly. The rainforest is about to be destroyed, unless a scientist can help to save it.

Getz, David. (1998). *Frozen Girl*. New York: Henry Holt.
   Frozen Girl discusses the discovery, history, and significance of an Incan mummy found frozen in the mountains of Peru.

Haynes, Tricia. (1999). *Colombia*. Philadelphia, PA: Chelsea House.
   This is an introduction to the South American country Colombia and how difficult the struggle has been to become a prosperous country. Many facts and information about Colombia can be found in this book.

Heinrichs, Ann. (1997). *Brazil*. Danbury, CT: Children's Press.
   This book describes the geography, vegetation, animals, history, economy, and culture of the South American country Brazil.

Heinrichs, Ann. (199)7). *Venezuela*. Danbury, CT: Children's Press.
   This is an introduction to the festivals, farms, geography, daily life, and history of the South American country Venezuela.

Hermes, Jules M. (1995). *The Children of Bolivia*. New York: Carolrhoda Books.
   This book provides the reader with an insight into the traditional festivals, dances, and dress of Bolivia. The diversity of people and geography are also covered throughout the book.

Hickox, Rebecca. (1998). *Zorro and Quwi: Tales of a Trickster Guinea Pig*. New York: Yearling Books.
   This Peruvian legend tells the story of how Quwi the clever guinea pig is chased night after night by Zorro the fox. Quwi decides to outwit the fox and make him look foolish.

Lourie, Peter. (1998). *Amazon: A Young Reader's Look at the Last Frontier*. Honesdale, PA: Boyds Mills.
   This is an introductory book to the destruction of the South American rainforests. Information about the Amazon cultures both past and present is also shared in this book.

Lye, Keith. (1998). *Take a Trip to Venezuela*. New York: Franklin Watts.
   This is a colorful introduction to the Venezuelan people and their everyday lives, school life, sports and recreation, crafts, festivals, money and stamps, transportation, etc.

Markham, Lois. (1997). *Colombia: The Gateway to South America*. New York: Benchmark Books.
   This colorful book introduces readers to historical, cultural, and geographical information about Colombia.

Reinhard, Johan. (1998). *Discovering the Inca Ice Maiden: My Adventures on Ampato*. Washington, DC: National Geographic Society.
   The author tells a tale of the discovery of a mummified Inca maiden who died five centuries ago on the summit of Ampato. The story is a day-by-day account of how the search unfolded and revealed the mummy.

St. John, Jetty. (1986). *A Family in Bolivia*. Minneapolis, MN: Lerner.
Terrific photographs in this book help tell the story of the lifestyles of a South American country. There are also books in this series that tell about the lifestyles of people living in Peru and Brazil.

Stiles, Martha Bennett. (1992). *James the Vine Puller: A Brazilian Folktale*. New York: Carolrhoda Books.
This folktale is about a turtle that outsmarts a whale and an elephant. This is a tale about brain over brawn.

Talbott, Hudson. (1996). *Amazon Diary: The Jungle Adventures of Alex Winter*. New York: Putnam.
Alex Winters is a sixth-grade student who details his trip to the Amazon through a handwritten journal that also includes illustrations and photographs. Alex observes the natural wildlife and religious practices and learns to eat the rusted grub. This book provides a glimpse into the life of the rainforest dwellers.

Van Lann, Nancy. (1998). *So Say the Little Monkeys*. New York: Atheneum.
Based on a tale from the Brazilian rainforest, in this book several tiny monkeys do not build a shelter because they are having too much fun. But when the night times comes, their wet and cold bodies remind them why it was important to build a home.

Activities and Projects

1. Divide the class into three groups. Have students pretend that they are reporters for a local newspaper. They must choose a topic such as traditions, festivals, dress, etc., that deals with one or more South American countries. Ask students to write stories and draw illustrations reporting the information found on their country.

2. Divide the class into several small groups and ask each group to take on the role of travel agents. Have students prepare travel plans for a specified country. The information can be gathered from the Web sites and literature listed above. Students should organize their information in the form of a travel brochure. When they have done this, ask students to obtain several travel brochures for selected South American countries from local travel agents. Encourage a discussion on the information presented in the student-created brochures compared with the travel agency brochures.

3. Using the Web site http://www.car.org/virtual_trip/bolivia/index.html, students can download and print pictures of Bolivia. Ask students to use the pictures to create their own homemade postcards. They should cut out photos and paste them onto rectangular pieces of oaktag. After making the postcards, students can pretend they were visiting Bolivia and write about their experiences there based on what has been presented in class.

4. Bring in copies of *USA Today* over a period of several days or several weeks, if possible. Ask students to create a temperature time line of selected cities in South America. For each city, students should list the high and low temperatures for a consecutive series of days. The information should be organized in the form of bar graphs or line graphs. Various groups should each develop a set of charts recording temperatures over an extended period of time. Later, engage students in a discussion about the similarities between selected North American cities and specific cities in South America.

Index